The Immoral Bible

D1598752

The Immoral Bible

Approaches to Biblical Ethics

Eryl W. Davies

t&t clark

Published by T&T Clark International
A Continuum Imprint
The Tower Building, 11 York Road, London SE1 7NX
80 Maiden Lane, Suite 704, New York, NY 10038

www.continuumbooks.com

British Library Cataloguing-in-Publication Data
A catalogue record for this book is available from the British Library

ISBN: 978-0-567-26162-5 (Hardback)
       978-0-567-30549-7 (Paperback)

Typeset by Fakenham Photosetting Ltd, Fakenham, Norfolk, NR21 8NN
Printed and bound in India by Replika Press Pvt Ltd

I nhad

OWAIN WYNN DAVIES

ac er cof am mam

GWEN ELUNED DAVIES

Table of Contents

List of Abbreviations

ANET	*Ancient Near Eastern Texts Relating to the Old Testament* (ed. J.B. Pritchard; Princeton NJ: Princeton University Press, 1950)
BZAW	Beihefte zur Zeitschrift für die alttestamentliche Wissenschaft
CD	Karl Barth, *Church Dogmatics* (13 vols; Edinburgh: T. & T. Clark, 1956–70)
CH	Code of Hammurabi
DOTT	*Documents from Old Testament Times* (ed. D. Winton Thomas; New York: Harper & Row, 1958)
EpRev	*The Epworth Review*
EvQ	*Evangelical Quarterly*
ExpT	*Expository Times*
HBT	*Horizons in Biblical Theology*
HTR	*Harvard Theological Review*
HUCA	*Hebrew Union College Annual*
*IDB*Sup	*The Interpreter's Dictionary of the Bible:* Supplementary Volume (ed. K.Crim; Nashville: Abingdon Press, 1976)
Int	*Interpretation*
JAAR	*Journal of the American Academy of Religion*
JBL	*Journal of Biblical Literature*
JBV	*Journal of Beliefs and Values*
JJS	*Journal of Jewish Studies*
JQR	*Jewish Quarterly Review*
JR	*Journal of Religion*
JSOT	*Journal for the Study of the Old Testament*
JSOTSup	Journal for the Study of the Old Testament: Supplement Series
JTS	*Journal of Theological Studies*
JTVI	*Journal of the Transactions of the Victoria Institute*
MAL	Middle Assyrian Laws
NRSV	*New Revised Standard Version*
N.S.	New Series
OED	*The Shorter Oxford English Dictionary* (2 vols, revised and edited by C.T. Onions; Oxford: Oxford University Press, 1983)
RevExp	*Review and Expositor*
RIDA	*Revue Internationale des Droits de l'Antiquité*
RSV	*Revised Standard Version*

SJT	*Scottish Journal of Theology*
TynB	*Tyndale Bulletin*
VT	*Vetus Testamentum*
ZAW	*Zeitschrift für die alttestamentliche Wissenschaft*

Preface

The present work has its origins in an article entitled, 'The Morally Dubious Passages of the Hebrew Bible: An Examination of Some Proposed Solutions', published in *Currents in Biblical Research* (vol. 3.2, April 2005, 196-228). I am grateful to SAGE Publications for permission to reproduce parts of the article, albeit in modified form, in this volume. I also wish to acknowledge my indebtedness to Professor Alan J. Hauser, Senior Editor of the periodical, for his encouragement and helpful comments as the article was being prepared for publication. Much of the volume was written during a sabbatical leave which I was granted in February-September 2009, and I am grateful to the authorities of Bangor University for allowing me this period to pursue my research, unencumbered by the duties of teaching and administration. I also wish to thank my colleagues in the School of Theology and Religious Studies for undertaking my university duties while I was away.

I wish to thank the staff at T. & T. Clark/Continuum, and, in particular, Anna Turton, Editorial Assistant, and Dominic Mattos, Senior Editor, for their interest in the volume and for their help, advice and guidance along the way. I am grateful to my wife, Eirian, who, as always, has been a constant source of support and encouragement, and to my children, Manon, Llinos, Gethin and Osian, who have provided me with some very welcome diversion from the often arduous tasks of writing and research. The book is dedicated, in gratitude, to my father and to the memory of my mother, who sadly passed away while the volume was being prepared for press.

Eryl W Davies
March 2010

Introduction

Numerous publications in recent years have drawn attention to aspects of the Hebrew Bible that are likely to offend the moral sensibilities of the contemporary reader[1], and the aim of the present volume is to examine some of the strategies that have been deployed by biblical scholars, past and present, in an attempt to come to terms with the ethically problematic passages of Scripture. Among the strategies discussed will be the evolutionary approach, the cultural relativists' approach, the "canon within the canon" approach, the canonical or holistic approach, the paradigmatic approach, and the reader-response approach. In order to provide some focus for the discussion, each strategy will be examined in relation to one of the most notorious passages of Scripture, namely, the account of Israel's conquest of Canaan as recorded in Josh. 6–11. These chapters depict Israel engaging in a "holy war" against the indigenous population of the land, a war in which the Israelites are commanded by God to kill all men, women and children. Of course, the presence of such passages in Scripture inevitably raises profoundly disturbing questions. How can such texts be reconciled with the Hebrew Bible's vision of a golden age of universal peace and justice? How can we interpret such acts in a way that is consistent with what the Bible tells us elsewhere about the nature and character of God? How can such passages that appear to openly advocate genocide and ethnic cleansing be reconciled with the fact that they appear in a book revered as sacred Scripture?

The issues raised by the presence of such passages in the Bible are not merely academic, for these texts have been interpreted, over the centuries, as providing theological justification for the oppression of various groups of people on the basis of religious dogma. The Bible has proved to be a useful weapon in the armoury of those who have sought to discriminate against race, colour, gender, class, religion or sexual orientation, and divine authority has been claimed for all kinds of abominable practices which have resulted in the marginalization and persecution of oppressed minorities. As Christopher Wright has observed, the crusades against Muslims, the genocide of North American Indians or Aboriginal Australians, the apartheid regime in South Africa, discrimination and violence against African Americans, and the expropriation of land from Palestinians, have all been perpetrated in the name of religion (2008:74; cf. Prior 1997; Brett 2008).

Of course, the idea of religiously motivated violence has become indelibly etched on the consciousness of the world following the attack on the World

---

[1] See, e.g., the studies by Carroll (1991); Lüdemann (1996); Schwartz (1997); Jones (1999); Brett (2008); and Thatcher (2008).

Trade Centre in 2001. A year later, John J. Collins began his Presidential
address to the annual meeting of the Society of Biblical Literature with the
following words:

> When it became clear that the terrorists of September 11, 2001, saw or
> imagined their grievances in religious terms, any reader of the Bible should
> have had a flash of recognition. The Muslim extremists drew their inspi-
> ration from the *Qur'an* rather than the Bible, but both Scriptures draw from
> the same wellsprings of ancient Near Eastern religion. While it is true that
> both Bible and *Qur'an* admit of various readings and emphases, and that
> terrorist hermeneutics can be seen as a case of the devil citing Scripture for
> his purpose, it is also true that the devil does not have to work very hard to
> find biblical precedents for the legitimation of violence … At a time when
> the Western world is supposedly engaged in a war on terrorism, it may be
> opportune to reflect on the ways in which the Bible appears to endorse and
> bless the recourse to violence, and to ask what the implications may be for
> the task of biblical interpretation (2003: 3–4).

The purpose of the present volume is to address this very issue. The way in
which scholars have dealt with the ethically problematic passages of Scripture
in general, and the accounts of biblical violence in particular, will afford an
opportunity to evaluate some of the current trends in biblical scholarship. It
will be demonstrated that each of the approaches discussed has its own advantages and problems, and an attempt will be made to draw something positive
from each strategy before subjecting it to detailed critique. In order to avoid
the accusation of being a cowardly fence-straddler, we have tended to favour
the reader-response approach to the biblical text (chapter 6), but it must be
emphasized at the outset that our ultimate aim has not been to recommend
or reject this or that approach, but merely to encourage a closer examination
of what we are actually doing when we appeal to Scripture in moral debate.
Indeed, it could well be argued that there is not a single hermeneutical key
for unlocking the biblical message and, in our postmodern age, many may
well feel that the convergence of as many different approaches as possible
is an inherently good thing, since the biblical text is too multifaceted to be
exhausted by a single interpretative strategy.

The volume was written in the conviction that the real issue is not *whether*
the Hebrew Bible can be used to provide ethical guidance for contemporary
communities of faith, but *how* it is to be used. The study is in no sense intended
to be exhaustive, and there are various other approaches to the ethically
problematic passages of Scripture that cannot be discussed within the compass
of the present volume, due to limitations of space. However, it is hoped that
what follows will shed some light on various trends in the study of the ethics of
the Hebrew Bible during the last century or so of academic study.

Chapter 1

The Immoral Bible

Anyone who has been concerned to apply the teaching of the Hebrew Bible to the needs and concerns of the present world has had to contend with the fact that it is, in many respects, a highly problematic volume. It is not merely that it contains many contradictions, improbabilities and errors of fact; it is not even that much of its teaching appears outmoded and to bear little relevance for contemporary Jewish and Christian faith and practice. The problem, rather, is that it often appears to advocate moral standards that seem to us to be offensive and unacceptable and, as Walter C. Kaiser has observed, nothing impedes the contemporary reader's appreciation and use of the Hebrew Bible more than the moral difficulties encountered within it[1].

Of course, it is important that the nature of the problem is not overstated, for the amount of material that is unedifying to an offensive degree is not great, and we would probably not trouble to read the Hebrew Bible at all if it did not embody a far greater proportion of acceptable norms than those we might want to oppose or question. But while it would be mistaken to magnify the ethically problematic passages of Scripture, it would be equally mistaken to minimize them, for their very presence has caused people, over the centuries, to raise questions concerning the canonical status of the Hebrew Bible, its underlying authority, and its continued use within contemporary communities of faith. The nub of the problem, of course, is that the Hebrew Bible is honoured as the sacred Scripture of Judaism and as part of the sacred Scripture of Christianity and, as such, it is regarded as possessing a normative and authoritative status within both religious traditions. Were it not for the fact that it had been granted canonical status and accorded a position of founda-tional significance within the synagogue and church, it could be regarded as simply another random collection of books from antiquity that could be read and valued just like any other body of literature. But the fact is that the Hebrew Bible is an authoritative document for both the Jewish and Christian faiths, and consequently Jewish and Christian believers might reasonably expect it to confirm and reinforce their beliefs and practices, and provide them with a valuable source of moral inspiration. They might also expect it to present standards of behaviour to be emulated, and images of God which show him

---

[1] Kaiser 1983:247. Much of Kaiser's volume is apologetic in tone, defending the Hebrew Bible against its perceived moral deficiencies.

to be a compassionate, caring and merciful deity. If so, it is likely that they will often be disappointed, for its teaching appears at times to be at best irrelevant and, at worse, morally perverse[2]. The problem is exacerbated by the fact that the morally questionable character of the Hebrew Bible is not limited to one book or genre, for material of dubious ethical value is encountered in the legal material and the narratives, in the prophetic literature and the psalms.

The Legal Material

Some of the laws and customs in the Hebrew Bible appear morally offensive to the modern reader. For example, polygamy seems to have been sanctioned in ancient Israel and appears to have survived, if only in exceptional cases, down to the Roman period[3]. The law sanctioned slavery, and although Hebrew legislation sought to regulate the treatment of slaves, there was no rejection of it as an institution, and it was evidently accepted within Israel as a given part of the social order[4]. Furthermore, the custom of blood-vengeance was recognized by the law, and although attempts were made to limit the abuses that could easily arise from the exercise of private justice, the next of kin (or $g\bar{o}$'ēl) was permitted to avenge the murder of his relative by finding and killing the person responsible[5].

Moreover, the sanctions attached to many of the laws appear, by our standards, to be harsh, cruel and intolerably vindictive. For example, the death penalty was laid down not only in cases of premeditated murder (Exod. 21:12; Lev. 24:17) but for those who struck, cursed or reviled their parents (Exod. 21:15, 17), or who abducted a man in order to make him a slave (Exod. 21:16)[6]. Capital punishment was demanded for abuses of sexual relationships, including adultery (Lev. 20:10), homosexuality (Lev. 20:13), incest (Lev.

---

[2] As Karl Barth observed, "at certain crucial points the Bible amazes us by its remarkable indifference to our conception of good and evil" (1928:38).

[3] Cf. Collins 1997:121–2. Judg. 8:30 suggests that polygamy was taken for granted in the domestic arrangements of early Israel, and both David (2 Sam. 5:13) and Solomon (1 Kgs 11:3) are reported to have had a number of wives.

[4] For a detailed discussion, see Swartley 1983:31–64. According to Mendelsohn (1949:23), the basic supply source of slavery in Israel, as in the ancient Near East generally, was the defaulting debtor; cf. Davies 1981:66–69.

[5] The Israelites were instructed to appoint six "cities of refuge" (i.e., places of asylum) to which a person who had killed another by accident could retreat (Num. 35:9–15). While the manslayer remained in the "city of refuge", he was legally protected from the "avenger of blood" until the proper judicial proceedings could be set in motion. Cf. Milgrom 1989:504–509; Davies 1995:359–68.

[6] Whether the death penalty was actually enforced in ancient Israel for such offences is a moot point. Kaiser claims that the death penalty was the maximum that was to be inflicted and that, in practice, a lesser penalty was imposed (1983:297–8). Certainly, various sanctions beside the death penalty seem to have been in force with regard to cases of adultery (cf. McKeating 1979:57–72).

20:11) and bestiality (Lev. 20:15–16). Death by stoning was the prescribed punishment for idolaters (Deut. 13·6–11), blasphemers (Lev. 24:14), and for a woman found not to be a virgin on her wedding night (Deut. 22:13–21). A man could even be stoned to death for the seemingly innocuous act of gathering wood on the Sabbath (Num. 15:32–36), and a particularly recalcitrant son could be stoned to death for persistently rebelling against his parents (Deut. 21:18–21). Death by burning was prescribed in the case of prostitution by a priest's daughter (Lev. 21:9), and the same penalty was imposed upon a man who had sexual intercourse with a woman and her daughter (Lev. 20:14). Bodily mutilation was deemed a perfectly acceptable and appropriate form of punishment in the case of a woman who seized a man's genitals, even in defence of her own husband (Deut. 25:11–12)[7], and the law of retaliation is expressed in all its crudity in the legislation which demands "life for life, eye for eye, tooth for tooth, hand for hand, foot for foot, burn for burn, bruise for bruise, wound for wound" (Exod. 21:23–24; cf. Lev. 24:18–21; Deut. 19:21)[8]. The curses that God threatened to inflict on those who disobeyed his laws and broke the terms of his covenant are also relayed in the most graphic and horrifying detail: "The LORD will afflict you with madness, blindness, and confusion of mind; you shall grope about at noon as blind people grope in darkness, but you shall be unable to find your way; and you shall be continually abused and robbed, without anyone to help" (Deut. 28:28–29). Even some of the positive motivations given for right conduct—riches, honour, and long life (Exod. 20:12; 23:26; Deut. 5:16; 33:18–19)—appear to us to be morally suspect, for instead of virtue being its own reward, obedience was predicated on the basis of a prudent assessment of the social and economic benefits that might accrue to the individual.

This is not to deny, of course, that there are many laws in the Hebrew Bible which are wholly admirable, such as the injunction to "love the LORD your God with all your heart, and with all your soul, and with all your might" (Deut. 6:5), and the command to "love your neighbour as yourself" (Lev. 19:18); nevertheless, it can hardly be doubted that it also contains many laws that will appear to the modern reader of Scripture as sub-Christian and of dubious moral and practical value.

---

[7] In contrast to other ancient Near Eastern Law codes (cf. MAL A 4–5, 8–9; *ANET* 180–1), this is the only specific case in Israelite law of physical mutilation being prescribed. Usually, assault was treated as a civil offence for which damages were paid to the injured party (cf. Exod. 21:18–19); see Phillips 1973:170; Wenham 1978:41.

[8] Whether the "lex talionis" was understood literally or viewed as an abstract principle is debated. A similar law occurs in the Code of Hammurabi; cf. CH 196, 197, 200; *ANET* 175. Later Jewish tradition reinterpreted the law to mean that the monetary value of a life or an eye must be recompensed (*Mekilta*, B. Talmud, Baba Kamma, 83b–84a). Daube (1947:102–53) argued that retaliation included a concept of compensation from the outset. See, further, Childs 1974:472; Phillips 1970:96–9.

The Narrative Tradition

Many of the narratives in the Hebrew Bible prove to be a further stumbling-block for contemporary readers of Scripture. The heroes of the faith are sometimes depicted as behaving in a less than exemplary fashion, for they lie (Abram in Gen. 12:10–20; 20:1–18), cheat (Jacob in Gen. 27:1–29), murder (Moses in Exod.2:11–15), curse (Elisha in 2 Kgs 2:23–24), and commit adultery (David in 2 Sam. 11). Other narratives raise disturbing questions concerning the very character and nature of God himself, for he is frequently depicted as acting in a morally questionable way. In the opening chapters of Genesis, he is depicted as a God who exhibits favouritism, accepting Abel's offering of the choicest of his flock, while rejecting Cain's offering of the fruit of the earth, for no apparent reason (Gen. 4:3–5). In the story of the exodus from Egypt he hardens Pharaoh's heart for his own self-glorification (Exod. 10:1–2), and inflicts diseases and plagues on the Egyptians (Exod. 7–11), killing every first-born in the land (Exod. 12:29), and completely destroying the Egyptian army (Exod. 14). Elsewhere, God is portrayed as meting out horrific punishments on an entire family or community because of the wrongdoing of individual members (cf. Num. 16; Josh. 7), and he strikes people dead simply because they accidentally touched a sacred object (Uzzah in 2 Sam. 6:6–8), or offered the wrong kind of sacrificial fire (the sons of Aaron in Num. 3:4)[9]. Moreover, the God who so often demands complete honesty and integrity from his people is occasionally depicted as capable of deception and duplicity himself. In Micaiah ben Imlah's vision, for example, he is described as seeking an effective strategy for enticing Ahab to his death, and resolves to send forth a lying spirit to deceive the king with promises of success (1 Kgs 22:19–23). In the exchanges between God and Satan in the opening chapters of the book of Job, God appears as a character prone to vanity, and not above wagering people's lives in order to settle a dispute. Sometimes, he is described as acting in a manner that contemporary readers of the Bible would regard as perverse or irrational: he orders Abram to sacrifice his only son, Isaac (Gen. 22), though the law prohibited human sacrifice and condemned those who ordered their sons to be offered to Molech (Lev. 18:21; 20:2); he causes Absalom to reject the good counsel of Ahithophel in order to bring ruin upon him (2 Sam. 17:14); he encourages David to conduct a census of the people, only to punish him for doing just that, and he slaughters 70,000 Israelites in the process (2 Sam.

---

[9] The precise meaning of the term rendered by the *NRSV* "illicit fire" (Heb. *'eš zārāh*) in Num. 3:4 has been much disputed. Haran (1960:115) suggests that Aaron's sons must have taken the fire for their censers from outside the altar-area, and in so doing were in breach of the command contained in Lev. 16:12–13; others suggest that the ritual error lay not in the fire but in the incense (Lev. 10:1), which had presumably not been compounded according to the instructions given by God to Moses in Exod. 30:34–38 (cf. Levine 1993:155–6). For a brief discussion of the various alternatives, see Davies 1995:27–28.

24:1–17)[10]; and he demands the life of David's newborn son in recompense for Uriah's life (2 Sam. 12:15–19).

Clearly, the existence of such texts within the Hebrew Bible must raise troubling questions in the minds of all contemporary readers of Scripture, for how can such narratives possibly contribute to the Christian's understanding of God, and how can they furnish normative guidance for ethical conduct in the twenty-first century? Far from providing examples of behaviour for the modern Christian to emulate, many of the stories recorded in the Hebrew Bible merely provide instances of human fanaticism, bigotry and intolerance. Not surprisingly, the existence of such texts in Scripture has led some to question the place of the Hebrew Bible in the canon, to reconsider its relationship to the New Testament, and to give serious thought to the principles that ought to govern its interpretation within the church and within the academy.

The Prophetic Tradition

Some of the texts in the prophetic literature similarly raise questions concerning the character of God. He commands one of his prophets to marry a prostitute and then, perversely, instructs him to repudiate her and her sons (Hos. 1:2–9; 2:2–4), and he sends another prophet on the seemingly pointless errand of deliberately closing peoples' minds to his will (Isa. 6:8–10)[11]. Ezekiel represents God as acting in a similarly perverse way by giving the people "statutes that were not good and ordinances by which they could not live" (Ezek. 20:25).

In some prophetic passages, God is depicted as capable of anger (Jer. 4:8), hatred (Mic. 1:2–3) and deception (Jer. 4:10), and he is described as leading the nations astray (Isa. 30:27–28), and pouring into their leaders "a spirit of confusion" (Isa. 19:14). The punishment which God inflicts upon his own people sometimes appears to be intolerably cruel, and in some prophetic passages the punitive intent of the divine will seems difficult to justify, for God's anger does not appear to be a just and proportional response to human sin. For example, the vanity and self-aggrandizement displayed by the women of Jerusalem may well have appeared unseemly to the prophet Isaiah (Isa. 3:16–17), but it surely did not warrant the punishment of sexual humiliation, rape and abuse ordained by God. In a similar vein, the self-indulgence of the rich who lay on beds of ivory and ate of the choicest meats may well

---

[10] That the biblical writers themselves were aware of the moral problem in this account is suggested by the fact that in the version recounted in 1 Chr. 21:1 it is Satan who incites David to conduct the census.

[11] As Andrew Davies has observed (2000:173–86), the account of Isaiah's call and commissioning as a prophet in Isa. 6:9–13 has caused commentators particular difficulty, for God here appears to initiate a procedure which will make repentance by his people ever more impossible, resulting in the "progressive crippling of Israel's spiritual awareness" (177).

have appeared to Amos as thoughtless and insensitive (Am. 6:4–7), but the punishment announced by the prophet (exile!) seems excessively harsh, and is clearly out of all proportion to the supposed "crimes" committed by the wealthy. Moreover, when God's fury is unleashed upon his people, he shows little self-restraint, and consequently the innocent are made to suffer as much as the guilty. Isa. 9:13–17, for example, contains a sweeping, universal condemnation by God in which the poor receive the same punishment as those who oppress them, and no compassion is shown even to the widow and orphan, who are usually depicted as particularly deserving of mercy and justice (cf. Davies 2000:132–4; Gray 2006:137–46). At times, the punishment inflicted by God appears to be unreasonable and even irrational. In Isa. 24:1–6, for example, God punishes humanity for defiling the earth, but in doing so he himself reduces the earth to a wasteland so that, ironically, "God's intended judgment for the initial offense will arguably cause more damage to the earth than the offense itself" (Gray 2006:149).

Moreover, the prophets appear to have no compunction about attributing evil as well as good to God. Isa. 45:7, for example, ascribes all happenings in nature to the personal agency of Yahweh: "I form light and create darkness, I make weal and create woe"; and Amos concurs that God is the originator of everything that happens on earth, for good or ill: "Does disaster befall a city unless the LORD has done it?" (Am. 3:6). Such pronouncements were, perhaps, an inevitable inference, given the belief of the prophets that God was the creator of everything; yet, the fact that Yahweh appears in the prophetic literature as the source of disasters and misfortunes (as well as blessings and prosperity) must surely give rise to serious ethical concerns.

Equally problematic for contemporary readers of the prophetic literature are the crude sexual metaphors used to depict the fate that awaits the people of Israel because of their wickedness. The idolatrous nation has acted like a harlot (Hos. 2:5) and therefore deserved to be punished, shamed and disgraced. The punishment inflicted upon her is described in the most lurid and graphic terms: she will be stripped naked, exposed and publicly humiliated (Hos. 2:3; Jer. 13:20–27); she will be abused, battered and raped (Ezek. 16:6–52), and she will be derided, mocked and ridiculed (Ezek. 23:32–34). Such retaliation was no more than the wife/nation deserved for betraying the trust of her husband/ God by indulging in sexual liaisons with other men. Indeed, in some cases, the wife is regarded as not only responsible for, and guilty of, her own violation, but as enjoying the abuse which she was made to suffer (Ezek. 23:5–8, 19–21)[12].

The existence of such passages within the prophetic corpus will no doubt be a cause of alarm and concern to readers, for the actions attributed to

---

[12] Not surprisingly, the sexual imagery deployed by the prophets is criticized by feminist biblical scholars because it presents a negative view of female sexuality by implying that women were by nature deviant and promiscuous, and that female desire was motivated not by love but by lust; cf. Brenner 1995:262–4.

God by the prophets are often ethically ambiguous and tend to offend our natural sense of justice and morality. Indeed, in many of the prophetic texts God appears to operate by moral standards of which humans would scarcely approve. This is not to deny, of course, that there are passages of profound ethical insight in the prophetic literature, but the presence of such sublime teaching should not blind us to the fact that there are other texts in the prophetic corpus which seem utterly inconsistent with the image of the morally beneficent and compassionate deity envisaged by Judaism and Christianity.

The Psalms

The book of Psalms, so often regarded as the high-water mark of Israel's faith, exhibits many elements which contemporary readers will find disturbing. In the first place, the psalmist is not averse to casting aspersions on God's character, for he is frequently depicted as an absent and remote deity, who is even capable of destructive acts against his own people[13]. Far from being helpful and attentive, he seems indifferent to the suffering and humiliation experienced by the very people who worship him (Pss. 22:1–2; 44:23–24). For their part, the psalmists claim to have done nothing to deserve the ignominy and ill-treatment which they are compelled to suffer, and they frequently strike an indignantly self-righteous note as they claim that their unswerving loyalty to God has gone unrewarded (cf. Pss. 40:9–10; 44:17–19).

There can be little doubt, however, that the most troublesome aspect of the psalms is the plea for God to wreak vengeance and retaliation upon the "enemies" or "evildoers" who are intent upon making the life of the psalmist a misery. Ps. 10:15–16 beseeches God to "break the arm of the wicked and evildoers", and expresses the hope that God will reign forever and that "the nations will perish from the land". A spirit of malice and vindictiveness is also reflected in Ps. 140:10–11, where the psalmist appears to give free rein to the hatred he feels towards his enemies:

"Let burning coals fall on them!
  Let them be flung into pits, no more to rise!
Do not let the slanderer be established in the land;
  let evil speedily hunt down the violent".

In some psalms, the imprecatory element is limited to a single verse as, for example, in Ps. 143, where eleven verses of elevated and noble thoughts are

---

[13] As Brueggemann has observed, the psalmist is not afraid to hold God to account, and does not flinch from truth-telling "even when that truth-telling is damaging to Yahweh's reputation and character" (1997:379).

followed in the final verse by a terse wish for God to "cut off my enemies and destroy all my adversaries" (v. 12). In other psalms, however, the curses feature far more prominently, as in Ps. 109:6–19, where the psalmist pleads for God to take vengeance upon the wicked and deceitful person who has spoken lies against him:

"May his days be few;
    may another seize his position.
May his children be orphans,
    and his wife a widow.
May his children wander about and beg;
    may they be driven out of the ruins they inhabit.
May the creditor seize all that he has;
    may strangers plunder the fruits of his toil.
May there be no one to do him a kindness,
    nor anyone to pity his orphaned children" (vv. 8–12).

Ps. 58 provides a further example of a psalm which invokes God's curse on the wicked who have shown themselves to be incorrigibly corrupt. The ungodly "go astray from the womb" and "err from their birth, speaking lies" (v. 3), and so they deserve to be duly punished:

"Let them be like the snail that dissolves into slime;
    like the untimely birth that never sees the sun" (v. 8).

The call for vengeance in this psalm is accompanied by the joy of seeing it realized, and there is an undisguised gloating over the fate that awaits the ungodly:

"The righteous will rejoice when they see vengeance done;
    they will bathe their feet in the blood of the wicked" (v. 10).

Perhaps the most notorious of the so-called "imprecatory psalms" is Ps. 137, which begins innocuously enough ("By the rivers of Babylon we sat down and wept when we remembered Zion"; v. 1), but ends with words of almost unparalleled vindictiveness:

"Happy shall they be who take your little ones
    and dash them against the rock!" (v. 9).

Biblical commentators, clearly embarrassed by the presence of such passages in Scripture, have been at pains to excuse these powerful negative emotions by emphasizing that such sentiments arose from the intense suffering which the psalmists had experienced at the hands of their enemy, and since they had no concept of an afterlife it was natural for them to demand some form of retaliation in the present. The fact is, however, that modern readers cannot condone or approve of such sentiments as those expressed above, and they are bound to wonder how these passages, which breathe a spirit of such malice and revenge, can be squared with Jesus' command to "love your enemies" and to "pray for those who persecute you" (Mt. 5:44). They might also wonder how such malicious thoughts can be present in a book which has nurtured the faith and piety of Christians over the centuries. Of course, this is not to deny that there are also many passages in the Psalms which are noble, profound and uplifting, and which continue to speak directly to the human condition; but there are also many other passages in the Psalter that are likely to offend our moral sensibilities, and it is certainly difficult to read some of the psalms without expressing horror at the sheer personal vindictiveness of the faithful as they pray for the doom and destruction of their enemies. It must be emphasized that this unbridled lust for revenge is not an incidental feature of the psalms; on the contrary, curses against the enemy abound in the Psalter, and there are numerous passages where the psalmist pleads for the vindication of the righteous and the destruction of the wicked. As Zenger has observed, "hatred, enmity, violence, retaliation, and even revenge are no sub-motifs in the Psalter: they are substantive parts of it" (1996:13), and it is the presence of these discordant notes within the canon of sacred Scripture which modern readers are bound to find disturbing and troublesome.

Violence and Warfare

Of all the ethically problematic texts in the Hebrew Bible, however, those that are most likely to offend the sensibilities of the modern reader are the ones which appear to sanction violence and warfare[14]. The historical books record countless instances of the brutality and barbaric treatment meted out by the Israelites to their enemies as they undertake their destructive and aggressive campaigns[15]. In 1 Sam. 15:3, God commands Saul to smite the Amalekites, killing them all, men, women and children, and sparing none. David is also said to have carried out a series of ruthless battles against the surrounding peoples: he is reported to have raided the Negeb, killing every single man and

---

[14] Rodd points out that "the Old Testament can easily appear to be the most bloodthirsty of all the sacred scriptures within the great religious traditions" (2001:185). He notes that only the book of Ruth and the Song of Songs are completely devoid of any references to battles or warfare, and even in the latter, imagery derived from warfare appears to be used (4:4; 6:4, 10; 8:9).

[15] The oft-quoted remark by Walter Benjamin to the effect that "there is no document of civilization which is not at the same time a document of barbarism" (1970:258) is no less true of the Hebrew Bible than for any other type of ancient literature.

woman (1 Sam. 27:8–12); on another occasion, he is said to have put to death two-thirds of the population of Moab (2 Sam. 8:2) and killed 22,000 Syrians (2 Sam. 8:5) and 80,000 Edomites (2 Sam. 8:13). Although the precise figures may be an exaggeration, this does little to reduce the ethical difficulty posed by such accounts, for there is no hint of any criticism in the narratives that such aggression and ruthlessness should have been exhibited; on the contrary, the narrators almost gloat over the large numbers of enemies who were slain (cf. Rodd 2001:187).

Of course, the violence depicted in Scripture is all the more offensive when God himself is depicted as a divine warrior who actively participates in battle to ensure Israel's victory[16]. Warlike epithets attributed to Yahweh abound in the Hebrew Bible: he is frequently depicted as a "man of war" (Exod. 15:3)[17], and as the "LORD of hosts" (2 Sam. 7:8, 26–27), which implies that he was in command of both the heavenly host and the armies of Israel. The wars of Israel were Yahweh's wars (Num. 21:14; 1 Sam. 18:17; 25:28), and the enemies of Israel were Yahweh's enemies (1 Sam. 30:26). The visible presence of God in war was the ark of the covenant, and when the ark accompanied the combatants into battle they could leave home with the certainty that Yahweh would deliver the enemy into their hands[18]. Even the Psalmists praise Yahweh as a divine warrior, "mighty in battle" (Ps. 24:8), who subjugates his enemies (Ps. 47:3), and in the prophetic literature God's character often exhibits traces of violence, vindictiveness and excess. In Isa. 34, for example, all the peoples of the earth are subjected to God's violent judgment:

"For the LORD is enraged against all the nations,
    and furious against all their hoards;
  he has doomed them, has given them over for slaughter.

[16] In a chapter entitled, "God the Warrior", in his volume, *The Old Testament and Theology*, G.E. Wright claims that "no attribute of the Biblical God is more consciously and almost universally rejected as this one" (1969:121).The centrality of the notion of God as warrior in ancient Israel is particularly emphasized by Miller: "One can only go so far in describing the history of Israel, or its religion, or the theology of the Old Testament without encountering the wars of Yahweh. In prose and poetry, early and late materials alike, the view that Yahweh fought for or against his people stands forth prominently. The centrality of that conviction and its historical, cultic, literary and theological ramifications can hardly be overestimated" (1973:1). Miller concludes that the imagery of the divine warrior "became a major factor in the formation of Yahwism and continued so throughout Israel's history" (64).
[17] Exod. 15:3 is part of the so-called Song of Moses, considered by some to be among the earliest passages in the Hebrew Bible. On the antiquity of the song, see Cross 1973:112–44; Freedman 1980b:176–8.
[18] In 1 Sam. 4:1–4, the defeat of the Israelites at the hands of the Philistines is specifically attributed to the absence of the ark. That the wars of Israel were won not so much through the prowess of the combatants but through the power of Yahweh is made abundantly evident in Judg. 7:2, where Gideon is instructed to reduce the number of his warriors so that it would be clear to all that the victory was Yahweh's, and his alone.

Their slain shall be cast out,
    and the stench of their corpses shall rise;
    the mountains shall flow with their blood" (vv. 2–3).

In Isa. 63:1–6 God is portrayed as returning from the battlefield, wading in the blood of his enemies, as if treading grapes in a wine-press. Even the brutality exhibited by other nations is regarded as having divine approval, and God seems perfectly content to see the Assyrians loot and pillage and engage in excessive violence and bloodshed (Isa. 10:5–6). But Assyria, too, will be punished by God for its blasphemous pride and arrogance, and the nation which had been the implement of divine judgment will soon feel God's anger directed towards their own destruction (Isa. 10:25).

Yahweh and the "Holy Wars" of Israel

Of all the passages in the Hebrew Bible that depict violence and bloodshed, however, the most abhorrent for the contemporary reader is undoubtedly the graphic and chilling account of the conquest of Canaan recounted in Josh. 6–11. Here, the Israelites are depicted as engaging in a "holy war" against the indigenous population of the land[19], and one of the essential elements of the holy war was the "ban" or *ḥērem*, which involved the ritual destruction of the cities and the complete annihilation of all their inhabitants, regardless of age, gender or military status[20]. Thus, after capturing Jericho, the Israelites are reported to have "devoted the city to the LORD and destroyed with the sword every living thing in it—men and women, young and old, cattle, sheep and donkeys" (Josh. 6:21). They then proceeded to capture and burn the city of Ai, killing all its inhabitants, a total of 12,000 people (Josh. 8:24–29). In conformity with the rules of "holy war", the inhabitants of Makkedah were also destroyed by Joshua and the invading army (Josh. 10:28), and a similar fate befell various cities in the southern region of the land, including Libnah (Josh.

---

[19] See von Rad (1951) for the classic treatment of the "holy war" tradition in the Hebrew Bible. Although von Rad used the term "holy war" to designate the conflicts commanded by Yahweh, the expression does not occur in the Hebrew Bible, and many scholars prefer the designation "Yahweh war" (see Jones 1975:642–58 for the distinction between the two expressions).

[20] Niditch (1993:29) refers to the "ban" as "this most shocking of ancient Hebrew ideologies of war", and Barr claims that the "ban" is "one of the supreme cases in regard to which people feel a moral revulsion against the Old Testament and its God" (1993:207). A Moabite inscription attests that the "ban" was not confined to Israel, for the identical term, *ḥērem*, occurs in the Moabite Stone dating from the second half of the ninth century B.C.E., which refers to the slaughter of all 7,000 inhabitants of Moab (*DOTT* 196–97; *ANET* 320–21). The "ban" is not attested elsewhere in the ancient Near East, although Malamat has suggested that the motif also occurs in 18th century Mari (1967:40–49). For a detailed study of the *ḥērem*, see Stern 1991.

10:29–30), Lachish (Josh. 10:31–32), Eglon (Josh. 10:34–35), Hebron (Josh. 10:36–37), and Debir (Josh. 10:38–39). In the northern campaign, Joshua took Hazor, killing the king and all the inhabitants of the city, before burning it to the ground (Josh. 11:10–11).

The feeling of revulsion that modern readers of the Hebrew Bible are bound to experience when reading such narratives of indiscriminate and wholesale killing is heightened by the fact that such atrocities were not only permitted or condoned by God, but were expressly commanded by him (Josh. 10:40). Indeed, the divine command was clear, categorical and uncompromising: "you must not let anything that breathes remain alive" (Deut. 20:16)[21]. Thus, the annihilation of the native inhabitants of Canaan appears to receive the highest possible legitimacy in the form of divine approval. Indeed, failure to carry out God's command to the letter would meet with bloody retaliation by God, as Achan discovered to his cost (Josh. 7:1–26)[22].

Almost as reprehensible for the modern reader as the accounts of the conquest of Canaan in Josh. 6–11 are the attempts elsewhere in the Hebrew Bible to justify the extreme cruelty involved in the mass extermination of the indigenous population. One of the reasons given for the complete annihilation of the native inhabitants was the utter depravity of the peoples who already occupied the land: "it is on account of the wickedness of these nations that the LORD is going to drive them out before you" (Deut. 9:4). It is made abundantly clear that if the Israelites failed to exterminate them completely, they would "teach you to do all the abhorrent things they do for their gods" (Deut. 20:18)[23]. The annihilation of the indigenous population was thus a means of rooting out from the very beginning what might prove damaging and destructive to the pure relationship that should exist between the people of Israel and their God. In this way, the *ḥērem* was, in effect, theologically rationalized, and regarded as the means appointed by Yahweh for ensuring the cultic purity of Israel. For the modern reader, however, this attempt to protect Israel from foreign influence at any price must be regarded as highly questionable,

---

[21] The evidence of the Hebrew Bible suggests that the "ban", or *ḥērem*, could vary in severity, from (a) the total destruction of all persons and property, as in Josh. 6:21, to (b) the total destruction of all persons but not property, as in Deut. 2:34–35, to (c) the destruction of all male citizens only, as in Deut. 20:12–14. For the lack of uniformity in the biblical traditions concerning the *ḥērem*, see Gottwald 1964:299–300, who suggests that the differences in the scope of the *ḥērem* injunctions may reflect varying interpretations at different periods in Israel's history or in different narrative circles, some tending towards a more lenient, others to a more rigid, approach.

[22] In 1 Sam. 15, Saul is condemned for failing to apply the "ban" with the utmost rigour, for he spared the life of Agag, king of the Amalekites. It was left to Samuel to fulfil God's will by hewing Agag to pieces at Gilgal (1 Sam. 15:32–33).

[23] The degrading aspects of Canaanite society are thought to have included sexual promiscuity and perversions associated with the fertility cults as well as collusion in child sacrifice (cf. Deut. 12:29–31).

for however great the ethical misdemeanours of the Canaanites, it could surely never justify genocide on the kind of scale envisaged in Josh 6–11.

Another way in which the biblical authors tried to justify the "ban" was by "sacralizing" it, regarding the slaughter of the indigenous population as a sacrifice to the deity who had made victory possible[24]. There was to be no material gain for the Israelites as a result of their conquest, for everything had to be dedicated to God himself. The people were merely surrendering to Yahweh all living beings and inanimate objects in recognition of the fact that he had exclusive rights over the spoil. In this way, the Israelites were, in effect, acquitted of moral responsibility for the mass destruction of the enemy, since they were only acting in accordance with their religious obligation. But clothing such activity in the garment of religion and piety merely makes the ethical problem more acute, for it begs the question as to what kind of God it is who demands such senseless killing? Moreover, it must have been little consolation to the victims to know that they had died as an offering to God by the aggressors in gratitude for their victory[25].

The biblical authors also attempted to justify the conquest on the grounds that God was fulfilling the promise he had made to the patriarchs: he would ensure that the people of Israel would take possession of the land in order "to accomplish what he swore to your fathers, to Abraham, Isaac and Jacob" (Deut. 9:5; cf. Gen. 12:7). When the Israelite farmer celebrated the harvest of the land, he was to declare that he had "come to the land the LORD swore to our ancestors to give to us" (Deut. 26:3); the conquest thus stood as a kind of monument to God's faithfulness to the promise he had made to the fathers. God had willed the territory to be the inheritance of his chosen people, and once ensconced in the land they were to become a blessing to the nations (cf. Gen. 12:3); indeed, only by annihilating the native population could the Israelites preserve their religious identity and mediate a blessing to the surrounding peoples[26].

[24] Cf. Niditch 1993:28–37. The root *ḥrm* denotes "separating" something, i.e., taking it out of profane use and reserving it for sacred use by consecrating it to God. The term later found its way into the general vocabulary of worship (cf. Lev. 27:21, 28; Ezek. 44:29), but it originally belonged to the ritual of "holy war".

[25] Cf. the wry comment of J.J. Collins: "The enemy is deemed worthy of being offered to God. One hopes that the Canaanites appreciated the honor" (2003:6).

[26] It is surprising how the biblical justification for the occupation of the land of Canaan has been accepted uncritically by biblical scholars. Christopher Wright, for example, poses the question (albeit tentatively): "Is it possible ... that in a fallen world where struggle for land involves war, and if the only kind of war at the time was the kind described in the Old Testament texts, this was the way it had to be if the land-gift promise was to be fulfilled in due course?... In view of his long-term goal of ultimately bringing blessing to the nations through this people Israel, the gift of land necessitated this horrific historical action within the fallen world of nations at the time" (2008:89).

Proposed Solutions to the Ethically Problematic Passages of Scripture

It is, perhaps, hardly surprising that various strategies have been devised over the centuries in order to counter the ethically problematic nature of the Hebrew Bible. The need for some such strategy was felt as long ago as the period of the Early Church, the members of which were only too acutely aware of the embarrassment caused by some of the morally dubious passages of Scripture. Some within the Early Church sought to overcome the moral difficulties of the biblical text by resorting to allegorical interpretation, and argued that only by applying such figurative exegesis could many passages in the Hebrew Bible be regarded as in any sense compatible with Christianity. However questionable some biblical texts might appear if understood in their literal sense, timeless truths could be elicited from them by applying an allegorical interpretation. Origen, the most notable figure in Christian scholarship in Alexandria during the second and third centuries C.E., argued that the interpreter should be encouraged to move away from the obvious, literal reading of the text and embrace, instead, a higher level of spiritual exposition[27]. In effect, Origen distinguished between the letter and the spirit of the Bible, and once priority was given to its spiritual meaning, the reader would find that even the most ethically problematic texts might yield a sense "worthy of God". Thus, for example, the notion of God as a divine warrior leading the faithful into battle was understood in a spiritual sense as a call to personal piety by opposing the forces of evil, and even the violence and brutality occasioned by the conquest of Canaan was sanitized for the purpose of spiritual exhortation[28]. Largely as a result of Origen's influence, the allegorical method of exegesis was applied whenever the natural sense of the text conflicted with the cherished beliefs of the Early Church concerning what was and was not consonant with the will of God and, in this way, the allegorical interpretation, in effect, "saved the Scriptures for the Church" (Tollinton 1929:xxxiv).

Some felt, however, that the allegorical method deployed by Origen was merely a device for seeking in Scripture a kind of truth that it was not meant to teach[29]; consequently, it was strongly rejected by the Antiochene Fathers (such as Chrysostom and Theodore; cf. Longenecker 1987:26–27) and was

---

[27] Origen acknowledged that it was the "stumbling-blocks and impossibilities" inherent in the biblical text that forced him to adopt the allegorical interpretation; see *De Principiis* 2.9.

[28] The story of the destruction of the Canaanites by Joshua and his army was interpreted as a symbol of the defeat of evil by another and greater "Joshua", the analogy no doubt suggested by the fact that the name Joshua was the Hebrew version of Jesus; cf. Brown 1999:70.

[29] Origen's detractors observed that the allegorical method deserved its name, for it made Scripture say something other (άλλο άγορευειν) than what it really meant. See Farrar 1886:193–4.

later repudiated (in principle if not in practice) by Luther. Nevertheless, in its day it represented for many the most plausible way of confronting biblical texts which might appear, on the surface, to be morally unacceptable.

One of those who firmly objected to the allegorical interpretation of Scripture was Marcion who, in the middle of the second century C.E., argued that such efforts to overcome the troublesome passages of the Hebrew Bible were merely a subterfuge that evaded the real issue. He insisted upon the literal meaning of the text, and argued that such a view necessitated a radical discontinuity between the Jewish Scriptures and the Christian New Testament. Consequently, the Hebrew Bible (along with several parts of the New Testament that he judged to be infected with Jewish concerns) should be discarded from the canon of Holy Scripture as an unnecessary and expendable burden which should form no part of Christian revelation. The Hebrew Bible constituted an inferior faith, and thus any ethical authority which it possessed for Christians was rejected *a priori*. Although the extent of Marcion's influence on the Christianity of Asia Minor in the second century C.E. cannot be denied[30], his radical rejection of the Hebrew Bible was itself rejected by the Early Church[31] and, indeed, his relentless attack on the Hebrew Scriptures was one of the factors which led indirectly to the defining of the limits of the canon of Christian Scripture, with the Hebrew Bible firmly included.

Although the above methods of dealing with the ethically problematic passages of Scripture were not unknown in the twentieth century[32], few today would regard such strategies as an effective solution to the problem at hand. While the allegorical interpretation may be regarded as a legitimate method of interpreting some biblical texts, notably the Song of Songs, it can hardly be viewed as a viable option to interpret such passages as the conquest of Canaan in Josh. 6–11. And while many may wish to sideline some of the ethically problematic texts of the Hebrew Bible, few would follow Marcion and advocate jettisoning it completely[33], for the Early Church regarded it as authoritative

---

[30] M.F. Wiles (1967:49) describes him as "a figure standing just off-stage but casting his shadow over every player on it" (cited by Longenecker 1987:22).

[31] Both Irenaeus and Tertullian wrote refutations of Marcion's position, Tertullian's *Adversus Marcionem* being "probably the most representative and certainly the most devastating polemic against Marcion of the day" (Longenecker 1987:24).

[32] Davidson noted that "a decidedly Marcionite tendency may be fairly traced in much modern discussion on Christian ethics" (1959:374), and he pointed to such volumes as W.R. Inge's *Christian Ethics and Modern Problems* (1930), R. C. Mortimer's *Christian Ethics* (1950), and R. Niebuhr's *An Interpretation of Christian Ethics* (1936), which virtually exclude the Hebrew Bible entirely from their discussion. In a similar vein, C.R. North observed that "many well-meaning Christians are to all intents and purposes Marcionite in their attitude to the Old Testament" (1946:149), while G.E. Wright claimed there had been "a widespread revival of Marcionism in the modern church" (1952:16). Such claims, however, were somewhat misleading, for the tendency was to ignore the Hebrew Bible rather than to demand its dismissal from the canon of Scripture.

[33] One notable exception was Adolf von Harnack, who wrote the standard book on Marcion, and who famously concluded in the oft-quoted last paragraph of his volume: "To reject

Scripture and it has always assumed a normative status within the community of faith.

It will therefore come as no surprise that biblical scholars during the past century or so have applied different hermeneutical approaches to the ethically problematic passages of the Hebrew Bible. While some of these strategies have waxed and waned during this period, others have persisted (in some form) throughout. Among the strategies examined in the present volume will be the evolutionary approach, the cultural relativists' approach, the "canon within the canon" approach, the "canonical" or "holistic" approach, the paradigmatic approach, and the reader-response approach. In order to provide some focus for the present discussion, each of these strategies will be examined in relation to one of the most notorious passages of Scripture, namely, the account of Israel's conquest of Canaan as recorded in Josh. 6–11. These chapters will serve as a convenient "case study" by which to adjudicate the success or otherwise of the various hermeneutical options which have been advocated to counter the ethically problematic passages of the Hebrew Bible.

Joshua 6–11 as a "Case Study"

The reason for isolating these particular chapters for consideration as we examine the merits of the various strategies under discussion is not difficult to justify. In the first place, such texts have made the Jewish and Christian faiths easy targets for those intent on lambasting the Bible and undermining belief. Typical is Richard Dawkins' belligerent depiction of the God of the Hebrew Bible at the beginning of the second chapter of his much-read volume *The God Delusion*:

> The God of the Old Testament is arguably the most unpleasant character in all fiction: jealous and proud of it; a petty, unjust, unforgiving control-freak; a vindictive, bloodthirsty ethnic cleanser; a misogynistic, homophobic, racist, infanticidal, genocidal, filicidal, pestilential, megalomaniacal, sadomaso-chistic, capriciously malevolent bully[34].

the Old Testament in the second century was a mistake the Church rightly repudiated; to retain it in the sixteenth century was a fate which the Reformation could not yet avoid; but to continue to keep it as a canonical document after the nineteenth century is the consequence of religious and ecclesiastical paralysis. To sweep the table clean ... is the action required of Protestantism today" (1921:248–9). For a discussion and critique of von Harnack's conclusions, see Barton 1997:35–62.

[34] Dawkins 2006:51. Dawkins' invective is only marginally less intemperate later in the chapter where he describes Judaism as "originally a tribal cult of a single fiercely unpleasant God, morbidly obsessed with sexual restrictions, with the smell of charred flesh, with his own superiority over rival gods and with the exclusiveness of his chosen desert tribe" (58). A briefer, but no less trenchant, indictment of God is found in the French writer Jules

While Dawkins' rhetoric is expressed in admittedly extreme and exaggerated terms, the fact is that there is no shortage of populist writers who will point to the malign influence of the Hebrew Bible on contemporary society, and in so doing perpetuate the stereotype of the Hebrew Bible as a predominantly violent book.

Secondly, of all the ethically problematic aspects of Scripture, it is almost certainly the "ban" or *ḥērem* which, in the words of James Barr, remains "uniquely and outstandingly a problem for Christian theology and ethical understanding" (1993:218). With regard to warfare in general, Christians may reasonably disagree among themselves, some advocating a pacifist approach, and others conceding that armed conflict is a necessary evil to ensure the long-term maintenance of peace. But with regard to the "holy war" described in Josh. 6–11, which involves the deliberate destruction of an entire population, there can surely be no room for disagreement, not least when our own time has witnessed the most horrific examples of genocide at work. While contemporary readers of Scripture may applaud its emphasis on the care of the widow and orphan, and the justice and compassion extended to the stranger and sojourner, it is likely that they will find it anomalous—to say the least—to read such passages as Josh. 6–11, which recount the Israelites engaging in a war in which defenceless civilians become victims as a result of the indiscriminate slaughter of men, women and children[35].

Thirdly, and perhaps most importantly, there can be little doubt that such texts as Josh. 6–11 have impacted negatively on the ethical beliefs and values of Jews and Christians over the centuries. The fact is that the conquest traditions have been deployed in support of barbaric behaviour and used to justify exploitation and domination in different regions of the world at different periods. Such traditions were invoked, for example, to justify the seizure by the invaders of the land of the Native Americans[36], and the expulsion of Palestinians from their land was defended on the basis of such passages as 1 Sam. 15, where Saul is instructed by God to exterminate the Amalekites[37]. As Niditch has remarked,

---

Renard: "I don't know if God exists, but it would be better for His reputation if He didn't" (cited by Julian Barnes 2008:46).

[35] The point is well made by Regina M. Schwartz (1997:xi): "Where the Bible both inspired me and seemed to fail me, then, is on ethics: a moving accountability for the widow, the orphan, and the poor and commitment to liberation from oppression is joined to obliterating the Canaanites... There is concern for the well-being of a neighbor up to a point, and that point is where the neighbor is regarded as posing a threat to the identity of ancient Israel—and that point is most often the very existence of the neighbor."

[36] Niditch (1993:3–4) refers to a sermon by Cotton Mather in 1689 as an example of the use of Scripture to encourage soldiers in their war against the native inhabitants of New England. For him, the native Indians were "a treacherous and barbarous enemy" who had to be subdued, as the Israelites subdued the Amalekites in the wilderness. See, further, Bainton 1961:167–8.

[37] Rabbi Moshe Segal compared the Palestinian residents of the West Bank and Gaza to the Amalekites whom Saul was instructed by God to exterminate (1 Sam. 15), and Rabbi Israel Hess of Israel's Bar-Ilan University published an article in which he compared the Arabs to

the war-like elements of the Hebrew Bible is a "burden the tradition must guiltily bear" (1993:168), for the violence inherent in Scripture has all too often inspired violence and served as a model for the persecution, subjugation and elimination of various peoples in a wide variety of contexts for over two millennia. Of course, it is not the Bible *per se* that has proved problematic, but its religious and political repercussions, and history provides ample witness to interpretations of the Bible that have been baneful in their effects.

Some will no doubt object that to focus on the narratives contained in Josh. 6–11 is misplaced, for the so-called "conquest model" presupposed in these chapters is now widely regarded as a literary fiction which was ideologically motivated[38]. In all probability, no such widespread annihilation of the Canaanites took place at the time of Joshua, and there was no mass genocide committed by the Israelites during this period. "Holy war" was simply a theoretical dogma and was never actually carried out in practice; indeed, the Hebrew Bible itself testifies that, far from being annihilated *en masse*, the Canaanites remained in the land to mix with the Israelites. However, that in itself does not relieve the moral difficulty posed by the story, for, as James Barr has observed, "the problem is not whether the narratives are fact or fiction; the problem is that, whether fact or fiction, the ritual destruction is *commended*" (1993:209). Thus, it is arguable that, even if the events recorded in Josh. 6–11 are a fiction, the narrative is no less problematic from the ethical point of view, for how should we regard a people who may not have perpetrated a massacre on a large scale and yet *claimed that they did*?[39] What kind of people would want to preserve such an ideology for its own sake? And if the Jewish editors of Scripture had any qualms about the reports of the annihilation of the Canaanite population, why were such stories preserved during the selection of material?

Conclusion

In this chapter, we have sought to outline, briefly, some of the ethically problematic texts within the Hebrew Bible. While many of the laws and

---

the Amalekites, and he stated bluntly that their extermination was mandated by the Torah. Such inflammatory statements inevitably incited some Jewish militants to use genocide to resolve the "Arab problem". See Ateek 1989:84–5.

[38] Although some scholars accept the basic historicity of the conquest account as recorded in the book of Joshua, it is now generally recognized that there are serious gaps in the archaeological data supporting the conquest as depicted in these chapters, and that the available evidence does not support the execution of any such widespread and violent intrusion by the Israelites. Collins claims that "all but conservative apologists have now abandoned the historicity of the Conquest story as found in Joshua" (2005:61), and Kang warns that such texts as Josh 6–11 "should not be taken as a battle report from a war correspondent" (1989:143).

[39] Cf. Bowden 1996:149. Barr observes that if the narrative was a fiction, "it seems it was a fiction of which people approved and one which parts of the Bible sought to inculcate as a good model" (1993:210).

narratives may seem morally suspect to the contemporary reader, and while even some of the passages in the prophets and the psalms may offend modern sensibilities, it was suggested that it was primarily the graphic descriptions of violence and brutality in the Hebrew Bible that is likely to provide the greatest stumbling-block for readers in the twenty-first century. As Kaiser has observed, it is "Yahweh's involvement with war in the Old Testament that poses the key problem for modern readers" (1983:176).

Of all the passages that depict violence and bloodshed, however, the account of the conquest of Canaan as recounted in Josh. 6–11 must be reckoned among the most troublesome, for here the entire indigenous population of the land is said to have been exterminated at the express command of God. Attempts by the biblical authors themselves to find some justification for the annihilation of the Canaanites do little to alleviate the ethical problem; on the contrary, if anything, they merely serve to compound the moral difficulties.

Clearly, there is nothing to be gained from minimizing the problems presented by the ethically unpalatable passages of the Hebrew Bible, or by closing our eyes and pretending that they do not exist. The fact is that these passages *do* exist, and the problems which they cause must be faced head-on. The following chapters will chart some of the strategies used by biblical scholars, past and present, to come to terms with these ethically troublesome texts, and an attempt will be made to offer a critical evaluation of their relative strengths and weaknesses.

Chapter 2

The Evolutionary Approach

One time-honoured solution to the ethically problematic passages of the Hebrew Bible is what may be termed the "evolutionary" or "developmental" approach, which was in vogue during much of the nineteenth century and the first half of the twentieth. During this period scholarly preoccupation with the historical-critical study of the Bible gave rise to the view that biblical faith had developed in stages, and that a gradual progression could be discerned in Israel's religious and moral perception. The more primitive concepts of Israel's early period gave way, in time, to more advanced and cultured ideas as God's people gradually developed in their moral perception and felt their way on matters of religious and ethical import. Israel's morality was seen as historically conditioned, and the Hebrew Bible was interpreted as bearing witness to a gradual refining and modification of the people's ethical understanding[1].

This development was frequently depicted in terms of a process of "education"[2]. Just as a child advanced in knowledge and discernment on the way to adulthood, so human beings progressed under divine guidance as they attained ever-higher levels of ethical and religious insight. God was likened to a skilful teacher who revealed his moral demands to his people only to the extent that they were able and ready to receive them[3]. The divine revelation was given "in many and various ways" (Heb. 1:1) as the exigencies of each age

---

[1] Two prominent exponents of this view during the nineteenth century were Thomas Arnold (1844) and F.D. Maurice (1855). For a discussion of these two writers and others who shared a similar view, see Rogerson 1984:188–96, and for a more detailed exposition of Maurice's contribution in particular, see Rogerson 1995:16–54. The idea that there were stages in the development of the divine revelation in the Bible was, in fact, mooted in the previous century in Johann Philipp Gabler's inaugural address at the University of Altdorf in 1787 (for a translation of the address and commentary, see Sandys-Wunsch and Eldredge 1980:133–58, esp. 153).

[2] In 1780, G.E. Lessing published his celebrated book on the "education of the human race", and F.D. Maurice saw the account of the fall in Gen. 3 as setting in motion a process of the divine education of man, "a means by which God will teach him more fully what he is, what he is not, what he was meant to be, and what he was not meant to be" (1855:61). Frederick Temple's essay, suggestively entitled, "The Education of the World" (1861:1–49), sought to emphasize the educative value of God's punishment of the Israelites for their acts of flagrant disobedience (cf., further, Rogerson 1984:209–12).

[3] Arnold expressed his conviction that "the revelations of God to man were gradual and adapted to his state at the several periods when they were successively made" (1844:328; cited in Rogerson 1982:76; 1984:191). The words of Chrysostom, to the effect that God "accommodates Himself to the weakness of men", and that he "often speaks and legislates,

demanded, and it was constantly being adapted to accommodate the stage of development of its recipients. God's revelation of himself at any given time was limited by the capacity of humans to comprehend and assimilate, for, as Frederick Temple remarked, the "whole lesson of humanity was too much to be learned by all at once" (1861:8; cf. Orr 1906:465–78). The Bible was regarded as none other than the record of the religious education of God's people, and the moral life of Israel was seen as one of constantly expanding ideals.

Since the customs, beliefs and mores of Israel emerged only gradually over a period of several centuries, due allowance had to be made for the fact that there were constant changes in Israel's ethical ideas and moral behaviour. The ethical apprehension of the people in the period of the Judges, for example, was bound to be inferior to that which existed at the time of the great prophets, just as the moral perception that existed at the time of the prophets was inevitably inferior to that which pertained at the time of Jesus. It was a gross oversimplification to suppose that all parts of Scripture could be regarded as equally true and valid simply because they were all the product of God's revealed will; rather, each injunction had to be evaluated and assessed in relation to its place in the development of biblical revelation as a whole. Elements in Israel's faith which were considered mistaken or offensive had to be considered in relation to the process of which they formed a part and not as isolated factors to be judged in and for themselves. Viewed in this light, the offensive passages of the Hebrew Bible did not prove quite such a stumbling-block for the Christian believer, for any dubious ethical pronouncements which it might contain simply reflected the misconceptions of the age, and were by no means to be considered as injunctions which were still morally binding. As Alan Richardson observed, the notion that biblical ideas were susceptible to historical development meant that "it was no longer necessary to believe that the divine command to Saul to slaughter the women and children of the Amalekites was as adequately revelatory of the character and purpose of God as the love-commandment of the Sermon on the Mount"[4].

Furthermore, adherents of the evolutionary approach insisted that the moral teaching of the Hebrew Bible must be viewed in terms of its eventual outcome in the teaching of Jesus[5]. The biblical text bore witness to a gradual refining and modification of peoples' ethical understanding, and it was only right that

---

not according to His own power but according to our capacity for hearing" (*Hom. on Ps. xcv*) are quoted with approval by Kirkpatrick (1908:9–10).

[4] Richardson 1963:302. A similar point was made by G. E. Wright, who argued that we cannot "expect to find the theology of Paul in the Books of Kings or that of Second Isaiah in the Song of Deborah" (1950:10).

[5] Although C.H. Dodd was generally critical of some aspects of the evolutionary approach to Israel's religion and ethics, he insisted that "the final product is definitely higher, richer, truer than the beginning" (1938:255), and that the Bible witnessed to "a progressive development of religion" (257) which led to a climax in the teaching of Jesus in the New Testament.

the biblical tradition be judged on the basis of the point at which it eventually reached, not the point at which it originally started. This argument was made very forcefully in the nineteenth century by J.B. Mozley, who contended that progressive revelation "must be judged by its end and not by its beginning" and that, in evaluating the morality of a progressive dispensation, "the test is not the commencement but the result"[6]. Of course, the consummation of the entire process was to be found in the New Testament, and this meant, in effect, that only those ethical pronouncements in the Hebrew Bible that were consonant with the teaching of Jesus could truly be regarded as normative; all else represented outgrown stages in human religious development and could therefore be quietly discarded with a clear conscience.

The Rise of the Evolutionary Approach

Perhaps the scholar whose work is most closely associated with the developmental approach to Israel's history and religion is Julius Wellhausen. In his famous *Prolegomena to the History of Israel* (1885)[7], Wellhausen sought to restore the documents of the Hebrew Bible to something approximating their proper chronological sequence, and he believed that once this task had been accomplished it would be possible to trace a development in Israel's religious and moral ideas. The acceptance of the Grafian hypothesis proved significant in this regard, for the source of the Pentateuch which had hitherto been recognized as the oldest came to be regarded as the most recent, and this naturally engendered a drastic change in the picture of the whole development of Israel's religious history[8]. Wellhausen was particularly interested in the interconnectedness of movements and events, and the task of the biblical scholar, as he saw it, was to bring the various sources into relation with each other and "seek to render them intelligible as phases of a living process, and thus to make it possible to trace a graduated development of the tradition" (1885:295). Wellhausen himself placed the Decalogue of Exod. 20 in the time of Manasseh, and regarded it as the product of the prophetic school of

---

[6] Mozley 1877:236–7. A similar observation was made by Curr, who maintained that "there can be no doubt about the familiar truth that things human must be estimated by their ends and not by their beginnings" (1951:6).

[7] For valuable discussions of various aspects of Wellhausen's *Prolegomena*, see the contributions of D.A. Knight, R. Smend, J.H. Hayes, P.D. Miller, L.H. Silbermann, and B.S. Childs in the volume of *Semeia* (25 1982) published to celebrate the centenary of the publication of Wellhausen's monumental work.

[8] Wellhausen's historical work was based on a careful analysis of the literary sources underlying the Pentateuch, whereby J, E, D and P were isolated and given relative dates. The investigation of the composition of the Pentateuch, however, was never regarded by Wellhausen as an end in itself, but was rather a means of solving the larger problem of the development of Israelite religion from the pre-exilic period to the beginnings of Judaism in post-exilic times. See Nicholson 1998:249.

thought. His insistence that the law was a late development in Israel and was ultimately dependent on the classical prophets inevitably forced a new interpretation of the way in which Israel's religious and ethical ideas developed. Wellhausen viewed the relation between Israel and Yahweh in the period of Moses as that of a natural bond which was only later replaced by a relationship based on conditions of a moral character. Indeed, it was only with the eighth-century prophets that a sense of awareness of the ethical dimensions of the relation between Yahweh and Israel began to emerge, and consequently these prophets came to be regarded as primarily ethical and moral reformers whose teaching represented the culmination of the religious development of Israel. Wellhausen's dictum that the law was, in fact, later than the prophets meant that these men could no longer be regarded as interpreters of a legal tradition originating in the time of Moses; on the contrary, they were to be regarded as great innovators and as the pioneers of ethical monotheism.

It is clear that Wellhausen's judgment of Israel's early history was predominantly a positive one, for although he recognized that the ideas which emerged at this time were somewhat primitive and naïve, this was more than compensated for by the freshness, naturalness and spontaneity which characterized the free spirit of this period (cf. Knight 1982:32). By contrast, Wellhausen was highly critical of the developments which emerged in Israel's later history, for, in his view, Second Temple Judaism was marked by a period of deterioration and degeneration, when the spontaneous religion characteristic of Israel's early epoch had been replaced by a narrow and stultifying legalism. Religion had moved from the simple to the formal, from the natural to the ceremonial, as priestly elements had entered the faith and narrowed the prophetic vision[9]. Among what Wellhausen regarded as the "unedifying features" of early Judaism was that it took "the soul out of religion", for the living God was made to give way to the law which "thrusts itself in everywhere" and which was to be obeyed simply for its own sake, a development which "rejoices neither God nor man" (1885:509). For Wellhausen, therefore, early Judaism denoted the end of religious spontaneity and was best viewed as "a mere empty chasm over which one springs from the Old Testament to the New" (1885:1). It represented a distinctly unattractive religious outlook in which the sublime ethical teaching of the classical prophets had been transformed into a system of minute regulations and restrictive devices designed solely for the avoidance of sin. As such, it advocated an insular, selfish morality "which scarcely requires for its exercise the existence of fellow-creatures" (1885:509)[10].

---

[9] In the Preface to the second section of the *Prolegomena*, entitled "History of Tradition", Wellhausen tellingly quotes Hesiod, "the half is greater than the whole", the implication being that the Hebrew Bible actually gains in stature when some of the post-exilic writings, such as the Priestly tradition and Chronicles, are omitted. Cf. Smend 1982:14.

[10] Wellhausen's view of early Judaism as "degenerate" was clearly a pejorative Christian judgment, and some scholars have argued that his starkly negative evaluation of this

In view of the enormous influence which Wellhausen exercised on subsequent biblical scholars, it is perhaps appropriate at this point to examine the assumptions which underlie his approach and to consider some of the intellectual and cultural developments that emerged during the nineteenth century which may have determined his presentation of Israel's religious history. One such development which was in vogue at the beginning of the century was that of Hegelianism. The notion of development occupied a significant role in the Hegelian system, though Hegel himself characterized it as a dialectical process by which advances in human thought were marked by a continuous movement leading from an idea (thesis) to its opposite (antithesis), the conflict being subsequently resolved by a higher union of both in the form of a "synthesis". The newly acquired insight then became another "thesis" to be superseded by another "synthesis" and so on.

Some scholars have concluded that Wellhausen's detailed description of the religious evolution of Israel (from a primitive naturalism, through henotheism, to a lofty monotheism) follows this strictly Hegelian dialectic, moving from thesis (the pre-prophetic period), to antithesis (the prophetic reaction), and finally emerging as a synthesis (in the nomistic stage)[11]. That Wellhausen was influenced by Hegel is thought to be further confirmed by his professed indebtedness to his teacher, Wilhelm Vatke, "from whom indeed I gratefully acknowledge myself to have learnt best and most"[12]. Now there is no doubt that Vatke was an ardent Hegelian[13] and, on this basis, it is sometimes assumed that Wellhausen, too, must have been influenced by the philosopher. Such "guilt by association" is clearly implied in Martin Kegel's oft-quoted remark: "Hegel begat Vatke, Vatke begat Wellhausen" (1923:10; cf. Smend:1982:14; Barton 1995:319). The fact is, however, that Wellhausen's work (unlike Vatke's) is devoid of explicitly Hegelian language and terminology, and any resemblance

---

period in Israel's history was an expression of a latent anti-Semitism. Blenkinsopp, for example, argues that Wellhausen's presentation of early Judaism "stands within a long tradition of denigration which ... made its modest contribution in due course to the "final solution" of the Jewish problem under the Third Reich" (1977:20). For a discussion of the so-called "anti-Judaism" bias in Wellhausen's work, see Silberman (1982:75–82), and for the widespread disparagement of post-exilic Judaism in nineteenth-century German scholarship in general, see Hayes and Prussner 1985:149–51.

[11] See, e.g., Albright 1964:137; 1968:1; Pedersen 1931:161–81; von Rad 1975:113.

[12] Wellhausen 1885:13. Wellhausen's effusive praise for his teacher is further confirmed by Robertson Smith, who quotes Wellhausen's judgment on Vatke's work as "the most important contribution ever made to the history of ancient Israel" (1912:602).

[13] Cf. Pedersen 1931:170–74. Vatke was one of the first exponents of Hegelian philosophy among German biblical scholars, and his work, *Die Religion des Alten Testaments nach dem kanonischen Büchern entwickelt* (1835), represented the first distinctly Hegelian interpretation of the religion of the Hebrew Bible, tracing a movement from primitive nature worship to a religion of spiritual individuality. However, his volume, though in many respects ahead of its time, was so abstrusely written, and so thoroughly imbued with forbidding Hegelian terminology, that it received only very limited attention and acclaim. See Hayes and Prussner 1985:100–103.

between the developmental schemes of the philosopher and the biblical scholar is, at best, superficial and perfunctory[14]. In fact, the influence of Hegel's philosophy waned fairly soon after his death in 1831, as philosophical trends moved in other directions, and Barton has suggested that Hegelianism was scarcely a viable intellectual option by the 1870s, and was more or less dead by the time Wellhausen was born[15].

Some scholars, rightly sceptical of the suggestion that Hegel's philosophy had an impact upon Wellhausen, have argued, instead, that he was influenced by the type of evolutionary thinking which had begun to pervade Western society following the publication in 1859 of Charles Darwin's *Origin of Species*[16]. Under Darwin's influence, scholars of the period argued that the whole sweep of human history should be interpreted in accordance with the evolutionary laws of science, and on this basis it was concluded that all cultures must have evolved gradually from a lower to a higher level of civilization. The crude, primitive, superstitious beliefs and practices of earlier epochs inevitably gave way with the passage of time to more advanced and sophisticated ways of thinking as human society continued on its upward spiral of growth and progress[17]. Indeed, it was believed that all cultures had passed through similar stages of social and religious development, as human nature progressed to ever-higher levels of achievement (Rogerson 1978:12–13), and it was regarded as perfectly justified to make cross-cultural comparisons in order to trace the developments in biblical thought[18].

---

[14] Hahn has argued forcefully that Wellhausen was uninfluenced by Hegelian principles of interpretation: "[W]hile Hegel interpreted the history of human culture in terms of progressive development, Wellhausen tended to emphasize the eternally valid nature of the natural, primitive forms of human society. Wellhausen was not a good Hegelian in his evolutionary doctrine. Whereas the Hegelian idea of development implied continuous progress, Wellhausen put a primary valuation on the initial stage in socioreligious development as the only genuinely significant stage" (1959:303). Clements concedes that while Hegelian ideas can be traced in Wellhausen's work, "they certainly did not determine his general method and approach" (1976:12)

[15] So Barton 1995:320, who refers to the detailed work of Perlitt (1965), which represents a comprehensive rebuttal of the supposed influence of Hegel on Wellhausen. R. Smend was similarly critical of the view that Wellhausen had been influenced by Hegel: "Wellhausen stood at as great a remove from Hegelian speculation as a German historian of the nineteenth century could without falling right out of context" (1982:14).

[16] Contrary to popular belief, it was not Darwin who introduced, or even popularized, the term "evolution"; indeed, the word did not even appear in the first five editions of his book *The Origin of Species*. It was only in the sixth and last edition of the volume, published in 1872, after Herbert Spencer (1862) had given the term wide currency, that the word finally found its way into Darwin's text, and even then its occurrence was comparatively rare. See Carneiro 1973:89 n. 2.

[17] Darwin himself gave some attention to the evolutionary basis of moral and social behaviour and concluded that moral laws developed because of their social utility (see Desmond and Moore 1991:262). Such was his influence that one commentator at the close of the nineteenth century claimed that the two most characteristic attitudes of the latter half of that century was "evolution and agnosticism" (cited by Nicholson 2003:5).

[18] One of the most notable attempts to provide such cross-cultural comparisons was that of

Such was the preoccupation with the idea of evolution and historical development during this period that it was inevitable that such factors should have
come to influence the way in which the Bible was interpreted. Viewed against
such trends, Wellhausen came to be regarded as an out-and-out evolutionist,
a kind of "theological Darwinian" (Barton 1995:319) who forced the biblical
sources into a mould of gradual evolution, with the Pentateuchal sources J, E,
D and P representing successive stages in the process[19]. Such a view, however,
has recently been refuted by scholars such as James Barr and John Barton, who
have argued that Wellhausen represented, if anything, the very opposite of the
evolutionary approach[20]. Far from it being the case that Wellhausen believed
in a unilinear evolution which proceeded gradually from lower to higher, with
the highest stage coming towards the end, Wellhausen argued that the fully
developed religion of Israel was found in the writings of the eighth-century
prophets, but that it degenerated with the passage of time to become the fixed,
hardened and rigidly legalistic movement characterized by the late Priestly
tradition. How such a misguided reading of Wellhausen's work came about can
only be conjectured, but Barton (1995:321–2) has suggested that it may have
been due to a confusion between the notions of "progress" and "progression":
Wellhausen undoubtedly believed that Israel's religion was characterized by
change, progression and development, and this may have led some to believe
that he shared the same assumptions as the evolutionists; the fact is, however,
that he turned the evolutionary schema on its head, and saw Israel's religion,
certainly from the exilic period onwards, as entering something of a downward
spiral and marked by regress rather than progress[21].

---

the Scottish anthropologist Sir James Frazer in his influential study, *The Golden Bough*, the
first edition of which appeared in 1890. Frazer advocated a particular scheme of cultural
development in which society was seen to move progressively through various stages, from
magic through religion to science. Frazer's theory, however, is frequently criticized for its
rather simplistic approach, and some of the anthropological assumptions underlying his
argument were somewhat outdated even in his own day. See Budd 1989:277.

[19] Delitszch, for example, considered Wellhausen's speculations about the development of
Israel's religious history to be "merely applications of Darwinism to the sphere of theology
and criticism" (quoted by the Reverend Smith 1882:368, cited by Smend 1982:14). More
recently, Brueggemann (1997:12–13) has suggested that Wellhausen's work reflected the
spirit of the age, which was strongly influenced by Darwin's evolutionary schema.

[20] Barton (1995:321) contends that Ewald's *History*, which purported to trace "the growth of
true religion, rising through all stages to perfection" (1869:5), was the kind of "History"
Wellhausen tried to *refute*. Barr maintains that any condemnation of Wellhausen for his
uncritical evolutionism is "almost grotesquely misdirected", and he contends that such
attacks are usually launched by those who have "taken little trouble to study his actual
works" (1977:147).

[21] While Barton may well be correct that the misunderstanding of Wellhausen's position
may have arisen out of a confusion of terminology, it seems more likely that the terms
which were confused were not so much "progress" and "progression", but "progress" and
"evolution". In the popular mind, progress and evolution seemed virtually synonymous,
both conjuring up a picture of things moving ever onwards and upwards and in no other
direction, whereas evolution need not, of itself, imply a gradual, continuous development

It is beyond the scope of the present chapter to seek to identify the precise nature of the influences upon Wellhausen[22]; it is sufficient here to note that Wellhausen's work to some extent reflected the intellectual climate of the previous generation of biblical scholarship. Certainly, the view frequently propounded that Wellhausen was the pathfinder of the developmental approach to the religion of Israel (cf. Wright 1950:15) needs to be reconsidered, for previous scholars had already expended considerable energy distinguishing the earlier from the later stages of tradition and tracing developments in Israel's religious and ethical thought. Thus, for example, the great Semitic grammarian and theologian Heinrich Ewald, under whom Wellhausen had studied at Göttingen, had already attempted to trace a "progressive development" in biblical thought, and had sought to determine how each concept had grown and matured until it reached its full and final form in the New Testament (1871–6), and Gustaf Oehler, whose *Theology of the Old Testament* appeared in two volumes in 1874, had similarly written in terms of the "progressive development" of Israel's faith, and had endeavoured to trace "the gradual progress by which Old Testament revelation advances to the completion of salvation in Christ" (1874:8). Furthermore, H. Schultz, whose influential two-volume work on the theology of the Hebrew Bible appeared in 1869, had already placed the biblical literature in what he regarded as its proper chronological sequence in order to provide "a history of the development of revealed religion as consummated in Christianity" (1909: I, 11). Of course, these works were dwarfed by the simplicity and elegance of Wellhausen's great synthesis, and he was undoubtedly able to pose the basic critical questions with far greater sharpness and precision; nevertheless, in advocating the view that Israel's religion *developed* (though not necessarily always in the direction presupposed by his predecessors), Wellhausen's work was, at least to some extent, reflective of the critical scholarship of his age.

Following the publication of Wellhausen's work there was no shortage of attempts to trace a developmental history of moral teaching within the canon. Volumes appeared in rapid succession which reflected a breezy optimism in the inevitability of progress, and scholars of the day oozed a certain confidence that their interpretation of biblical morality was self-evidently correct, convinced, as they were, that the "tide of history" was with them. "Progressive revelation" was regarded as the key to understanding Scripture, just as "progress" and "evolution" were the keys to understanding human history (cf.

---

in Israel's religious pilgrimage. C.S. Lewis (1967:82–93) classified as a "great myth" the notion that evolution necessarily implies progress and improvement.

[22] Barton (1995:325–8), following Perlitt (1965), suggests that the two main influences on Wellhausen were nineteenth-century German historiography, and Romanticism, compared with which Hegel and Darwin were "quite insignificant influences" (327). See, also, Blenkinsopp 1977:20. Hahn traces Wellhausen's interests back to Rosseau and Herder (1959:304–5).

Curr 1951:1–11). Although Wellhausen's work ought to have put paid to any idea of "progressive revelation" (since, in his view, regress rather than progress marked the later post-exilic period), biblical scholars continued to believe that Israel's religion was capable of being charted according to an evolutionary pattern which began with a primitive stage of natural religion and progressed to a higher form of ethical monotheism. Such a theory was regarded as fully in accord with the spirit of the age and with a firm belief in the capacity of humans to grow, develop, and mature with the passage of time. It seemed perfectly natural to assume a development in Israel's moral understanding and to presuppose a movement from simpler to more sophisticated forms of belief and practice. S.R. Driver, whose commentary on Genesis was published in 1904, reflected the typical view of his time when he commented that "progress, gradual advance from lower to higher, from the less perfect to the more perfect, is the law which is stamped upon the entire range of organic nature, as well as upon the history of the civilization and education of the human race"[23].

During the first quarter of the twentieth century, the evolutionary approach continued to command the acceptance of the majority of scholars, at least in general outline. The idea of the development of religious and ethical ideas had become firmly entrenched in the common psyche and had been absorbed into the mainstream of biblical interpretation. Indeed, so deeply rooted was the idea that Israel's religion and morality had progressed gradually from the simple and rudimentary to the more complex and sophisticated that attempts were occasionally made to arrange the chronological order of the various traditions according to the stage of moral progress in Israel's history that they were thought to reflect. The more primitive the religious teaching, the earlier was deemed to be the source. For example, the cultically oriented "ritual decalogue" of Exod. 34 (assigned by Wellhausen to the early J source) was widely regarded as older in origin than the later "ethical decalogue" of Exod. 20 (assigned to E) with its overwhelming emphasis on moral norms (cf. Wellhausen 1889:332–3). To the mind of the day, influenced as it was by the theory of evolutionary progress, such an approach to Israelite morality was regarded as so self-evident that it was rarely even questioned in scholarly circles[24].

Among scholars of this period who saw the morality of the Hebrew Bible in developmental terms, special mention may be made of the works of A.B. Davidson (1904), H.G. Mitchell (1912) and J.M.P. Smith (1923), all of whom

---

[23] Driver 1904:56. Writing a quarter of a century later, R.S. Cripps, commenting on Amos' imperfect conception of God, observed that "one of the mistakes which the Christian Church has made, issuing in damage impossible to calculate, has been to standardize as eternal and ultimate truth that which was but a stage—however lofty—in the slow process of its revelation and discovery" (1929:25).

[24] Cf. Fosdick, who claimed that the Hebrew Bible reflected twelve centuries and more of "deepening and enlarging spiritual experience and insight", and that such a view of Scripture had "become the common property of the well-informed" (1938:ix).

were firmly convinced that it was not in the nature of an historical religion to be static, and that the development of Israel's religion and ethics was one of constantly expanding ideals[25]. Davidson argued that the growth and development of moral and theological ideas in the Hebrew Bible were inseparably connected with the progress of Israel as God's people. According to him, the revelation of moral and spiritual truths "were not made sporadically, but were given in continuous connection with the national life and experience, and so the truths are interlinked with one another in the same way as the successive stages of evolution in the national history are" (1904:12). In order to trace the development of Israel's morality, it was necessary to place the biblical material in its proper historical context "so that we may correctly perceive how ideas arose and followed one another in Old Testament times" (1904:5). A similar concern to trace the progress of Israel's ethical values characterizes the volume by H.G. Mitchell, for he believed that, by rearranging the biblical books in chronological sequence and distinguishing within them the varying strata of composite writings, it would be possible to provide a "connected historical survey" of the ethical teaching of the Hebrew Bible and to determine "whether and to what extent the Hebrews made progress during the period covered by the Old Testament" (1912:11, 18). On the basis of his study, Mitchell concluded that the outstanding characteristic of the Hebrew ethic was its capacity for growth and development, and J.M.P. Smith concurred that "nothing is more noteworthy than the great progress made by the Hebrews in their thousand years of moral discipline"[26]. It was readily conceded that there were occasionally some minor setbacks in the development of Israel's moral and religious thinking, but this did not shake their basic conviction that this development could be traced in broadly evolutionary terms. Thus, for example, although it was recognized that the achievement of the great classical prophets was followed in the post-exilic period by a more ritualistic and legalistic emphasis, this was usually viewed as nothing more than a temporary aberration, since the highest levels of moral discernment in the Hebrew Bible were not reached until later times, as witnessed, for example, in the book of Job (Smith 1923:320). Of course, the climax of the entire development was seen as lying beyond the Hebrew Bible in the New Testament, for the

---

[25] The roster of leading evolutionists during this period also included such scholars as A.S. Peake (1913); Oesterley and Robinson (1930); and E. Sellin (1933).

[26] Powis Smith 1923:viii. The term "progressive revelation" is eschewed in his volume in favour of the terms "moral progress" or "ethical progress" (38, 40, 67–8, 83, 124, 257), for what was being described was not a progress in revelation *per se* but a development of religious ideas and practices. C.H. Dodd was similarly aware of the problems inherent in the concept of "progressive revelation", and he preferred to use the expression "progressive discovery", by which people "advance from the erroneous to the true" (1938:269). Other scholars, however, appear to have used the term "progressive revelation" without any qualms (North 1946:147; cf. Kaiser 1983:11). For the theological difficulty posed by the term, see Smart 1961:79–80.

teaching of Jesus far transcended anything that could be found in the Hebrew Scriptures. Indeed, so profound were the ethical injunctions contained in the Gospels that they were regarded as the norm against which everything else in the Bible could be measured[27].

The evolutionary approach to Israel's ethics may be said to have received its classic formulation in H.E. Fosdick's popular and lucidly written volume, *A Guide to Understanding the Bible*, significantly sub-titled *The Development of Ideas within the Old and New Testaments* (1938). The six "ideas" which engaged Fosdick's attention (God, Man, Right and Wrong, Suffering, Fellowship with God, and Immortality) were traced in their progress through the Bible with the aim of providing "a genetic survey of developing Biblical thought" (1938:xii). Fosdick contrasted what he regarded as the primitive ideas and practices evident in the early traditions of the Bible with the more developed ideas found in later texts, and he argued that the latter presupposed a much higher level of ethics and a much more advanced conception of God. Such a view merely reaffirmed the conclusions he had reached in an earlier volume in which he had argued that "every idea in the Bible started from primitive and childlike origins and, with however many setbacks and delays, grew in scope and height toward the culmination in Christ's Gospel"; as such, the Hebrew Bible should be regarded as "the record of an amazing spiritual development" (1924:11–12).

The Ethically Problematic Passages of Scripture

For many biblical exegetes in the nineteenth and early twentieth century, the evolutionary approach afforded a plausible and satisfying solution to the problem posed by the ethically troublesome passages of Scripture, for it provided a framework within which its primitive elements could be seen in their proper perspective. In effect, the method served the same purpose for nineteenth- and early twentieth-century scholarship as the allegorical method had served for the early and medieval church: it explained away ethical injunctions and practices that no longer commended themselves to more enlightened sensibilities. The method was a way of preserving the best of the ethical teaching of the Hebrew Bible without having to dismiss it wholesale, as Marcion and his followers had done, and it relieved people of

[27] Cf. Kennett 1925:385–6; Bewer 1930:16–21. Many scholars quite consciously regarded the spirit of Jesus' teaching as a kind of benchmark by which to judge everything else in Scripture, so that "whatever is in harmony with that spirit is true, whatever cannot stand this test must go" (Bewer 1930:19). Sometimes, of course, such judgments were made entirely subconsciously, as was observed by Kirkpatrick, who claimed that, if there were jarring notes in the Psalms, "silently we transform or accommodate them to the standard of the Gospel" (1908:20).

the embarrassment caused by the presence in Scripture of passages which not only seemed to offer little by way of edification and guidance but which often appeared to be positively offensive and immoral. Moreover, the strategy was based on a principle that seemed perfectly sound and irrefutable, namely, that ideas of morality in every culture were subject to the corrections of time, and the same, *mutatis mutandis*, must have been true of the culture of ancient Israel. The ethically unpalatable parts of Scripture could thus be explained away as the product of Israel's primitive mentality, and as reflecting an early stage in the nation's religious development.

Among biblical scholars who applied the evolutionary approach to the ethically problematic passages of Scripture, special mention may be made of W.S. Bruce, who devoted an entire chapter of his volume on the ethics of the Hebrew Bible to the moral difficulties inherent in the biblical text. Bruce recognized that such difficulties had "brought perplexity to many a tender Christian conscience" (1909:5), but he believed that they could be satisfactorily resolved once it was acknowledged that the people of Israel had undergone "a long curriculum of education" and that their moral training "began at the very lowest stage" (6). It was not part of God's providential purpose to raise humankind all at once to its highest stage of moral perfection; on the contrary, as a patient and judicious teacher, he would only impart knowledge that was appropriate to the educational progress of his pupils. "The course of training was long", he wrote, "but it was steadily onward and upward; and rudimentary precepts were laid aside when the principles that underlay them had been clearly evolved" (275). The dubious laws and barbaric customs which characterized Israel's early period were "*but moments in the disciplinary process*" (276; his italics); they were mere scaffolding, temporarily useful, but requiring to be laid aside when the structure was complete. Of course, that structure was only finally completed with the coming of Jesus, and for that reason the focus of attention should not be on the "imperfection of the rudimentary stages" (277), but on the perfect revelation of God's will as reflected in the Gospels.

For Bruce, the notion of the gradual training of humankind was reason enough to account for the more unpalatable aspects of the Hebrew Bible, for laws and customs which were later to be regarded as immoral were constantly being adjusted and adapted to accommodate the particular stage of Israel's moral progress. Thus polygamy, for example, though seemingly permitted in some passages of the Hebrew Bible (cf. Gen. 29:21–30; Judg. 8:30; 1 Kgs 11:3), was a phenomenon that characterized the early period of Israel's history; as the nation advanced in her ethical perception, the custom gradually fell into desuetude and was later replaced by the more acceptable practice of monogamy. Similarly, such practices as human sacrifice, divination and sorcery belonged, for the most part, to Israel's early period and were later prohibited (cf. Deut. 18:10–11) as a more enlightened and sophisticated outlook began to replace the twin evils of ignorance and superstition. The laws concerning

slavery in the Hebrew Bible evinced a movement towards greater moral sensi-
tivity[28], and the barbaric practice of blood vengeance which existed in early
Israel (cf. Deut. 19:4–13) was abrogated in later times[29]. The evolutionary
strategy even managed to account for some of the more dubious aspects of
God's character by claiming that the early depiction of Yahweh as a cruel,
capricious deity gave way, with the passage of time, to one that emphasized the
moral consistency of his nature. Thus, the ethically problematic passages of
Scripture were to be seen in the context of the divine education of the chosen
people, and once we "admit that the Revelation of God is progressive, and that
as a result Israel's education is progressive...such difficulties disappear" (276).

Of course, Bruce did not argue that the primitive ideas of the Hebrew Bible
should be rejected or dismissed out of hand; he merely pleaded that such ideas
should be acknowledged for what they were: necessary stages on the route to
a deeper and more profound understanding of human ethical obligation. If
biblical teaching was to be taken seriously as a source of moral guidance, due
allowance had to be made for the fact that its moral norms evolved gradually
over a period of time, and it was only reasonable and logical that its ethical
values be judged accordingly.

Criticisms of the Evolutionary Approach

A significant backlash against the evolutionary approach was marked by the
publication in 1933 of Walther Eichrodt's magisterial two-volume *Theology of the
Old Testament*[30], which appeared to be a conscious repudiation of the developmental historical perspective espoused by earlier scholars. In the Preface to the
first edition of his work, Eichrodt made little effort to disguise the polemical
nature of his undertaking, criticizing previous attempts to articulate such a
"Theology" for their inability to free themselves from "the structure–patterns
of developmental theories" (I 12). Instead of viewing Israel's religious and
ethical ideas in some kind of chronological sequence, Eichrodt favoured a
systematic ordering of the material which emphasized the inter-relationship

---

[28] In the older Book of the Covenant (Exod. 20:22–23:33), the time limit set for servitude
pertains only to the male slave (Exod. 21:2), but the later injunction of Deut. 15:12 extends
the rule to include female slaves; and while in the earlier legislation of Exod. 21:2–11 there
is no mention of any obligation to provide gifts for the freed slave, such benevolence is
commended in the later provision of Deut. 15:14. See, further, Rogerson 2004:19.

[29] In early Israel, murder was regarded as a private matter to be settled between the families
of the two parties concerned, and the murderer would be handed over to the "avenger of
blood" (usually one of the relatives of the victim), who had the right—and, indeed, the
duty—to take his life. Later, such family feuds were no longer entertained, and laws such
as those in Num. 35:9–34 were designed to control personal vendettas by ensuring that
public justice arbitrate between the slayer and the "avenger of blood". See, further, Davies
1995:359–68.

[30] The two volumes appeared belatedly in English translation in 1961 and 1967.

of its component elements. He regarded the "covenant" as the integrating principle for his synthetic approach, and claimed that this concept might usefully illuminate "the structural unity and the unchanging basic tendency of the message of the OT" (I 13). It was quite in keeping with this view that Eichrodt, in a review of Fosdick's *A Guide to Understanding the Bible*, criticized the author's "evolutionary historicism", and claimed that the volume marked a "period of biblical scholarship which is now drawing to an end", and represented "the obituary of a whole scholarly approach and method of investigation" (1946:205).

But despite Eichrodt's powerful criticism of the evolutionary schema and his insistence that "developmental analysis must be replaced by systematic synthesis" (I 28), it is clear that he failed to free himself completely from the shackles of the developmental approach. His view that the religion of Israel exhibited "a constant basic tendency and character" (I 11) is frequently undermined in the course of his two-volume work by constant references to the progress and development of Israelite religious and ethical viewpoints, and despite his strenuous efforts to distance himself from the advocates of the evolutionary theory, he betrays a subconscious sympathy with their general approach. For example, Eichrodt detected a distinct refinement of moral judgment in the so-called Elohist source in the Pentateuch, as witnessed by this tradition's omission of references to gross sexual immorality, its sterner condemnation of lying and stealing, and its more sophisticated view of the value of the female (II 325). The later Priestly writers similarly evinced a higher sense of moral propriety by ensuring that, in their version of the patriarchal stories, everything that might be regarded as unacceptable or offensive had been "omitted or adjusted" (II 336–37). The problem with the earlier popular morality encountered in the Hebrew Bible was that it left everything to the free discretion of the individual, and "refused to accept the progressive influence of the divine revelation" (II 322–23). The early notion of the "fear of God" gave way in the classical prophets to an emphasis on the love and compassion of God, as witnessed especially by Hosea and Jeremiah (II 290–301). For Eichrodt, the external trappings of the earlier period were gradually replaced by an emphasis on a deeper, internalized faith as the people of Israel struggled "for the profounder comprehension of the ethical norms" (II 322). According to Eichrodt, later Israel exhibited *"a refining and deepening of ethical understanding"* (II 336; his italics), and in the post-exilic community one finds a comprehensive *"repair of the deficiencies of early Israelite morality"* (II 338; his italics). Indeed, Eichrodt concluded that behind the historical development of the Hebrew Bible there was, throughout, a powerful and purposive movement, and while Israel's religion may, at times, appear to be stale and static, there was always another forward drive "reaching out to a higher form of life and making everything that has gone before seem inadequate and incomplete" (I 26)[31]. Thus, while ostensibly appearing to repudiate the evolutionary approach, Eichrodt was unable to divest himself completely of the notion of the progressive influence of divine revelation[32].

A much-needed refinement of the evolutionary schema was proposed by W.F. Albright in his seminal volume, *From the Stone Age to Christianity*, published in 1940. Albright did not, as Brueggemann has suggested (1997:26, 48), seek to resist the evolutionary understanding of Israel's history; on the contrary, his approach was decidedly developmental in outlook and, as James Barr has observed, even the title of his volume smacks of an evolutionary approach[33]. Indeed, Albright argued that it was no longer possible to construct a philosophy of history without assuming some kind of evolutionary schema, "whether it be the naturalistic progressivism of eighteenth-century rationalists, the metaphysical unfolding of Spirit which we find in Hegel, or nineteenth-century biological evolution" (1940:49). It is clear that what Albright objected to was not the idea of evolution *per se*, but an exaggerated emphasis on the evolutionary principle which presupposed that there was a smooth, unilinear development in Israel's thought, and that its entire moral and religious ideas could be neatly categorized according to a gradually ascending scale of values[34]. The problem with such a system, as Albright saw it, was that all social and religious phenomena were forced to fit a Procrustean bed: if a particular religious idea was deemed to be advanced and sophisticated, it was automatically assigned to a later stage in Israel's development, regardless of any extrinsic evidence; conversely, if it was deemed to be crude and primitive, it was pushed back into an earlier period. By adopting such an evolutionary schema, the history of Israel's moral progress was reconstructed to suit *a priori* hypotheses concerning the direction of development, and any suggestion of a higher level of ethical thought in earlier sources (or primitive concepts in later sources)

---

[31] Significantly, Eichrodt believed that this movement did not come to rest "until the manifestation of Christ, in whom the noblest powers of the OT find their fulfilment" (I 26).

[32] In this regard, Barr has rightly observed that the polemic of the so-called "anti-evolutionists" was rife with contradictions and was generally ill-thought out and confused (1999:94). The ambiguity inherent in Eichrodt's own approach is clearly illustrated by the radically different assessments of his work offered by Walter Brueggemann and Brevard Childs: while the former contends that Eichrodt's exposition "broke decisively with rationalistic developmentalism" (1997:31), the latter argues that Eichrodt represented a later modification, albeit more sophisticated, of the type of approach adopted by H.G. Mitchell and J.M.P. Smith (1992:674).

[33] Barr 1999:88. That Albright thought in "developmental" terms is abundantly evident by his remark that fifth-century B.C.E. Israel had "reached the summit of its spiritual evolution", while the fourth century B.C.E. "marks a major interruption in the continuity of Jewish evolution" (1940:256, 265). Elsewhere, Albright claimed unashamedly that "I am an evolutionist, but only in an organismic, not in a mechanical or amelioristic sense" (1964:141).

[34] Albright claimed that his own treatment of Israel's religious and moral ideas presupposed "the ascending curve of human evolution, a curve which now rises, now falls, now moves in cycles, and now oscillates, but which has always *hitherto* recovered itself and continued to ascend" (1940:309–10).

had somehow to be explained away or regarded as a later interpolation. The fact was, however, that all such simple evolutionary formulae were misleading, for, as G.E. Wright observed, "many phenomena are at their finest degree of development when first encountered" (1969:84). That there were changes in Israel's religious and moral outlook over the centuries was readily conceded; the point was, however, that the movement was not always in one direction, pointing towards ever higher ideals. Religious phenomena were too complex in origin and too fluid in nature to allow for such a simple and straightforward pattern of development.

Yet, although Albright accepted, in principle, that the Hebrew Bible could be viewed as one long continuum of tradition which inevitably reflected a growth and development in religious ideas and moral outlook, he believed that the extent of such development was, in fact, very limited, and that the changes observed between each period of Israel's history were relatively minor and insignificant in character. Thus Albright was able to make the controversial claim that "Mosaism...did not change in fundamentals from the time of Moses until the time of Christ"[35]. The reason for this lay in Albright's belief that practically everything that was important for Israel's faith was already present, *in nuce*, at the time of Moses, and so there was little scope for any substantive development in subsequent centuries. The concept of monotheism, for example, could be traced back directly to Moses, and thus Wellhausen's thesis that the religion of Israel unfolded gradually from primitive naturalism to a lofty ethical monotheism was regarded as misconceived and completely without foundation[36].

While there is much of value in Albright's trenchant critique, it should be noted that by no means all the so-called "evolutionists" advocated a smooth, uniform development in Israel's religious and ethical values. Many—like Wellhausen himself—recognized that there was an element of regress as well as progress in Israel's faith, and they openly acknowledged that the Hebrew Bible did not always represent what Northrop Frye called "a vision of upward metamorphosis" (1982:76). Even Fosdick, who was convinced that a "coherent development" (1938:ix) in moral ideas could be traced within the Hebrew Bible, was aware of what he called the "chronological fallacy", which assumed

---

[35] Albright 1940:309. Although Albright's statement was much criticized at the time, he repeated it almost verbatim in his volume *History, Archaeology and Christian Humanism*, published more than twenty years later (1964:57). Indeed, in the later volume he expressed his view even more vehemently, adding that "only the most extreme criticism can see any appreciable difference between the God of Moses in JE and the God of Jeremiah, or between the God of Elijah and the God of Deutero-Isaiah" (1964:154).

[36] Albright claimed that "Moses was as much a monotheist as was Hillel" (1940:309). Albright's pupil, G.E. Wright, similarly rejected the notion that Israel's religion evolved from animism through polytheism to henotheism and monotheism. According to Wright, the faith of Israel, even in its earliest and most basic form, was so utterly different from that of contemporary polytheisms that it was not possible to explain it fully in evolutionary, developmental terms (1950:7; 1952:20–21).

that later in time always meant superior in quality; on the contrary, he admitted that there were occasional retrogressions in biblical thought which served as a constant reminder that "ethical insight cannot be graded on the basis of the calendar" (1938:xiii).

The more serious indictment of the evolutionary approach, rather, was that it tended to disparage—at least by implication—much of the ethical values enshrined in the Hebrew Bible. By making the Christian gospel the yardstick by which all else was to be judged, and accepting only the ethical insights which comported fully with those of the New Testament, adherents of this strategy, in effect, made the injunctions of the Hebrew Bible appear outmoded and irrelevant. After all, what point was there in tracing Israel's blundering, faltering steps when one's time could more profitably be spent contemplating the divine revelation in its purest and most perfect form in the teaching of Jesus? Of course, there was no suggestion that the Hebrew Bible should be completely abandoned but, as far as its *ethical* teaching was concerned, it was viewed merely as a prelude to the gospel, and consequently as a source of secondary importance[37].

By thus relativizing the Hebrew Bible, adherents of the evolutionary approach were not, as is sometimes suggested, exhibiting Marcionite tendencies[38], for there was no overt rejection of its contents or even a *conscious* attempt to devalue its teaching. Their attitude appears to have been one of apathy, rather than antipathy, towards the Hebrew Bible. There was no desire to renounce or discard it; it was merely quietly ignored and viewed with a studied indifference. It represented a preliminary stage in Israel's ethical development which had now been surpassed and therefore could no longer be regarded as normative for the Christian believer.

Before concluding the present chapter, it may be salutary to consider how the evolutionary strategy has been applied to the "holy war" traditions of the Hebrew Bible, for such an examination well illustrates both the strengths and weaknesses of this particular approach to the ethics of the Hebrew Bible.

The Evolutionary Approach and the "Holy War" Traditions

The evolutionary approach was regarded as a particularly useful strategy to explain, if not to excuse, the kind of atrocities perpetrated by the Israelites against their enemies in the book of Joshua[39]. It was emphasized that the

[37] Cf. J.D. Smart, who notes that "the theory of progressive revelation has left in many minds the impression that once we have reached the Christian level of revelation the earlier stages are no longer of more than an antiquarian interest" (1961:80).
[38] Cf. Wright 1952:16–18. Bright suggests that there was a distinctly Marcionite element in this approach, although it was "not consciously recognized or explicitly admitted" (1967:100).
[39] Cf. North 1946:147–8. Even more recent scholars have appreciated the value of the

accounts of such violence and brutality are found primarily in the earlier traditions contained in the Hebrew Bible; as the centuries advanced, a more humane and pragmatic attitude to war began to emerge[40]. Indicative of this development was the fact that some of the classical prophets were prepared to condemn the atrocities associated with war (cf. Am. 1:3–2:3), and by the time of Deuteronomy various limitations were imposed upon the practice of warfare, so that excessive killing and wanton destruction could be avoided. The concept of the "ban" was considerably modified with the passage of time: cattle and booty were exempt (Deut. 2:34–35; 3:6–7), as were women and children (Deut. 20:12–14; Num. 31:7–12), and it was possible for prisoners of war to be dedicated to the service of the sanctuary (Josh. 9:23; cf. Eichrodt I 140). Enemies were permitted to surrender and thus save their lives (Deut. 20:10–11), and special rules were prescribed for female captives enabling them to be taken as wives by the Israelites (Deut. 21:10–14). By the later period of the monarchy the custom of the "ban" seems to have disappeared altogether, and Israelite kings tended to show clemency in the waging of war, and they appear to have enjoyed a reputation for being merciful and compassionate towards the enemy (cf. 1 Kgs 20:31)[41]. Of course, the development in Israel's attitude towards warfare was inevitably slow and gradual, and the pinnacle was not reached until the time of Jesus, who openly renounced all forms violence, and enjoined a more conciliatory attitude towards one's enemy (cf. Hobbs 1989:230–32). It was ultimately in the light of his pronouncements, especially as reflected in the Sermon on the Mount (Mt. 5–7), that the more primitive and brutal aspects of warfare in the Hebrew Bible were to be judged.

evolutionary approach in order to overcome the ethical problem posed by Israel's conquest of Canaan. Thus, for example, Ateek, referring particularly to God's injunction to destroy Jericho and its inhabitants (Josh. 6:17, 21), argues that it "reveals a human understanding of God's nature and purpose that was superseded or corrected by the revelation in Christ"; such passages, he continues, are "revelatory of a stage of development of human understanding of God that we must regard, in light of Christ's revelation, as inadequate and incomplete" (Ateek 1989:83). Gottwald conceded that the idea of "holy war" did Israel no credit and should be regarded as "one of the vestiges of ancient Semitic religion that remained chaff amidst the wheat of ancient Israelite faith"; consequently, such violent texts "must be frankly taught as pages from the preparatory history of Christian faith" (1964:308, 310).

[40] The evolutionary approach to warfare in the Bible has been succinctly summarized by D.N. Freedman: "The Old Testament itself, with its interminable litany of battles and bloodshed … has been seen as the archive of primitive violence, a record of man's crude and violent beginnings, which the species happily has outgrown, its finer sensibilities and pacific objectives being expressed and articulated in the words of the classical prophets and reaching a pinnacle of universal harmony in the teaching of Jesus of Nazareth" (1980a:13).

[41] Gottwald (1964:306) observes that there is little evidence that the notion of "holy war" was taken literally by any of the kings of Israel from Saul onward. Even Josiah, who was at pains to enforce the strictly cultic aspects of Deuteronomic legislation (cf. 2 Kgs 22:8–23:25), did not regard the injunctions of holy war in Deuteronomy as prescriptive, for there is no evidence of his imposing the "ban" on apostate or pagan nations. Gottwald therefore concludes that "rejection of holy war concepts was in fact the mature view of Israel's own representatives (e.g. Isaiah 2:1–4; 19:18–25)" (308).

Closer examination of the biblical texts relating to warfare, however, suggests that the evolutionary approach to the problem has only a spurious plausibility. The Deuteronomic laws, for example, do not uniformly suggest that attitudes in Israel became less brutal and more humane with the passage of time. Indeed, Rofé has convincingly argued that the more humane attitudes to war encountered in Deuteronomy (e.g. 20:10–11, 14; 21:10–14) belong to the earliest layers of tradition; the total "ban" predicated in such passages as Deut. 20:16–18, which demands the complete destruction of the enemy, is the result of the interpolation of a later editor and must be viewed as something which "nullified the tolerant and humane spirit that imbued the original series" of laws relating to conduct in warfare[42]. Furthermore, as late as the sixth century B.C.E., Jeremiah called upon God to impose the "ban" on Babylon the "plunderer", and to "utterly destroy her entire army" so that "they shall fall down slain in the land of the Chaldeans" (Jer. 51:3–4). Similarly, the book of Esther (belonging perhaps to the fifth century B.C.E.) has been viewed by some as reflecting a return to "a primitive ethic of war rich in bloodthirsty vengeance" (Niditch 1993:120; cf. Esther 8:11; 9:5–10).

Moreover, some of the narratives contained in the Hebrew Bible suggest that warfare was no less aggressive during the period of the monarchy than it was in earlier times. The account contained in 2 Kgs 10:24–25, for example, describes how Jehu, in an attempt to bring about a religious reform, slaughtered the worshippers of Baal, putting them all to the sword, ḥērem-style, with a warning to his men that whoever let anyone escape would forfeit his own life. In this regard, it is interesting to observe that Hosea's disapproval of the bloody revolution that Jehu brought about at Elisha's request (Hos. 1:4) is *earlier* than the apparently approving tone of the Deuteronomic account preserved in 2 Kgs 10. Similarly, the non-militant rending of the Zion theology in Isa. 2:2–4 (cf. Mic. 4:1–4), where swords are beaten into ploughshares, gives way in the later text of Joel 3:9–12 to a militant nationalism, where the ploughshares are beaten back into swords (cf. Brenneman 1997:111–135). This is significant, for it is the very opposite of what one might expect if the "evolutionary" principle had held sway.

The fact is that nowhere in the Bible can a *development* be discerned which envisions pacifism as the ultimate divine purpose for Israel; rather, the image of God as divine warrior extends throughout the Hebrew Bible, and even receives a new impetus in later prophetic and apocalyptic writings. A recurring image in exilic and post-exilic prophecy, for example, is that of the bloody victory banquet which would follow Israel's final defeat of her enemies. In Jer. 46:10 God makes a sacrificial feast of the slain, and in Ezek. 38–39 the beasts and birds of prey gather to drink the blood of the princes of the earth, and it is the young men killed in war who become the sacrificial feast (Ezek. 39:17–20). The

[42] Rofé 1985:37–8. Fishbane (1985:200) agrees that the more lenient ideology is the earlier.

violent aspects of God's character are also seen in such passages as Isa. 34:2–7, where he is depicted as having devoted the nations to destruction and given them over to slaughter, so that "their slain shall be cast out, and the stench of their corpses shall rise" (v.3), and in Isa. 63:3, where Yahweh is depicted as a warrior splattered in blood like a person who has been treading the wine-press. As Niditch has observed (1993:46), such passages clearly indicate that the ideology of the "ban" is not an ancient or primitive view of warfare that was later totally rejected; on the contrary, there are numerous passages which testify to its presence in comparatively late poetic texts. The Hebrew Bible contains various ideologies of war, but these cannot be traced in a simple chronological sequence from the intolerably cruel to the more compassionate and humane; rather, different—and sometimes contradictory—ideologies coexisted during various periods in Israel's history.

Nor does it follow that the New Testament regularly eschews violence by providing a benign vision of uninterrupted peace and harmony[43]. While Jesus' teaching may have been predicated on non-violence and love of enemy, it must not be forgotten that he is also depicted as one who came not to bring peace but a sword (Mt. 10:34)[44]. Moreover, extreme violence is anticipated at the end of the present age, as is clear from some of the escha-tological passages in the New Testament, which deploy language derived from battle (cf. Mk 13:7; Rev. 6:1–11; 19:11–21). Rev. 14:14–20 describes the torment of judgment that awaits the ungodly, when the one like the Son of Man appears seated on a cloud with a sickle in his hand, which he uses to strike the earth (vv.14–16). The imminent fall of Rome is heralded in gloating terms in Rev. 19, which depicts a rider on a white horse, whose robe is "dipped in blood", and from whose mouth appears a sharp sword "with which to strike down the nations" (vv.11–16)[45]. Such examples could easily be multiplied, but it is suffice here to note that the violence depicted in the New Testament is hardly less brutal than that encountered in the Hebrew Bible, and the evidence at our disposal can hardly support the view that Israel's ethics of warfare evolved in a gradually ascending scale of values.

---

[43] Among recent scholars who have questioned the pacifist credentials of the New Testament, mention may be made of Desjardins (1997) and Punt (2003), the latter of whom states that "the focus has traditionally been placed on the violence inflicted upon Jesus often to the exclusion of his contribution to it" (152).

[44] Longman and Reid (1995:91–135) have explored the use of the "divine warrior" motif in the Gospels, and they regard it as an element that has been so subtly woven into the narrative that it has not been widely recognized by biblical commentators.

[45] For the view that the book of Revelation is replete with echoes of imagery associated with divine warfare, see Longman and Reid 1995:180–92, and for a discussion of the concepts of persecution and vengeance in Revelation, see A.Y. Collins 1983:729–49.

Conclusion

Before concluding the present chapter, it may be appropriate to consider whether the evolutionary approach is one that simply belongs to a bygone age and is currently no more than an "historical curiosity" (Smart 1961:250). After all, has not the model by now outlived its usefulness and been all but abandoned by the scholarly community? Indeed, Barr has even suggested that scholars who continue to adopt this approach are in danger of leaving themselves open to ridicule: "Anyone who uses the word "evolution" in a scholarly paper has to be ready to be laughed at as behind the times, indeed as a dinosaur which has itself miraculously escaped the forces of evolution" (1999:92). Yet, Barr himself recognizes that the notion continues to exercise considerable influence among some leading biblical scholars, albeit in a modified form.

One scholar who has attempted to analyze and interpret the biblical material with the help of evolutionary categories is Gerd Theissen, whose book, *Biblical Faith: An Evolutionary Approach*, was published in 1984. Theissen is careful to avoid any suggestion of naïve optimism and progress in human development, for he is aware that the "evolutionary theory, too, has undergone evolution" (1984:xi). Nevertheless, he believes that the Darwinian concept of evolution and natural selection can usefully be applied to the Bible, not because its teaching follows an evolutionary pattern, but precisely because it turns the traditional evolutionary theory on its head, and thus illustrates what was new, radical and distinctive in biblical teaching. Whereas the evolutionary principle advocated the survival of the strong, the teaching of the classical prophets completely undermined all such systems of domination by emphasizing that God was on the side of the weak, the oppressed and the downtrodden. This "counter-tendency" to the evolutionary theory is seen most clearly in the teaching of Jesus, who completely reversed the principle of natural selection with its emphasis on the solidarity of the in-group (such as the family), and aggression towards the "outsider"; Jesus' disciples, on the contrary, were to make a radical break with their families and love the "outsider" or the "enemy". In Jesus' teaching, the first would be last and the lowly exalted, and the kingdom of God would belong to the meek and despised of the earth. Such teaching was anti-evolutionistic in its approach, for it blatantly contradicted the natural process of selection, with its emphasis on the "survival of the fittest". Jesus' concern was for the survival of the *weak*, i.e., the very ones who would have gone under according to the evolutionary schema (1984:157–60). It is not our concern here to discuss the merits of Theissen's approach, merely to indicate that the view that the evolutionary theory is an out-of-date phenomenon, eschewed by all respectable biblical scholars, is one that may need to be reconsidered.

Despite the criticisms levelled against the evolutionary approach, the fact is that evolution is a reality with which both biblical theology and biblical ethics must reckon. After all, no living culture is static, and just as there were changes and developments in Israel's social and political organization and structure, so there must have been changes and developments in Israel's theological and ethical thinking. Views and judgments propounded in any given period are always subject to the corrections of time, and it would be foolish not to admit that changes in thought, perspective and practice must have occurred during the thousand years or so of Israel's history covered by the Hebrew Bible. While Israel's moral pronouncements were changed, modified, refined and clarified with the passage of time, such changes probably occurred in zigzag fashion, with periods of ethical advance followed by periods of ethical regression. Provided we do not think in terms of a gradual, unilinear development, there is nothing unscholarly about using the term "evolution" to describe the progress in Israel's ethical thinking, and there is no reason, in principle, why the evolutionary model should not be applied to the Hebrew Bible. Indeed, the work of Gerd Theissen, discussed above, shows how a nuanced application of the evolutionary approach to the Bible can prove to be most instructive and illuminating (cf. Barton 1988:50–58).

It was recognized, however, that the evolutionary model was not without its potential drawbacks, not the least of which was the tendency of some of its adherents to downgrade the Hebrew Bible and focus only (or predomi- nantly) on the elements in it which seem consonant with the spirit of the New Testament. Unfortunately, echoes and reverberations of some of the negative aspects of the evolutionary approach are still perceptible in recent scholarly literature (cf. Barr 1971:24–40). This is manifested primarily in the way in which, in discussions of biblical ethics, the canon of the New Testament is often accorded a privileged hermeneutical function, and the Hebrew Bible is read in the light of the normative principles drawn from the teaching of Jesus. Thus, for example, J.D.G. Dunn claims that the New Testament witness to Christ serves as the "canon within the canon by which to measure and interpret the rest of the canon—the Old Testament" (1982:216, cited in Goldingay 1987:125), and R.B. Hays argues that if irreconcilable tensions exist between the moral visions of the two Testaments then, as a matter of principle, "the New Testament vision trumps the Old Testament" (1997:336). Such views of the absolutist claims of Christian theology have had the unfortunate consequence of leading some to stress the uniqueness and superiority of one religion over the other, a sentiment hardly conducive to fostering meaningful dialogue between Jews and Christians.

Chapter 3

The Cultural Relativists' Approach

Another strategy that has been deemed helpful to overcome the issue of the ethically problematic passages of the Hebrew Bible is the approach adopted by the cultural relativists[1]. According to this view, the customs, beliefs and practices of people vary enormously across cultures, and they cannot be properly understood without taking account of the social and historical context out of which they emerged. Since ethical values are part and parcel of any culture, it follows that various cultures will often adhere to widely different moral systems, and so the fact of *cultural* relativism is often taken to imply *ethical* relativism[2]. Ethical relativists claim that morality is not an absolute or universal phenomenon; rather, it is always relative to the culture and period out of which it emerges. Norms which may be valid in one culture may not be so considered in another; practices which are legally and morally permissible in one society may be regarded as illegal and immoral in another. It follows that each culture must be viewed as a self-contained entity, right in its own period and by its own standards, and there can be no absolute or objective moral norms which are binding on all peoples at all times. There is thus no independent basis or overarching standard by which the morality of another culture can be judged; indeed, to impose our own high-minded ethical principles on another society would merely be to indulge in what social anthropologists would regard as an unhealthy ethnocentrism. Instead, each culture should be judged by its own standards, and the theory of ethical relativism should instil in the individual a measure of tolerance towards all cultures and an appreciation of their rich diversity.

---

[1] Among anthropologists, two of the most notable exponents of the theory of cultural relativism are Ruth Benedict (1935) and Melville Herskovits (1972; 1973:58–77), though neither is particularly concerned with problems arising directly from the biblical material.

[2] As cultural anthropologists have observed, there is something paradoxical and almost self-destructive in the very notion of ethical relativism as a theory, for once we ask whether the theory itself is relative or absolute we are immediately faced with a conundrum: if it is deemed to be absolute then the notion of an "absolute relativism" seems to be something of a contradiction in terms; on the other hand, if it is claimed that it is only relative, then this only serves to undermine the value and credibility of the theory, making it appear rather trivial and hardly worth bothering with. See Trigg 1973:2–3.

Cultural Relativism and the Hebrew Bible

Now scholars who apply the cultural relativists' approach to the Hebrew Bible emphasize that the biblical texts evolved out of a particular historical, social and cultural situation, and must be understood in the context of the society for which they were written. The biblical writers lived in an agrarian, slave-based, patriarchal, polygamous society, and they presupposed beliefs about the physical world and social relations that we can no longer accept. They expressed their insights in terms appropriate to the times in which they were writing, and it was therefore inevitable that they should reflect the attitudes, outlooks and beliefs of the people of their age. It would thus be a gross distortion to try to wrest the moral teaching of the Hebrew Bible from its historical moorings and transport it across the centuries with the aim of applying it to a totally different cultural situation. Rather, it must be recognized that the ethical values of the Hebrew Bible are historically and culturally conditioned, and they cannot be pressed into the service of a different world-view, nor can they be 'normalized' to accommodate our own particular standards and values. The Hebrew Bible was promulgated for a particular people at a particular time in a particular place, and it would be disingenuous to attempt to absolutize its claims and permit its ancient values to masquerade as universal norms[3]. The Hebrew Bible is an ancient book, and no interpretative sleight-of-hand can make it anything else.

Once the biblical material was viewed in this light, the so-called 'ethically difficult' passages were seen to be far less troublesome and problematic. In effect, the approach adopted by the cultural relativists allowed religious believers to read and understand Israel's moral code without necessarily having to adopt it as their own. Modern readers of the Hebrew Bible were reassured that they need not be in the least perturbed by the morally dubious nature of some of its commands, for the ethical norms which it presupposes were not designed to serve as a model or pattern for the pious of subsequent ages to emulate. The principles enshrined in Scripture had a limited validity, and were ultimately binding only upon the society for which they were originally intended.

This meant that Christians and Jews were not required to accept the biblical legitimation of practices such as slavery, polygamy, and blood-revenge, merely to recognize that these were social customs which were regarded as perfectly acceptable and valid in their time. Moral systems were always being tailored to cultural needs, and in this respect the morality of the Hebrew Bible was

---

[3] This was the view taken, for example, by Karl Barth, who argued that to apply the biblical commands to people other than those to whom they were originally addressed was a methodologically misguided approach. Rather, God's command "is always an individual command for the conduct of this man, at this moment and in this situation" (*CD* iii/4:11), and so the Bible contained no universalizable ethical commands (*CD* ii/2:673–4).

no exception. The biblical writers functioned, of necessity, within the limitations imposed by their context, and it was inevitable that they should accept as
normative certain rules and customs which we might regard as grossly offensive
and objectionable. The corollary of this, of course, was that we cannot blame
the biblical authors for perceived ethical shortcomings that we ourselves would
almost certainly have exhibited had we been living in their time and place. To
condemn the biblical writers for not seeing the world as we see it would be to
violate not only their integrity but our own. Our moral judgments are determined by the cultural heritage to which we belong, and we cannot blame the
ancient Israelites for condoning slavery or blood-revenge any more than we
can blame our forefathers for believing that the world was flat.

Such an approach to the text of the Hebrew Bible has been welcomed
by—among others—some feminist biblical critics who have been concerned
with the secondary status of women as depicted in many of the biblical texts.
The offending passages, it is argued, are merely a reflection of the beliefs and
customs of people who had very different frames of reference from our own,
and who belonged to a cultural system far removed from the one which we
inhabit[4]. The so-called 'sexism' of which the biblical writers are often accused
was simply the inevitable product of the male-dominated world to which they
belonged, and the subordinate position of women that they appear to advocate
merely reflects the social and cultural conventions of the time. We may well
feel that the biblical writers have been unfair to women, but the fact is that *we*
would be unfair to *them* if we failed to see them in the context of their own
predominantly patriarchal society. The biblical statements that appear to be
demeaning to women must be read in historical terms, and should not be
regarded as permanently prescriptive for all time (cf. Davies 2003b:20–23).

Among mainstream biblical scholars, one of the leading exponents of
the cultural relativists' approach during the twentieth century was Dennis
Nineham, whose volume, *The Use and Abuse of the Bible* (1976), raised some
important questions concerning the way in which the Bible should be
understood and interpreted by contemporary communities of faith[5]. At the
beginning of the volume, Nineham expresses his conviction in the following
words:

[4] Carol Meyers, for example, contends that gender differences that might strike us as
oppressive or hierarchical may not have been so perceived in ancient Israelite society.
She argues that the exclusion of women from the priesthood may not necessarily have
been regarded as a denial of their rights or a sign of their inferior status; rather, it was
a recognition that their energies might more profitably be directed to the crucial tasks
of child-bearing and child-rearing (1988:36, 163). Meyers criticizes scholars who use
"contemporary feminist standards ... to measure the cultural patterns of an ancient society
struggling to establish its vitality under circumstances radically different from contemporary western conditions" (26).

[5] For a discussion of Nineham's views, see Barton (1979:103–109; 191–9) who, while critical
of some of Nineham's arguments, concedes that cultural relativism is "an attractive and
persuasive theory" which "had better be taken seriously" (109).

[P]eople of different periods and cultures differ very widely; in some cases so widely that accounts of the nature and relations of God, men and the world put forward in one culture may be unacceptable, as they stand, in a different culture, even though they may have expressed profound truth in their time and expressed it in a form entirely appropriate to the original situation (1976:1).

Nineham concedes that it had long been recognized that the Bible was 'involved in all the problems of cultural relativity familiar to historians and literary critics' (1976:29), but he insists that the implications of this had seldom been adequately analyzed and defined by biblical scholars. The problem for interpreters of the Bible, as he saw it, was that the beliefs, assumptions and presuppositions of the biblical authors differed considerably from those embraced by people in the twentieth century and, indeed, from those of theologians who had attempted to expound the biblical text during the greater part of Christian history. The interpretative difficulty had been exacerbated by the rapid cultural changes which, since the Enlightenment, had produced radical and revolutionary transformations in attitude and outlook in virtually every sphere of life. Such cultural shifts meant, for example, that what were once regarded as 'nature miracles' were now considered to be the results of irregularities in the natural world which had previously been unrecognized or imperfectly understood; similarly, certain illnesses, which were once regarded as the result of 'demon possession', were now recognized by the medical profession to be the result of mental and psychological abnormalities (32–3). Assumptions which were largely taken for granted by the biblical authors and regarded by them as patently self-evident were questioned by contemporary readers of Scripture, who inevitably had a very different understanding of the nature of the universe. The Hebrew Bible expressed its insights in terms appropriate to the times in which it was written, and its teaching could not be culturally updated without impugning the very essence and integrity of its message. Consequently, the values expressed in the Hebrew Bible could not simply be transposed as they stood into our modern belief-system, and the only way to do justice to the biblical authors was to understand them 'in the cultural circumstances of their own day'[6]. Nineham's volume may thus be regarded as a conscious attempt to distance the biblical world from our own[7], and to

---

[6] Nineham 1976:35. Nineham argued that the same held true in the realm of philosophy, since Plato's thought makes full sense only when understood in the cultural context of ancient Athens. It was, of course, possible to embrace Platonism today, "but only in the sense that one finds one's understanding of reality in one's *own* totality illuminated and moulded by Plato's understanding of it in *his*" (1976:102).

[7] According to Nineham, the starting-point for any interpretation of the Hebrew Bible must be the recognition that it represents "the developing religious tradition of a community which belonged to a totality or totalities other than our own" (1976:137). He argues that the same holds true of the New Testament, for attempts to determine the impact that Jesus'

highlight the limitations of our understanding of what can only be regarded as an alien culture[8]. Nineham does not argue that modern culture was completely incompatible with the Bible—that, he concedes, would be too sweeping and simplistic a statement, given the heterogeneous nature of contemporary society—but he does contend that Christians should not have to be committed to the outlook of the Bible, or let its pronouncements stand in judgment on the beliefs and values espoused by our own culture.

Clearly, Nineham's views raise important hermeneutical issues, and have significant and far-reaching implications for all who look to the Bible as a normative statement of their beliefs and practices. After all, if the ethical pronouncements of the Hebrew Bible were inextricably bound up with the cultural milieu out of which they arose, and were relative to that culture, could it afford any guidance at all to contemporary communities of faith? Nineham gently prepares his readers for the inevitable conclusion by stating in very general terms that 'it is characteristic of a period of rapid technological change such as ours that in many spheres it can no longer rely to any great extent on the practice or opinions of the past for guidance on how things are best done in the present' (1976:9)[9]. Much later in the volume, this principle is applied directly to the biblical tradition: 'we have to ask how far attitudes and teaching deriving from the biblical and early post-biblical totalities, however appropriate or profound they may have been in their settings, are capable of determining in any direct way what our beliefs and attitudes should be in our very different cultural totality' (236). This did not necessarily mean that the morality enshrined in the Bible was irrelevant for the Christian believer, but it did mean that the biblical pronouncements could not simply be transposed as they stand to a completely different culture, nor could the biblical faith be assimilated, unchanged, into contemporary belief-systems[10]. Because

---

    teaching had on his contemporaries foundered on the "failure to take seriously enough the differences between totalities" (189).

[8] Nineham maintains that "the thoughts, beliefs, words and actions of any culture are essentially related to the other elements in it and cannot be understood, let alone actively reproduced, except in the context of that culture" (1976:106).

[9] According to Nineham, even the teaching of Jesus cannot be exempt from the general principle that it is relative to the cultural context in which it occurred, for his words and actions were conditioned by the prevailing outlook and perceptions of the culture of first-century Palestine (1976:190). Liberal theologians had misrepresented Jesus' teaching about the fatherhood of God precisely because they had neglected its context in the educational and ethical world in which his teaching was delivered and meant to be understood (102).

[10] Throughout the volume, Nineham seems unduly pessimistic about the possibility of making the biblical ethic relevant for contemporary society, mainly because of the difficulties which arise in attempting to lift the Bible "out of its original totality in order to offer it, more or less neat, for assimilation by our totality" (1976:108). He clearly betrays the period in which he was writing when he continues: "an element from a past totality, or series of totalities, cannot be transplanted into another, any more than one person's heart can as yet be transplanted into someone else's body and [be] fully or permanently assimilated" (108).

much of the Bible stood in basic conflict and discontinuity with current beliefs and assumptions, 'it is no way of settling ethical problems for people in the twentieth century simply to try to behave in ways which may have seemed natural—and may indeed have been right—in the first' (229).

Paradoxically, it was only when Christians were aware of the 'pastness' of the Bible and its distance from themselves that its relevance could properly be appreciated[11]. Readers of Scripture must be challenged to think 'the thoughts of the biblical writers after them', for 'the meaning of words is always relative to the situation and experience of the person who wrote them' (207). Furthermore, they must seek to identify with the biblical authors and be aware of the hopes, fears, outlooks and presuppositions which they shared with their contemporaries, for, ultimately, their ideas could only be understood in relation to their cultural context[12]. We must enter into the minds and attitudes of past periods and accept their standards for what they were, deliberately excluding the intrusions of our own preconceptions. Once readers were helped to contextualize the text of Scripture, they would realize that they were not bound by a literal acceptance of any part of it; on the contrary, they would be led to consider how the meaning declared in the events of the Bible could best be expressed in their own culture. Of course, to enter the minds of the biblical authors and attempt to understand their belief-systems and values required an effort of imagination and an empathy with a past age, for such belief-systems and values would almost certainly appear alien to contemporary readers of Scripture, who may well feel that they were 'sailing in strange waters' (257). Nevertheless, once they had entered into full imaginative identification with this alien culture, they would discover that the Bible revealed undertones and overtones never before suspected.

Before examining the arguments of Nineham in detail, it will be convenient to consider the views of Cyril Rodd, whose volume, *Glimpses of a Strange Land* (2001), may be regarded as a more recent application of the cultural relativists' approach to the Hebrew Bible. Nineham's work receives surprisingly little attention in Rodd's volume, though he is given due credit for drawing our attention to the enormous gap that exists between the biblical world and our own (2001:203, 271). That gap grows ever wider in Rodd's own study as he

---

[11] Nineham quotes with approval the words of Lionel Trilling: "It is only if we are aware of the reality of the past as past that we can feel it as alive and present. If, for example, we try to make Shakespeare literally contemporaneous, we make him monstrous. He is contemporaneous only if we know how much a man of his own age he was; he is relevant to us only if we see his distance from us ... In the pastness of these works [viz. Wordsworth's *Immortality Ode* and *The Prelude*] lies the assurance of their validity and relevance" (Trilling 1951:186; quoted in Nineham 1976:192–3; cf. 238).

[12] There seems to be something of an inconsistency here in Nineham's argument, for while he constantly emphasizes our remoteness from the people of biblical times ("it is doubtful how far it is possible to enter fully into the mind of another age"; 1976:101), we are evidently not too remote to be able to identify imaginatively with them.

attempts to show how far removed from our modern secular society are the ideas and perceptions enshrined in the Hebrew Bible[13]. His discussion of purity and pollution (5–18), for example, or his examination of the concepts of honour and shame (19–27), are designed to highlight the 'sharp divide' that exists 'between ourselves and the ancient Israelites' (158). Similarly, the notion of divine punishment encountered in the prophets, and the ways they are reported to have obtained their messages through visionary experiences, 'should alert us to the distance that separates them from us' (295)[14]. Indeed, even to speak of 'ethics' in an abstract sense is alien to the thought of the Hebrew Bible. The text of Scripture leads us into a 'strange land' (328), and one can hardly view the biblical landscape without noticing 'how foreign the country looks' (158).

Rodd displays a distinct impatience with all scholars who fail to appreciate the distinction between the biblical world and our own[15], and he argues that the problem with current discussions of biblical ethics is that 'the gap between the biblical world and our own...has been pushed aside' (271)[16]. His impatience is rooted in his deep-seated conviction that such neglect inevitably leads to a distorted view of the ethical values of the Hebrew Bible. He maintains that our current ethical concerns are often allowed to determine not only the nature of the evidence presented but the very subjects selected for discussion. Rodd notes that volumes dealing with biblical ethics tend to focus on issues of contemporary concern, such as poverty, war, or care for the environment, issues which, although highly problematic from our point of view, were not necessarily so envisaged in the world of the biblical authors. According to Rodd, it is our awareness of poverty in the developing world that makes it a moral issue in contemporary society; it is the wars fought during the twentieth century, and the threat posed by weapons of mass destruction,

---

[13] Rodd never tires of reminding his readers of the profound differences that exist between the culture of the ancient Israelites and our own. For example, in discussing the rape of Dinah in Gen. 34, he comments that "we are within a totally different culture here" (2001:266), while Tamar's reaction to her rape in 2 Sam. 13 "shows us that the Israelite culture was not the same as our own" (266).

[14] Rodd emphasizes the foreignness of the prophets' visionary experiences to our way of thinking by commenting that "we would give no credence at all to a political speaker who declared that his criticism of some economic or social scandal came from God through a vision" (2001:296).

[15] Among the many scholars who, in Rodd's view, failed to take seriously the social and cultural differences between our world and that of ancient Israel, mention may be made of David M. Gunn, whose volume, *The Story of King David* (1978), is criticized because "he has not given sufficient place to the distance between Israelite culture and our own" (2001:290); and Katharine Dell, who is similarly rebuked for showing "little appreciation of the gap between ourselves and ancient Israelite society and culture" (233 n. 84).

[16] Part of the blame for this is attributed by Rodd to modern literary approaches to the Bible, which have tended to sever the link between history and the text, thus encouraging us to read the Hebrew Bible "as if it were written today rather than at least 2,200 years ago" (2001:271).

that makes war such a highly-charged issue in the present day; and it is current concerns about global warming that bring environmental issues to the top of our agenda (159–60). In ancient Israel, on the other hand, poverty was simply 'a misfortune not a problem' (180); war was 'a normal fact of life' (272) which was largely 'taken for granted' (205); and environmental concerns were simply not an issue (249)[17]. Scholars who, in Rodd's view, move too quickly from the Bible to the present day, and fail to rid themselves of the assumptions and interests of the modern world, are roundly rebuked. Thus, Norman Whybray's discussion of the poor in the book of Proverbs (1990) is found wanting, since he has discussed the book 'from a modern position which sees existence of the poor as a condemnation of society' (178); Robert Murray's volume, *The Cosmic Covenant* (1992), is condemned because he interprets the Hebrew Bible in ways that happen to fit in with his own environmental concerns (240–3); John Barton's attempt to discern a principle of *imitatio Dei* in the Hebrew Bible is a case of 'approaching the text with twentieth-century eyes' (66)[18]; A.E. Harvey is a 'good scholar' who has unfortunately been 'misled by modern attitudes' (196 n. 29); Gordon Wenham is criticized for implying that any of the biblical writers 'could so leap out of their own culture as to become supporters of a twentieth-century "Christian" ethic', (42)[19]; and nearly all the scholars discussed in his chapter on 'Nature' (234–49) have attempted to 'turn the Old Testament writers into late twentieth-century environmentalists' (249). By contrast, Rodd maintains that his own study manages to remain completely aloof from current

---

[17] Such statements, of course, raise the thorny issue of the extent to which the biblical text can be regarded as a reliable guide to the social and economic structure of ancient Israel. Rodd himself is clearly aware of this problem and frequently warns against overconfident claims to understand the ethos of ancient Israelite culture, claiming that "too much about ancient Israel is unknown and can never be known" (2001:160), that it is "doubtful if ancient Israelite culture can ever be recovered" (139), that it is "difficult to know what the feelings, ideas and values of a people brought up in a culture which is foreign to us will be" (286), and that it is "extremely difficult to imagine what it was like to live in such a society as that of ancient Israel" (263). Yet Rodd appears to be able to transport himself to that society with comparatively little difficulty, for his volume is replete with unwarranted assumptions and sweeping generalizations about the outlook, attitudes, conceptions, prejudices and underlying assumptions of the ancient Israelites. He presumes to know not only what would and would not have constituted a "problem" for the ancient Israelites, but that rape in ancient Israel was probably "far less common than in modern society" (269); that it never occurred to anyone in ancient Israel that animals had any rights or that there was anything morally wrong with killing them (213); and that the demand to care for the environment is not found in the Hebrew Bible because "it did not occur to anyone in ancient Israel to make such a plea" (249). Christopher Wright has roundly rebuked Rodd for making such unfounded *a priori* statements and asks, quite properly, "How does he know?" (Wright 2004:104 n.2).

[18] Rodd's chapter on *imitatio Dei* (2001:65–76) contains a sharp rebuke of the present writer, who may be added to the roll call of scholars who have imported modern ideas into the biblical text (Davies 1999:99–115). For a response to some of the criticisms levelled by Rodd, see Barton 2007:35–46.

[19] Rodd does, however, make the generous concession that once Wenham's "idealism is seen for what it is, useful insights can be derived from his study" (2001:42).

concerns, and is an attempt to examine the Hebrew Bible as it is, in its own terms, without imposing upon it his own construction of reality: 'We need to leave the Old Testament where it is, in its own world—or rather worlds, for it stretches across different periods of history and contains the ethics of many different human groups' (327).

Not surprisingly, perhaps, those who particularly elicit Rodd's scorn are feminist biblical scholars, who have devised various strategies in an attempt to 'excuse' the Hebrew Bible of its predominantly patriarchal bias[20]. Such strategies are summarily dismissed by Rodd because he believes that they result from contemporary concerns about the equality of the sexes, and merely serve to distort the biblical evidence by importing modern ideas about the role and position of women into an alien culture. In what many will regard as a deliberately provocative decision, Rodd uses the *RSV* translation throughout his volume, since it (unlike its successor, the *NRSV*) deliberately avoids the use of gender inclusive language; by reproducing the masculine forms which regularly occur in the Hebrew, English readers are thereby constantly reminded of the patriarchal nature of the culture which produced the biblical text (2001:x). The Hebrew Bible is a 'strange land', and Rodd regards the use of gender inclusive language in modern translations as merely a ploy designed to remove its 'strangeness' and make the biblical text fit more neatly into our own culture and speak more directly to readers in the twenty-first century. He argues that, instead of trying to 'modernize' the biblical text, we should recognize that Israelite culture differed greatly from our own, and that we do the Bible a gross disservice if we fail to respect those differences[21]. We should simply acknowledge that the Hebrew Bible promotes oppressive patriarchal structures, and that the biblical faith is hopelessly misogynistic, and—in a rebuke clearly aimed at feminist biblical scholars—he warns that 'it is no use to rail against the type of society that is found in the Old Testament simply because it offends our modern susceptibilities' (279). Women are perceived and valued very differently in our own egalitarian society, and 'what must not be done is to judge Israelite cultural and ethical norms by those of feminists in the modern world' (270). There is therefore little to be gained by reading the biblical text in a less sexist way, importing into it modern ideas in an attempt to make it accord with our own beliefs and values. Rather, the biblical view of women must be seen in the context of ancient Israel's predominantly patriarchal culture, and the challenge facing feminist biblical critics is to 'appreciate how the situation in ancient Israel would have looked to those living at the time' (160).

---

[20] For a discussion of the various strategies deployed by feminist biblical scholars, see Davies 2003b:17–35.

[21] Nineham clearly concurs with this when he states that "cultures *do* differ widely and it *is* very difficult for a member of one culture to understand the thought of another, let alone know how it should affect his own thought when he has understood it" (1976:17).

The Advantages of the Cultural Relativists' Approach

Now, in some respects, the strategy deployed by the cultural relativists seems eminently plausible, and it cannot be denied that it has a certain logical appeal. After all, we are people of the twenty-first century, and we cannot pretend that we still live in the first millennium B.C.E. and embrace the norms and customs of that period as though they were completely compatible with our own[22]. We instinctively accept that what is regarded as right and proper conduct varies from society to society and from one age to the next. We willingly recognize the worth of moral values to those who live by them, and concede that those values can often only be understood in the context of the culture from which they emerged. Moreover, our familiarity with the historical-critical method has made it natural to view the Hebrew Bible as an ancient book which must be studied in its appropriate cultural setting[23]. Indeed, we would probably concede that if the biblical laws and institutions were *not* considered in the light of their original context they could well be open to misinterpretation or misunderstanding[24]. The cultural relativists could thus claim that the effect of their strategy was merely to formalize what most readers of Scripture tended to do in any case, namely, to view the Hebrew Bible against its historical background, and to see its ancient thought-patterns and alien institutions as the products of a bygone age which can no longer be regarded as binding upon a more secular, pluralist society.

For these reasons, the application of cultural relativism to the Hebrew Bible will not in itself cause undue anxiety to many contemporary Christian readers of Scripture; indeed, the view that the Bible is a culturally conditioned phenomenon will seem to most to be perfectly reasonable and self-evident. Human situations change and the issues and problems of one culture will not necessarily be those of another. Most readers of the Hebrew Bible would therefore probably concede that some of the biblical laws are, indeed, relative to the culture from which they emerged, and can no longer be regarded as

---

[22] As James Barr has wryly observed, "when the modern church-goer is solemnly assured that he is in essentially the same situation as the Prophet Moses, or Nicodemus, or Cornelius, he ought to burst out laughing" (1973:47).

[23] Curiously enough, the strategy deployed by the cultural relativists is likely to appeal both to adherents of the historical-critical approach and to those who embrace a post-modern perspective, for on the one hand it recognizes the time-conditioned quality of both the form and content of Scripture and its distance from the world of modern rationality, while on the other hand it is in keeping with post-modernism, which seems to spend much of its time assailing absolute truths and questioning the notion of objective, timeless, universal values.

[24] The so-called "lex talionis" is frequently cited as a case in point. The law of an "eye for an eye" and "tooth for a tooth" (Exod. 21:23–25) may ostensibly appear as cruel and barbarous, but, viewed in the context of its time, it was probably intended not to justify retaliation but to limit the extent of the punishment that might be inflicted by a capricious judge or a vengeful relative.

binding in our own age and culture. After all, nobody today would seriously entertain the prospect of putting to death a man who indulged in homosexual activities (as demanded by such texts as Lev. 20:13), nor would they ask a woman suspected of adultery to prove her innocence by drinking a noxious potion prepared by a priest (as was the custom in ancient Israel, according to Num. 5:11–31)[25]. We fully accept that these are ancient laws and customs designed for peoples of ancient times, and know that it would be nothing short of ridiculous to take them as they stand and apply them to our contemporary society.

Moreover, we recognize that moral values necessarily yield to changed circumstances, and it is obvious that rules and regulations designed to control ancient agricultural communities are bound to be inadequate if applied to a modern post-industrial society. For example, according to the law of Exod. 22:25, it was unlawful to practise usury (i.e., the taking of interest on money lent) in ancient Israel; however, with the rise of capitalism in the West and the enormous increase of commerce and growth in industry, the practice gradually lost its moral stigma and slowly eased its way into respectability. Thus, what was repudiated in the agrarian economy of ancient Israel came to be condoned (and even recommended) in the commercial economy of the modern age.

Despite the obvious attractions of the theory of cultural relativism, however, the strategy as applied to the Hebrew Bible is not without its problems, and it will be convenient at this point to consider some of the drawbacks of this particular approach.

The Drawbacks of the Cultural Relativists' Approach

While most readers of the Hebrew Bible would probably readily concede that some of the biblical laws and practices are relative to the culture from which they emerged, and that not everything in Scripture is normative for modernity, they would surely expect the Bible to retain at least *some* relevance for modern society. For this reason, they would probably reject the view advocated by some of the diehard relativists, who claim that even the supposedly 'universal laws' of the Hebrew Bible are no more than time-conditioned, situational statements that cannot easily be applied to contemporary concerns[26].

---

[25] For a discussion of the so-called "trial by ordeal" reflected in Num. 5:11–31, see Davies 1995:48–57; Brichto 1975:55–70; Frymer-Kensky 1984:11–26.

[26] Rodd concedes that some of the ethical injunctions in the Hebrew Bible, such as the condemnation of adultery, remain valid across time and culture, but even these are regarded by him as problematic, since the Israelites were enculturated to a different kind of family structure. Whereas adultery for us is seen as disloyalty to a marriage partner by indulging in sexual relations with a third person, in the Hebrew Bible it is viewed merely as an offence against the rights of the husband over his wife (2001:328).

In this regard, Rodd's discussion of the Decalogue of Exod. 20:1–17 seems particularly pertinent, for it clearly demonstrates the logical conclusion to which a thoroughgoing relativism must lead. Rodd notes that whereas the Ten Commandments are commonly viewed as 'universal laws' designed to apply to all peoples at all times, the commandments, in their original setting, were 'directed to a narrow section of Israelite society' (2001:88). Referring to the work of David Clines (1995:26–45), he notes that the commandments, in fact, envisaged only the adult male Israelite, who was married, owned a house, was wealthy enough to own slaves, and important enough to give evidence in a lawsuit. On this basis, Rodd questions the universality of these laws and poses a provocative question: 'Is it not time to abandon the idea that in the Ten Commandments we possess a set of absolute laws which apply to all human beings in every society and in every age?' (91–2). It is clear from Rodd's discussion that, once we begin to contextualize the biblical text and recognize its time-conditioned and culture-bound quality, its applicability to the contemporary situation is immediately compromised.

A further example may be seen when Rodd turns to examine in some detail the laws governing lending at interest (Exod. 22:25; Lev. 25:35–38; Deut. 23:19–20) in the Hebrew Bible (142–57). His conclusion—hardly controversial—is that they belong 'to a particular society and culture, and cannot be fitted into an entirely different one' (157). As we have seen above, most readers of the Hebrew Bible would probably have no qualms in agreeing with such a view. But having made this statement, Rodd becomes suddenly aware of its far-reaching implications for any wider discussion of the relevance of biblical ethics: 'Does it imply that law is entirely relative to the society in which it functions? Can distinctions be made between laws which have a permanent validity in all human societies and those which are culture bound? If so, how can it be determined which fall into the class of universally relevant laws?... More broadly still, do the Old Testament laws and the Israelite ethic have any continuing force?' (157).

This failure to appreciate the abiding relevance of the biblical injunctions arises, at least in part, from the tendency of the relativists to exaggerate the difference between our own world and that of ancient Israel, and to over-emphasize the incommensurability of the two cultures[27]. Thus Rodd, for example, argues that the cultural setting of Israel's laws "was so different from anything that exists in modern society that comparisons are impossible"

---

[27] Rodd claims that "the gap between ancient Israel and the totally different society in which we live ... make it impossible to apply the ethical teaching directly to today" (2001:325 n.56; cf. Rodd 1995: 6–7). This seems an unduly pessimistic view, for, as Malina has observed, advances in sociological theory, accompanied by a judicious use of cross-culturally based models deriving from the social sciences, can provide invaluable help in our quest to comprehend texts that emanate from an ancient culture and make them relevant to our own; see Malina 1982:229–42; 1986.

(138). Nineham goes even further, declaring that 'primitive man' differed 'so much from us in his understanding of himself, his gods and his world that it is at least as misleading as it is illuminating simply to lump us both together under the category "human beings"' (1976:95). According to this approach, the problem of historical distance cannot simply be by-passed, and the sense of rupture between the two cultures is greater than the sense of continuity. We can never bridge the cultural divide that separates us from the people of biblical times, nor can we wave a magic wand and find that what Karl Barth called 'the differences between then and now' (1933:1) have somehow miraculously been erased. The cultural relativists claim that the Bible, like all literary works, is the deposit of the cultural milieu in which it was written, and that the biblical writers held assumptions which made events meaningful for them in ways which may not appear meaningful in the same way for us[28]. No matter how hard we train ourselves to become part of the audience for whom the biblical texts were written, time and distance have intervened to such an extent that we inevitably become aware of the foreignness and remoteness of the biblical world.

In words reminiscent of Nineham, Rodd tries to make a virtue out of a necessity by claiming that it is in the very 'strangeness' of the landscape of the Hebrew Bible that its appeal lies for the modern reader; its value resides in the fact that it opens our eyes to the completely different assumptions, presuppositions and aims of what for us must remain an alien culture. What it does *not* do is provide us with rules which can be applied directly to the modern world. Indeed, if the biblical ethic chimed in exactly with the dominant norms and standards of the western world, it would have nothing new to offer that could not be found elsewhere. Consequently, far from trying to make the Hebrew Bible relevant to contemporary concerns, and draw out ethical lessons for the present era, Rodd is highly critical of all who engage in what he clearly regards as a futile and self-defeating exercise[29].

For contemporary readers of Scripture, however, such an approach will seem decidedly unhelpful, suffused, as it is, with a kind of exultant negativity. It will appear to many as a counsel of despair, for it will merely have the effect of making the Bible appear outmoded, obsolete and irrelevant, having little or no bearing on issues of contemporary concern. Far from responding to the needs of our world, the Hebrew Bible comes to be regarded as a document of

---

[28] In the words of James Barr, their view was that "any work or text composed in an ancient time and an ancient culture has its meaning in that time and that culture, and in our time or culture may have a different meaning, or indeed may have no meaning at all" (1973:39).

[29] Rodd criticizes Waldemar Janzen's discussion of the Phinehas episode in Num. 25 because "it is too much an attempt to extract features which have an abiding value for ethics" (2001:284).

purely antiquarian interest, reflecting how the people of a particular period responded to the issues of the day[30].

The problem with such an approach is that no framework seems to exist by which to move from the world of ancient Israel to the contemporary world, and consequently the ethics of the Hebrew Bible remains firmly rooted in the past. Emphasis is placed on the gulf that separates the modern reader from the world of the Bible, and there is no attempt to make the transition between them[31]. But while it is true that a chasm separates us from those who wrote the biblical texts, the divide is not necessarily unbridgeable, for behind the different cultural patterns between our society and that of ancient Israel there lies a striking uniformity. The people of ancient Israel, like ourselves, lived in a multi-cultural and multi-religious society, and the two cultures are held together by certain shared beliefs and common values, such as an abhorrence of incest, disapproval of rape, opposition to oppression, respect for innocent life, and the distinction between murder and manslaughter. The continuity between the two cultures may even be seen in the way in which modern theories of "justice" have, to some extent, already been anticipated in the Hebrew Bible. Thus, the theory of "retributive justice", for example, which is commonly appealed to in order to justify calls for the death sentence in cases of murder, is already anticipated in the so-called "lex talionis" ("an eye for an eye, a tooth for a tooth, a life for a life"; Exod. 21:23–25); similarly, the theory of "compensatory justice", in which injured parties (or their families) have a monetary claim against the wrongdoer, is anticipated in the laws of Exod. 21:32–36. Such examples, which could easily be multiplied, merely serve to emphasize that there are cultural "constants" as well as cultural differences between our society and that envisaged in the Hebrew Bible, and that they do not differ significantly with regard to what are considered to be the ultimate ethical goals. The two cultures are not mutually incomprehensible entities, as the cultural relativists would have us believe, and there is sufficient analogy between the biblical world and our own to make it possible to apply the former to the latter. Scholars writing from the perspective of the developing world, for example, have found meaningful cultural connections between the values and struggles of the ancient Israelites and their own (cf. Mosala 1995:239), and

[30] Rodd, while praising T.R. Hobbs' study of warfare in the Hebrew Bible for placing Israel's military practices in the context of their time, notes that "the main conclusion which seems to be drawn is that at heart the Old Testament has little to say to today, so embedded is it in the social conditions of its time" (2001:203). Much the same, of course, could be said of Rodd's own study of the ethics of the Hebrew Bible.

[31] Many scholars have been much exercised with the problem caused by the cultural gap between the Bible and the modern world, but they have usually made suggestions as to how the gap can successfully be bridged. R. Bultmann, for example, drew a sharp distinction between the culture of the Bible with its mythological outlook, and that of the modern scientific age, and he found Heidegger's existential analysis helpful to bridge the gap (cf. 1958:45–59; 1984:1–43).

liberation theologians have demonstrated how some of the traditions reflected
in the Hebrew Bible can be applied to new situations.

Moreover, it is possible that some of the perceived differences between the
two cultures are not as striking as Rodd and Nineham would have us believe.
Rodd, for example, claims that such concepts as honour, shame, and purity
were significant for the Israelites in ways that they are not for us; but it is
arguable that the concept of shame still functions as a powerful sanction in
contemporary society, and Brueggemann has demonstrated that the purity
laws of the Torah are not without relevance for the contemporary church
(1997:193–6; cf. Cosgrove 2002:44–6). We must not, therefore, over-emphasize
the remoteness of the biblical world from our own, nor exaggerate the inability
of the modern reader to enter into the cultural ethos of the biblical authors,
for although we inhabit different worlds of moral discourse, we are, nevertheless, inheritors of the Judaeo-Christian tradition, and thus stand in some
degree of continuity with the people of biblical times (Goldingay 1990:53).

The fact that the provisions of the Hebrew Bible were addressed to a
particular situation does not mean that they cannot be used and applied to
others. Indeed, we may decide, having contemplated its message, to change
our own moral stance with regard to a particular issue, and be persuaded
that *its* ethical judgment is superior to our own. By entering into constructive
dialogue with the Hebrew Bible, we may be able to augment our own culture's
collective wisdom and morality, and bring forgotten or long-neglected insights
back into view. Certain concepts, originally at home in one culture, may find
a niche in a different one, perhaps combining with our own moral ideas in
new and unexpected ways. It is this very dialogue that is in danger of disap-
pearing with the cultural relativists' approach, for its unyielding emphasis on
the remoteness of the biblical commands has the effect of distancing the moral
requirements of the Hebrew Bible from ourselves, and the inevitable result is
that its contemporary relevance becomes an item which quietly and impercep-
tibly slips off the ethical agenda.

Cultural Relativism and the "Holy War" Traditions

At this point, it may be salutary to consider how this strategy might be applied
to such passages as those encountered in Josh. 6–11. Adherents of this
approach emphasize that the violence perpetrated by the Israelites against
the native inhabitants of Canaan must be viewed in its proper historical
perspective. Whereas such atrocities would be regarded by ourselves as "war
crimes" and "crimes against humanity", the cultural relativists insist that such
traditions should not be judged by modern standards of what constitutes
human rights. As Christopher Wright has remarked, "we must understand the
conquest within the context of ancient Near Eastern culture (and not by the

standards of the Geneva convention)" (2008:87). T.R. Hobbs, in particular, has argued that warfare in the Hebrew Bible must be examined in its historical, social and cultural context, and that such an examination must form the "prerequisite for any ethical or theological reflections which might be made on the general topic" (1989:208)[32]. Before we rush to condemn the actions perpetrated by the people of Israel as depicted in the book of Joshua, it behoves us to remember that "the personages found within the pages of the Old Testament and the writers who record their stories cannot be treated simplistically as 'people like us'" (1989:17). In his discussion of leadership qualities in warfare, Hobbs makes the following telling remark: "One of the dangers of studying the Old Testament material ... is that of reading back into the past standards of our own day and culture. It is the danger of westernization and modernization ... [W]e need to be aware of the kind of society in which these leaders functioned, and further, the values and standards which are contained within the literature of the society" (93). For the ancient Israelites, the annihilation of the Canaanites would have been viewed simply as an inescapable part of life and would not have been regarded as a moral problem, or even as a necessary evil[33]. A similar view is expressed by Rex Mason, who notes that wars in the ancient world were, by their very nature, unspeakably cruel and brutal, and that it must therefore be recognized that the kind of actions attributed to the Israelites, however reprehensible they may appear to us, were "normal in the social, political, religious and cultural context of the time" (1997:75). It would thus be "hopelessly anachronistic for us to pass moral judgments about the severe cruelty in war ... in the light of what we would want to claim as the more humane feelings of a modern, educated, liberal conscience" (1997:74).

Furthermore, it is argued that when such passages as Josh. 6–11 are placed in the context of their time and culture, they may not be quite as reprehensible as they might ostensibly appear, for the wholesale destruction of the Canaanites recounted in these chapters was not intended as a sanction for hatred, violence and vindictiveness; rather, it was part of a set ritual—referred to in the Hebrew Bible as the "ban" (Heb. *ḥērem*)—according to which the population of captured cities and even their animals and belongings had to be destroyed, since they were regarded as a kind of offering or sacrifice to God (cf. Lüdemann 1997:40; LaSor, Hubbard and Bush 1996:148). However abominable these texts may appear to us, the point is that various cultures during the first millennium B.C.E. engaged in sacrificing humans to their gods, and

---

[32] Gottwald emphasizes that we must put the belief in the "ban" "in its proper context", and, in doing so, "we may illuminate the belief and even palliate it somewhat by showing that other contemporaries, such as the Moabites, thought and did likewise" (1964:307).

[33] Hobbs objects to the title of P.C. Craigie's volume, *The Problem of War in the Old Testament* (1978), because it sees the biblical texts from *our* perspective; for the ancient Israelites, war was simply taken for granted as a fact of life and was not regarded as a "problem" as such. See Hobbs 1988:461; 1989:16–17; cf. Rodd 2001:198.

such practices were regarded as morally acceptable, often even as morally
commendable.

Such arguments, however, seem highly questionable from an ethical point of
view, for it is surely disingenuous to try to excuse the wholesale destruction of
the Canaanites by saying, in effect, "Not to worry! This was normal practice at
the time, and this is how all enemy nations were treated during the period in
question". As James Barr has rightly remarked, there "can be no moral extenu-
ation on the grounds that Israel simply fitted in with what was normal in the
environment" (1993:211). Moreover, it is questionable whether the kind of
genocide practised by the Israelites in Josh. 6–11 was, in fact, "normal" in the
ancient Near East at the time, for there is no indication that any other culture
(apart from the Moabites) placed the enemy under a "ban" and massacred
them in the way in which the Israelites are reported to have exterminated the
Canaanites (cf. Brekelmans 1959:128–45; Kang 1989:80–82). Furthermore,
although the cultural relativists abjure us to be tolerant of the ways of other
peoples in other cultures, the historical conditioning of Israel's way of waging
war should not deter us from a radical condemnation of such practices, for
there can surely be no room for divergence of opinion about the deliberate
elimination of whole populations, either at that time or in our own.

Conclusion

As we have seen, the cultural relativists try to resolve the issue of the ethically
problematic texts of the Hebrew Bible by claiming that the moral values of
ancient Israel are simply the product of the social and economic framework of
that particular culture and that particular period. Elements that may appear
to us as unacceptable or reprehensible—such as patriarchy, polygamy, slavery
or the atrocities associated with "holy war"—are merely the hallmarks of the
Bible's historical conditioning, and reflect the cultural situatedness of the
people of ancient Israel. It would clearly be wrong, therefore, to abstract the
values enshrined in the Hebrew Bible from their context in ancient Israel's
institutions and practices and try to make them relevant for ourselves in a
very different cultural situation. However binding the biblical injunctions may
have been to those to whom they were originally addressed, they cannot serve
directly as a model for contemporary communities of faith. The Hebrew Bible
should not be regarded as the deposit of timeless, universal principles; what it
contains, rather, are historically specific texts which were intended to address
some of the burning issues of the day. Failure to recognize this merely leads to
a distortion of the Hebrew Bible and encourages biblical scholars to "twist it
into shapes that it never held" (Rodd 2001:329).

But the fact that the Hebrew Bible is the product of a particular cultural
situation does not mean that it cannot be relevant and authoritative in a

decisive way for other cultures in other periods. Liberation theologians and scholars from the developing world attest to the fact that, although many of the assumptions of the biblical writers may no longer be tenable, there can be a community of understanding between their culture and our own. The text can resonate profoundly beyond its immediate context, and can open itself up to an unlimited number of readings, themselves situated in different socio-cultural conditions. "Distanciation"—the byword of the cultural relativists—need not necessarily imply alienation, since it is possible for the Hebrew Bible to transcend its historical and cultural limitations and address the concerns of the present in a meaningful and dynamic way. By exaggerating the differences between the biblical world and our own, the cultural relativists have managed to exaggerate the problem of the appropriation and application of the text to the contemporary world. In so doing, they have succeeded only in turning the Hebrew Bible into an historical relic, an antiquarian artifact, fit only to be consigned to the academic and ecclesiastical ghetto. The fact is that the ethical values of the Hebrew Bible *can* be disentangled from their cultural wrappings, so that people in the twenty-first century can still find in the biblical text a message that speaks to their particular circumstances. Because that message is one that at times disturbs and challenges, at times comforts and reassures, and at times encourages and inspires, it still has continued relevance and appeal. However remote and alien the cultural relativists conspire to make the culture of ancient Israel appear, and however much they emphasize its ancient thought-forms and archaic references, it *is* possible to reach out to what Karl Barth called "the strange new world within the Bible" (1928:28–50) and to find within it values that transcend their cultural limitations.

Another aspect of the cultural relativists' approach that must be seriously questioned is its denial of the legitimacy of cross-cultural judgments. Time and again they emphasize that the biblical writers must not be criticized disdainfully from our lofty and superior vantage-point, for in passing judgment on the naïve ideas and barbaric practices encountered in the Hebrew Bible we merely flatter ourselves that we have achieved a degree of sophistication that has enabled us to outgrow the primitive taboos of the biblical period[34]. But to criticize the ethical injunctions found in the Hebrew Bible need not imply an intellectual arrogance on our part, or a condescending attitude towards the biblical writers. Indeed, such a reading of Scripture would rapidly degenerate into an arid exercise in self-congratulation. But why should we accept that all values and principles are justified by virtue of their cultural acceptance? And while cultural relativism encourages an element of tolerance and understanding of another culture, why should we accept aspects of Israelite culture,

---

[34] Barton defends Nineham on this score, arguing that nowhere does he imply that our own ideas are superior to those of the past; Barton does concede, however, that Nineham sometimes conveys a tone of superiority (1979:104–5).

such as slavery and polygamy, which we find unacceptable? The unfortunate effect of cultural relativism is to nullify in advance any possible objection to behaviour or values which we find indefensible.

The fact is that it is all too easy, in discussing the ethically dubious passages of Scripture, to retreat into the safe haven of cultural relativism, stressing how time-bound and culturally-dependent the writings of the Hebrew Bible are. The strategy associated with the cultural relativists gives the impression of being merely a convenient way of side-stepping the problems caused by biblical commands and customs that happen to conflict with our own rational and moral judgments.

Chapter 4

Canonical Approaches

Two very different—one might say mutually exclusive—strategies have been advanced to deal with the ethically problematic texts of Scripture, both firmly based on the notion of the "canon". According to one view, usually labelled the "canon within the canon" approach, readers are invited to sift through the biblical texts in search of what they may find useful and valuable as a source of ethical guidance in their lives[1]. They are encouraged to balance the moral statements of Scripture in their own scales of ethical judgment, extracting the principles that they consider to be instructive and enlightened from those that they might regard as dubious and questionable. The material that they deem to be edifying can be retained, while that which they find objectionable can be discarded. "Use what you can" appears to be the slogan of this approach, with the implicit corollary that what turns out to be unusable or unsuitable can be jettisoned without any qualms. In effect, this strategy invites readers to form their own "canon" of texts based on the wider canon of Scripture, and by adopting this approach they are encouraged to focus upon those features of the biblical tradition that are more central and relevant to their faith.

The other strategy, which in many respects is diametrically opposed to the above, may be termed the "canonical approach". According to this view, to single out some texts, while rejecting others, is merely to distort the biblical witness and to demean its very essence. If justice is to be done to the message of the Hebrew Bible, readers must take the entire canonical evidence into consideration and eschew any attempt to privilege any particular portion of it. They must constantly bear in mind the meaning and import of the biblical message as a whole, for this will inevitably influence the way in which they will interpret individual texts. Scripture is viewed as a vast canvas in which the individual details are not as significant as the picture as a whole. Just as we cannot properly appreciate a masterpiece if we stand too close, so we cannot properly

---

[1] The phrase "canon within the canon" will be used in this chapter for convenience, though whether it is an appropriate or exact expression to refer to a particular collection of texts is a moot point. Barr claims that the expression should only properly be used to refer to groups of *books* within the canon (such as the Pentateuch or the Gospels) rather than to "groups of favourite passages, preferred because they are thought to express regulative theological conceptions" (1999:385). Ironically, however, Barr himself later in the same volume uses the expression "canon within the canon" to refer to "a set of basic passages to which one must turn again and again" (449).

interpret Scripture if we focus exclusively on particular passages. Individual incidents and isolated precepts must be measured in the context of the entire thrust of biblical revelation, for reading the Bible involves the elucidation of the whole in relation to its parts and the parts in relation to the whole. Thus the plea of those who adopt the canonical approach is quite straightforward: let us not try to elicit ethical norms from isolated texts but look, rather, at the broader picture and go by the general impression of the biblical message as a whole. Scripture establishes certain norms and values as acceptable and others as unacceptable, and whatever impression is left by individual incidents or provisions, there is a "general drift" to be discerned which makes it abundantly clear what is required and what is prohibited. Unlike the "canon within the canon" approach, therefore, this strategy does not reject the unpalatable parts of the Hebrew Bible; it merely allows us to view them in a broader perspective, and enables us to read Scripture untroubled by some of its more unsavoury aspects.

Both of the above canonically-based approaches recognize that readers are bound to find in the Hebrew Bible material that many will regard as offensive or unpalatable, but each strategy has a very different method of tackling the issue. In this chapter, an attempt will be made to analyze the strengths and weaknesses of both approaches, and to consider to what extent they have succeeded in diffusing the offence or embarrassment caused by some of the ethically problematic passages of Scripture.

The "Canon within the Canon" Approach

The "canon within the canon" approach is by no means new[2]; indeed, its roots may be traced back to the Bible itself. As is well known, Jewish tradition accorded the Torah pride of place, regarding it as more authoritative than other parts of Scripture, and in this sense the Pentateuch may be said to have formed a sort of pre-canonical "canon within the canon" (Wright 1969:179–80; Barr 1983:72). Moreover, the writers of the New Testament, in quoting from the Hebrew Scriptures, tended to focus on a select number of books, and made no attempt to appeal to a representative sample from within the Hebrew Bible as a whole[3]. Medieval theologians drew careful distinctions between the moral laws of the Hebrew Bible, which they regarded as authoritative, and

---

[2] Barr wonders whether there ever was "a time or a place where church and exegesis were governed by the one canon of scripture and no interior selection" (1999:386). G.E. Wright makes a similar point when he states that the selection of texts or themes within Scripture "appears to have been the method by which the canon has been used as such throughout the history of the western world" (1969:180).

[3] It is estimated, for example, that approximately half the explicit quotations in the New Testament come from Isaiah and the book of Psalms (Barr 1983:61; Evans 2002:186).

the ceremonial and judicial laws, which they considered to be inferior and no longer binding upon Christian believers (Aquinas *Summa* 1a2a, 98–105). In the period of the Reformation, Luther conceded that not all portions of Scripture possessed equal authority, and by emphasizing the importance of some books and relegating others to the side-lines, he effectively formed his own "canon" within the wider canon of the Bible[4]. Even today, many churches have some kind of "stepped canon" in the sense that some books are regarded as central, while others are considered to be more peripheral[5].

During the twentieth century the "canon within the canon" approach has been more influential in scholarly circles than is often realized, and it has proved a useful hermeneutical tool in the hands of both liberation theologians and feminist biblical critics.

(a) Liberation Theology

Liberation theologians in Latin America and South Africa have tended to accord the book of Exodus pride of place in their interpretation of Scripture, and it was regarded as a privileged text which was taken to reflect the essential core of the Bible's message[6]. The exodus event itself symbolized the quest for political transformation and social justice, and the story of the release from captivity of a group of slaves against formidable odds clearly had resonance for the poor and marginalized in the developing world, who felt similarly oppressed and downtrodden. They were able to empathize with the suffering of the ancient Hebrews and with their desire for freedom, and the exodus story demonstrated that, through the power of God, it was possible for the disadvantaged and persecuted to throw off the yoke of oppression and break free from established institutions in order to refashion a new life for themselves (Fierro

---

[4] In the preface to his translation of the New Testament, Luther regarded the Gospel of John, I John, Romans, Galatians, Ephesians, and I Peter as representing the noblest books of the New Testament, and he relegated James, Hebrews and Revelation to a secondary status on the grounds that they did not support the concept of "justification by faith". With regard to the Hebrew Bible, Luther singled out Genesis and the prophetic writings as especially inspired. See, further, Farrar 1886:335–7; Lønning 1972:72–115.

[5] The central Pauline letters, for example, are regarded as particularly important in Lutheran churches, whereas the Gospels are accorded a supreme position in many currents of Anglicanism (cf. Barr 1983:40–41). Käsemann argues that the canon legitimizes different denominations and teachings, and claims that every branch of the church and every theological tradition in practice operates with its own canon, that is, with its own selection of legitimate texts (1964:95–107).

[6] Thiselton observes that the story of the exodus from Egypt "becomes a recurring theme in all liberation hermeneutics" (1992:416). The Peruvian theologian Gustavo Gutiérrez was one of the first to apply the "exodus" to the oppressive political situation in Latin America (1974), and the same text was regarded as primary among theologians in black South Africa. For a survey of liberation theology as reflected in different parts of the world, see the various contributions in the volume edited by Rowland (1999).

1977:144–5). Although the exodus account was regarded by liberation theologians as one which was firmly anchored in the history of ancient Israel, its value lay in its adaptability and in its potential to transcend its original historical and ethnic setting, and to speak in a meaningful way to contemporary groups of people who suffered racial, economic or gender oppression. As such, it offered an attractive paradigm for those who were themselves engaged in a struggle with authority and facing up to the reality of persecution and death.

In addition to the exodus, some of the prophetic oracles were regarded as significant, primarily because of the prophets' uncompromising defence of the poor, and their vigorous denunciations of social injustices (cf. Isa. 1:16–17; Am. 5:10–12). The divine preference towards the poor was also evident in the ministry and teaching of Jesus, especially in his condemnation of the rich, and his insistence that the poor and oppressed would be the first to inherit the kingdom of God (cf. Lk. 6:20; cf. Mt. 19:23–24; Cone 1986:110–28). Another text which proved useful in the armoury of the liberation theologians was the book of Revelation (cf. Rowland and Corner 1990:131–55), for its portrayal of the state as oppressor, and its depiction of a society that had grown rich on the basis of exploitation (cf. Rev. 13, 17, 18), was one which clearly chimed in with the experiences of the poor in the developing world. The book offered inspiration to those who opposed an attitude of supine accommodation to the powers that be, and it provided hope and encouragement to all who looked for the fulfilment of God's righteousness in human history, and who believed that God, the liberator, would free them from the shackles of economic and social degradation (Boesak 1987:28–39).

These above-mentioned texts, among others, were regarded by liberation theologians as the hermeneutical key which opened up the core of the Bible's message. Indeed, they believed that their own experience of living among the poor and underprivileged had enabled them to glimpse interpretative insights which had largely eluded the sophisticated approach of First World exegesis. The task of theology, as they saw it, was none other than to "explicate the meaning of God's liberating activity so that those who labor under enslaving powers will see that the forces of liberation are the very activity of God" (Cone 1986:3). Of course, by focusing almost exclusively on texts which depicted the poor as the victims of injustice and exploitation, liberation theologians laid themselves open to the charge that their interpretation of the Bible was based on a "canon within a canon", for their concern was with a relatively small sample of pertinent biblical texts (cf. Rowland and Corner 1990:51, 87–8); nevertheless, they believed that such a strategy was more than justified if it served to bring hope and comfort to those engaged in the tortuous struggle against imperialism and dictatorship.

(b) Feminist Biblical Criticism

The "canon within the canon" strategy has also proved attractive for feminist biblical critics who are offended by the deprecatory attitude towards women exhibited in much of the biblical material. This approach allows them to sideline the more objectionable statements of Scripture and to highlight, instead, those which view the female role in a positive light, and which offer a welcome alternative to the predominantly patriarchal perspective[7]. Indeed, feminist biblical scholars who deploy the "canon within the canon" approach make little attempt to disguise the fact that they have their own favourite passages of Scripture. Such texts might include Prov. 31:10–31, where the woman is praised as trustworthy, skilful, generous and wise, and depicted as directing the work of her servants, educating her children, and even engaging in commercial transactions, seemingly on her own initiative; or Num. 27:1–11, where the daughters of Zelophehad petition Moses for a change in the laws regarding inheritance, and do so with such force and persuasion that the justice of their case is generally recognized; or the Song of Songs, where the voice of the female (in contrast to that of her male counterpart) is direct, articulate and enterprising, and where there is no suggestion of male domination or female subordination[8]. Among other texts that have frequently served as a kind of "inner canon" for feminist biblical critics are those which deploy female images to depict the deity (cf. Isa. 42:14)[9], and narratives which emphasize the prominent role played by women of courage, independence and initiative in a man's world[10]. The fact that such passages exist in Scripture is said to indicate

---

[7] Phyllis Trible's influential volume, *God and the Rhetoric of Sexuality* (1978), provides a good example of this method of salvaging non-patriarchal fragments from the biblical text and highlighting positive images of women as recorded in the Hebrew Bible; her study thus invites a "selective" reading of the Bible in an attempt to show that Scripture does not present a uniformly patriarchal perspective. Cf. Davies 2003b:26–9.

[8] See Trible 1978:144–65. Some feminist biblical critics have drawn attention to the fact that the military metaphors in the Song of Songs are associated not with the male, as might have been expected, but with the female, thus inverting the conventional or stereotyped biblical view of gender roles. See Meyers 1988:178–9.

[9] Cf. Trible 1973:31–34; 1978:22–23, 31–59. A significant proportion of the passages in which God is described as having female attributes is found in the book of Isaiah; cf. Sawyer 1996:198–219; Gruber 1983:351–9. On the concept of God as "mother" in Hosea, see Schüngel-Straumann 1986:119–134.

[10] Among the women usually singled out for special mention are Huldah, the prophetess, whose wise counsel was sought and heeded by the king, and whose authentication of the scroll discovered in the Temple effectively precipitated a religious reformation (2 Kgs 22:14–20); or Miriam, the prophetess, who had the temerity to rebuke Moses for his exclusive claim to receive divine revelation (Num. 12:1–2); or Deborah, the military strategist who (along with Barak) led an army into battle and delivered the Israelites from the Canaanite general, Sisera (Judg. 4:4–16; 5:1–22). The fact that such women have survived the androcentric records as individuals who achieved fame and distinction in their own right is regarded as providing a welcome corrective to the Hebrew Bible's predominantly patriarchal perspective. Cf. Davies 2003b:27–8.

that the Hebrew Bible is not devoid of a feminist perspective, and while the overwhelming patriarchal stamp of Scripture is not denied, this "inner canon" of texts is regarded as indicating that there are fundamental impulses in the biblical tradition that are representative of more inclusive ways of thinking.

The Advantages of the "Canon within the Canon" Approach

The adoption of the "canon within the canon" approach has many obvious advantages. The first, of course, is its basic simplicity, for it involves the easiest of all tasks: that of winnowing the ethically acceptable material from that which is morally unpalatable. By means of this process, the Hebrew Bible is immediately divested of all the antiquarian elements that are no longer regarded as valid, and of all the laws and customs that might be regarded by contemporary readers as abominable or abhorrent. After all, *some* line has to be drawn between that which is valid and authoritative, and that which is obsolete and outworn, and, according to adherents of this strategy, this seems as good a way as any to draw it.

In the second place, the strategy has the merit of acknowledging openly what everyone (except the most ardent purist) takes for granted, namely, that everything contained in the Bible cannot be regarded as equally binding upon the Christian[11]. Most of us, for example, would happily endorse the commands of the Decalogue concerning murder, adultery and theft (Exod. 20:13–15), but would entertain serious qualms about putting to death a particularly recalcitrant son (Deut. 21:18–21). Most would probably wholeheartedly endorse the admonitions of Lev. 19 not to pervert justice (v. 15) and to love one's neighbour as oneself (v. 18), whereas few would regard as equally binding the injunctions contained in the same chapter to refrain from wearing a garment made of two kinds of cloth (v. 19), or from trimming the edges of one's beard (v. 27). This approach recognizes, in a reassuringly honest and forthright way, that not all the admonitions of Scripture carry equal weight or have equal authority, and that we are bound to accept some of its provisions while rejecting others. Furthermore, while we may pay lip service to the *idea* that all the books of the Bible are equal, we innately feel—to paraphrase Orwell—that some books *are* more equal than others. In the Hebrew Bible, for example, the Song of Songs would hardly be regarded as on a par with the book of Isaiah, or, in the New Testament, the Gospel of John would surely be considered more important than the Epistle of Jude[12]. We accept in practice—whether consciously or

---

[11] As Barr (1983:122) has observed, Christians might be forgiven for doubting whether Methuselah actually lived to the grand old age of 969 years, but not if they failed to believe that Christ had died and risen for the forgiveness of sins.

[12] Barr makes a similar point when he states that "no one really supposes that Esther or Ecclesiastes draws the same interest or plays the same role within fundamentalist Christianity as the letters of St. Paul or the gospel of St. John" (1977:62).

not—a certain grading of the biblical material, and readily recognize that the Bible in its entirety cannot be regarded as uniformly authoritative (cf. Melugin 1988:49; Birch and Rasmussen 1989:156–8).

Moreover, from a purely practical point of view, the "canon within the canon" strategy can claim to be one which is entirely necessary, for we cannot reasonably be expected to be familiar with the entire content of the biblical teaching; the sheer quantity and variety of material which the Bible contains makes it inevitable that readers will have to be selective in their approach and prioritize certain passages over others[13]. By inviting us to regard as binding only those parts of the Bible that we find ethically acceptable, this approach permits us to adopt the biblical passages of which we approve, while allowing us to reject—with a clear conscience—passages that might conflict with our deeply ingrained sense of what is right and proper.

Finally, this strategy may justly claim at least some measure of support from within the Scriptural tradition itself. As we have seen, Jewish tradition regarded the Torah as the authoritative core of the Hebrew Bible, and the writers of the New Testament were highly selective in the choice of books from which they quoted in the Hebrew Scriptures. Indeed, the Gospel narratives suggest that Jesus himself occasionally affirmed the priority of some passages of Scripture over others[14]. Thus, Scriptural tradition itself appears to have questioned the notion of a flat, level canon that had equal authority in all its parts, and it could be argued that there is, therefore, a biblical warrant for the selective approach to the Hebrew Bible advocated by the proponents of this strategy.

Before considering the possible drawbacks of the "canon within the canon" approach, however, it will be convenient to examine briefly the way it has been deployed to deal with the "holy war" traditions in the Hebrew Bible.

The "Canon within the Canon" Approach and the "Holy War" Traditions

It perhaps goes without saying that this particular strategy has proved especially amenable to scholars who have sought to construct a theology of peace on

---

[13] Dunn maintains that Christians have always adopted this approach in their reading of Scripture: "We must observe first the historical fact that no Christian church or group has in the event treated the NT writings as uniformly canonical. Whatever the theory of canonicity, the reality is that *all Christians have operated with a canon within the canon*" (1977:374; his italics).

[14] In Mk 10:2–9, when Jesus is asked about his attitude to divorce, he appears to prioritize Gen. 1:27 and 2:24 (which imply that marriage is a life-long monogamous institution) over the law of Deut. 24:1–4 (which permits and regulates divorce; cf. O'Donovan 1976:63–4). Similarly, in Mk 2:23–28, when the question is raised concerning work on the Sabbath, Jesus responds by referring to the example of David, who committed an apparent breach of the law but was not condemned for it (1 Sam. 21:1–6), thus implying that human need must take precedence over ritual obligation. See Goldingay 1995:96–99.

the basis of the Hebrew Bible. Faced with the numerous accounts of violence and brutality in Scripture they have, of necessity, been "highly selective in their choice of material" (Hobbs 1989: 14), highlighting those passages which commend pacifism, while ignoring or devaluing those which appear to promote violence. Thus, passages such as Josh. 6–11, which describe the complete annihilation of the Canaanites at the express command of God, are conveniently shunted to one side, allowing us to focus instead on texts which contain lessons of a more salutary nature, such as the importance of beating "swords into ploughshares" and "spears into pruning hooks" (Isa. 2:4). Laws that command the Israelites to massacre the native inhabitants of the land (cf. Deut. 7:1–2) are overlooked in favour of those that demand care and respect towards the sojourner and resident alien (cf. Exod. 22:21).

Perhaps nowhere is this strategy of deliberately ignoring such ethically problematic passages better illustrated than in the liturgy of the Church[15]. The preferred option of the Roman Catholic Church for dealing with such unsavoury passages is to exercise a certain degree of restraint in their liturgical use. Thus, while Deut. 7:6–11 ("for you are a people holy to the LORD your God …") is read on the Feast of the Sacred Heart (celebrated on the Friday following the second Sunday after Pentecost), vv. 1–5 of the same chapter, which demand that the Israelites destroy the nations that inhabit the land of Canaan, are omitted. Nor are such passages as Deut. 9:1–7; 12:29–30; 20:16–18—all of which promote ethnic cleansing as an act of obedience to God—used in the liturgy (Prior 1997:273–78). With regard to the book of Joshua, the liturgical readings skip from Josh. 5:12 to Josh. 24, thus omitting the accounts of the conquest completely, and thereby ensuring that "church-going Catholics encounter virtually none of the land traditions which are offensive" (Prior 1997:275). Such careful selectivity is also evident in the Revised Common Lectionary used by the Anglican Church, which similarly skips from Josh. 5:9–12 to Josh. 24.1–2a, 14–18, thus entirely omitting the ethically troublesome account of the conquest of Canaan. Now it cannot be denied that the use of a lectionary in Christian worship has some obvious advantages, for it introduces the congregation to the diversity and richness of the canon, and ensures that its members are exposed to a wider range of canonical material than they might otherwise hear. But it also has its disadvantages, for it is arguable that the process of ruling out of court all material which might be regarded as sub-Christian is a less than honest way of dealing with the text of Scripture, for the congregation is thereby introduced to an incomplete and expurgated version of the Hebrew Bible[16]. Of

---

[15] Nineham observes that this has been a particularly favourite strategy of liturgists, who have used it to free themselves from what has sometimes been called the "curse of the canon" (1976:230).

[16] Cf. Davidson 1999:365–8. Bailey (1977:139–53) helpfully draws attention to the advantages and disadvantages of using lectionary texts in Christian worship. I am grateful to my colleague, Professor Gareth Lloyd Jones, for drawing my attention to these articles.

course, given that the Church's purpose in selecting readings from Scripture is to enlighten, deepen and stimulate faith, it is perfectly understandable that it would want to pass over Scriptural passages, such as Josh. 6–11, that might be regarded as offensive or objectionable, but such a strategy simply illustrates the embarrassment caused by the existence of passages in the Hebrew Bible that the community of faith wish were not there.

The Drawbacks of the "Canon within the Canon" Approach

While the "canon within the canon" strategy, as we have seen, has some obvious advantages, this "pick and choose" approach to the ethics of the Hebrew Bible must be viewed with considerable reserve. In the first place, it gives the impression of regarding the reading of Scripture as an exercise rather akin to visiting a restaurant, where the individual is invited to select from the menu what appears to him or her to be most appetizing; by adopting such a strategy, nobody need come from the Bible (any more than they need leave the restaurant) without finding at least something to suit their particular taste. But it is doubtful whether such an eclectic and selective approach to biblical morality can be defended, for there is something vaguely spurious about a strategy that invites us merely to ignore those passages of Scripture of which we do not approve. The clear danger of such an approach is that the ethical values that we derive from the Bible will turn out to be no more than expressions of our own personal preferences, and that the biblical passages that we embrace will be those that happen to conform to our own instinctive assumptions about what is right and proper.

Another drawback of the "canon within the canon" approach is that it inevitably produces a somewhat reductive and truncated reading of the Hebrew Bible. After all, a high degree of selectivity is required to carve out of the biblical text an ethically acceptable viewpoint, and such selectivity is bound to leave a residue of unused material larger than that chosen. Of course, adherents of this strategy would not wish to advocate the formal expurgation of any part of the Hebrew Bible—they recognize that there is too much of value even in its less edifying parts for it to be excised completely—but, on the practical level, large parts of Scripture effectively lose their place in the canon. It is this subtle demotion of biblical texts that causes the main concern among those opposed to the "canon within the canon" approach. Their objection to the strategy is not that some texts are elevated above others, for that is regarded as almost natural and inevitable, given the diverse interests and viewpoints of readers; rather, what appears unacceptable is the concomitant downgrading of certain passages to a secondary position, for this (they fear) could turn out to be the thin end of the wedge, leading eventually to the downgrading of entire books within the Hebrew Bible or even the Hebrew Bible as a whole[17].

A further weakness of this strategy is that it can so easily lead to a distortion of the biblical message. The above discussion of the approach advocated by liberation theologians illustrates how passages from the Bible can be used as "proof texts" to support pre-established positions. The passages selected by liberation theologians are clearly those that happen to be congenial to the particular viewpoint which they embrace and the particular cause which they wish to advance. As we have seen, the exodus from Egypt is regarded by them as the supreme event in the Hebrew Bible which should serve as an incentive for involvement in the contemporary task of human liberation from oppression. However, recent scholars, writing from a Palestinian perspective, have highlighted the hermeneutical problem that such a focus on the exodus entails, for the freedom of the Hebrews from Egypt was secured precisely so that they could conquer another's territory (Ateek 1989; cf. Pleins 2001:168–70). Gutiérrez refers to the oppression suffered by the Hebrews in "the land of slavery" (Exod. 13:3; 20:2) and emphasizes their repression (Exod. 1:11) and humiliation (Exod. 1: 13–14), but says nothing about the oppression and humiliation suffered by the indigenous population of Canaan at the hands of those very slaves[18]. He claims that the "liberation of Israel is a political action … and the beginning of the construction of a just and comradely society" (1974:88). But a "just and comradely society" for whom? Certainly, not for the Canaanites, who, according to the biblical tradition, were annihilated by the invading Israelites. This one-sided emphasis on the liberating agenda of the Hebrew Bible has led liberation theologians to overlook—or perhaps deliberately ignore—its oppressive aspects. As Michael Prior has rightly observed, if the exodus theme had been combined with the conquest theme we would have been left not with "a paradigm for liberation, but for colonial plunder"[19].

---

[17] Barr, in particular, has expressed serious concerns about the tendency by those committed to the "canon within the canon" approach to deprecate elements in the Hebrew Bible: "People often do not want to read genealogies, geographical and tribal lists, or obscure passages from some prophets. The neglect of the Old Testament as a whole in many Christian traditions usually has this character: people do not want to change the canon so as to remove it; they simply let it fade out from sermons, from liturgies, from general usage" (1999:386).

[18] Gutiérrez 1974:88. Thiselton wonders, not without some justification, whether the hermeneutical strategy adopted by liberation theologians functions "*pragmatically to filter out from the biblical text* any signal which does anything other than affirm the hopes and aspirations of a given social sub-group" (1992:410; his italics). Whitelam has argued that biblical scholarship generally has paid scant attention to the indigenous population of Canaan, and that such an omission is tantamount to a denial and silencing of Palestinian history. He reaches the controversial, if rather over-stated, conclusion that "biblical studies is, thereby, implicated in an act of dispossession which has its modern political counterpart in the Zionist possession of the land and dispossession of its Palestinian inhabitants" (1996:46).

[19] Prior 1997:283. Thiselton has rightly criticized liberation theologians for manipulating the biblical text to provide only positive signals for the aspirations and desires of those whom

Of course, such careful selection of biblical texts suits well the agenda of the liberation theologians, for by focusing almost exclusively on the exodus, the repressed people of Latin America and South Africa were "encouraged to assume the fortunes of the liberated slaves without being burdened with the guilt of dispossessing others" (Prior 1997:279). Clearly, the work of the liberation theologians serves as a timely reminder that unless great care is used in the selection of passages, the "canon within the canon" approach can lead to the rather embarrassing recognition that what we imagine to be a "biblical ethic" is, in fact, nothing of the sort; it is merely a distillation of our own particular predilections and prejudices[20].

A further problem with the "canon within the canon" approach is that the teaching of the Hebrew Bible concerning various issues is often vague, nebulous and even self-contradictory, and in such cases the Bible can be cherry-picked for quotations in support of both sides of an argument[21]. Nowhere is this more evident, perhaps, than in discussions of the role and status of women in the Hebrew Bible. As we have seen, some feminist biblical critics have adopted the "canon within the canon" approach as a means of focusing on biblical passages that portray women in a positive or favourable light, but the problem is that this strategy is one that can be used both ways. Against those who cite (often with a certain undisguised relish!) passages such as Gen. 2:21–23 in support of the subordination of women, feminist biblical critics respond by pointing to the more egalitarian view presupposed in Gen. 1:26–27; against those who quote Paul's injunctions regarding the submission of women to their husbands (1 Cor. 11:3–12; 14:34–35), feminists draw attention to the apostle's more positive statements regarding the equal status of male and female in such passages as Gal. 3:28[22]. The value of such arguments, however, must be regarded as highly questionable, for as Plaskow has observed, there is

they represent: "Any merely selective use of texts to encourage those who are oppressed can be perceived in principle to represent precisely the same strategy of hermeneutical method as the oppressors who use texts to legitimize their own programmes ... Without some *critical* hermeneutical tool, both sides in the struggle can continue to appeal to different texts to re-enforce and re-affirm their corporate identity and interests" (1992:429).

[20] Rowland and Corner have sought to defend the selective use of the Bible by liberation theologians, claiming that only thus is it possible to make any sense of the disparate collection of material which it contains (1990:87–8). However, there can be little doubt that such a procedure can lead to a gross distortion of the Bible's message, and the consequences of neglecting certain traditions (such as those of the conquest) can be deeply troubling.

[21] Cf. Wright 2004:17. As Schwartz has observed, during the Civil War in the United States, Lincoln invoked the exodus to free slaves, while the South invoked the conquest to justify the perpetuation of slavery (1997:58).

[22] Schüssler Fiorenza (1984:61) has observed that "throughout the centuries Christian feminism has claimed Galatians 3:28 as its Magna Carta, whereas the patriarchal church has used 1 Corinthians 14 or 1 Timothy 2 for the cultural and ecclesiastical oppression of women". Schüssler Fiorenza and others have conceded that the method, typified by such scholars as Trible, of isolating the liberating traditions of the Hebrew Bible from the patriarchal traditions, is far from satisfactory.

something overly simplistic about adding up the sexist and non-sexist passages of the Hebrew Bible and declaring that the non-sexist has won (1990:xiii). The danger of such an approach is that readers may give up on the Bible altogether and lapse into a kind of moral nihilism, believing that one position is as good as any other because there are arguments that can be advanced on all sides of the moral issue. There undoubtedly *are* ways of dealing with the deprecatory attitude towards women exhibited in the Hebrew Bible, but scanning the biblical text for positive images of the female, and using them to form what Alice Bach has called a "prettified canon" (1993:197), is not one of them.

Finally, the criteria used by adherents of the "canon within the canon" approach to decide which parts of Scripture may be deemed acceptable and which may not often appear to be ill defined and arbitrary. For example, those opposed to homosexuality on the basis of the Bible will have little difficulty in quoting biblical verses in support of their position, but it is by no means clear why they accept the validity of the Bible's *prohibition* of the act but not of the *penalty* that should be inflicted (death, according to Lev.20:13)[23]. Nor is it clear why they should privilege these particular prohibitions while neglecting others (such as the prohibition against lending at interest; cf. Rodd 1995:5–6). Those who insist on the normative authority of the Hebrew Bible when dealing with sexual morality often ignore it when it comes to teaching on other issues which they feel cannot and perhaps should not be observed[24].

The fact is that there is something fixed, final and definitive about the concept of the "canon", but once we start tinkering with it and raising the possibility of a "canon within the canon", the floodgates are immediately opened, and Scripture can be plundered to provide authority for a whole raft of subjective opinions and individual fancies. Moreover, if one is going to choose biblical passages according to the whim of the moment, or according to one's own particular prejudices and dispositions, in what sense can the Bible be regarded as in any meaningful way *authoritative*? If one is going to select particular biblical passages and reject others, then surely some strict herme-neutical guidelines must be developed in order to prevent the selection from becoming completely arbitrary.

Some such guidelines have occasionally been suggested by biblical scholars, though the criteria advocated to enable the individual to choose between the diverse moral traditions of the Hebrew Bible are usually less than satis-factory. Kaiser, for example, follows a long tradition in drawing a distinction between the moral and ritual requirements of the Hebrew Bible, and argues

---

[23] Cf. Rogerson, who notes that "people who cite Gen. 9.6 in support of capital punishment do not normally add that the Old Testament requires the death penalty not only for homicide, but for cursing one's parents, for blasphemy and for adultery" (2004:15).

[24] Thatcher observes that "almost all Protestants who are unwilling to abandon their biblical literalism about homosexuality become closet revisionists over divorce and remarriage (whatever Jesus might have said)" (2008:30).

that the former should be retained while the latter may be discarded[25]. Thus, such moral enactments as those concerning fairness in the judicial process, or respect for one's neighbour (Lev. 19:15, 18), are still regarded as relevant and acceptable, while ritual regulations, such as those concerning the types of sacrifice that had to be offered, or the various festivals that had to be observed (Num. 28–9), are clearly no longer valid or applicable.

The difficulty with this suggestion, however, is threefold. In the first place, the Hebrew Bible itself draws no such distinction between its moral and ceremonial laws; all were given by divine command and all were considered equally binding[26]. Secondly, the divisions between the moral and ritual laws of the Hebrew Bible are not as clear-cut as we might imagine (cf. Lalleman 2004:45–6; Wilson 1988:66–67). For example, the injunction to observe the Sabbath may be regarded as a moral law (as it is in Exod. 23:12; Deut. 5:12–13, where the slave has the right to rest on the Sabbath on the grounds that God rested on the seventh day of creation), or as a ritual or ceremonial law (as it appears in Lev. 23:1–3, where it is mentioned in the context of the observance of festivals; cf. Rogerson, 2004:33). Thirdly, it is by no means clear that all the moral laws in the Hebrew Bible can be regarded as acceptable as they stand, nor is it clear that all the ritual or ceremonial laws are to be regarded as outmoded or irrelevant. For example, no one today would uphold the "moral" requirement to impose the death penalty on those who commit adultery (Lev. 20:10; Deut. 22:22) or who curse their parents (Exod. 21:17; Lev. 20:9); on the other hand, the principle of "tithing" advocated in the "ritual" law of Lev. 27:30–33 is still accepted in some churches, and adopted by many Christians as an ideal by which to measure their giving (cf. Bright 1967:53–4). Thus any criteria based on the distinction between the ritual and ethical laws of the Hebrew Bible is fraught with problems and cannot properly be applied to justify our selectivity of certain passages.

---

[25] Kaiser 1983:312. Some of the early Church Fathers, such as Origen, Irenaeus, Tertullian, and the Alexandrians generally, drew a distinction between the ritual or ceremonial laws of the Hebrew Bible, on the one hand, and the moral laws on the other. See Longenecker 1987:26. Later, Aquinas was to follow suit, arguing that the moral laws were to be observed by all humans, whereas the ceremonial and ritual laws were directed to the specific circumstances of the ancient Israelites, and were no longer universally binding. See Rogerson 2004:33.

[26] Thus, for example, Lev. 19, which is usually regarded as part of the so-called "Holiness Code", contains a mixture of ethical commands (such as the injunction to "love your neighbour as yourself"; v. 18) and ritual commands (such as the injunction to destroy meat left over on the third day after a "sacrifice of well-being to the LORD"; vv. 5–8), and both types of legislation are indivisibly bound together within the same chapter (cf. Rodd 2001:5–6). Gray observes that in the prophetic literature, also, the ethical and ritual aspects are closely intertwined, for the prophets continually emphasize that cultic worship must be informed by a concept of justice that includes a moral and ethical dimension. He points, for example, to Isa. 1:16–17 ("wash yourselves; make yourselves clean"), which has clear ritual and cultic associations (cf. Lev. 14:8; 15:13) but which, in the Isaianic context, is given a moral content by being linked to the adoption of ethical behaviour (2006:30–2).

For these reasons, many have expressed considerable reservations concerning the "canon within the canon" approach as a method of dealing with the morally dubious passages of Scripture (e.g., Goldingay 1995:105–6). It is regarded as a convenient way of glossing over the more objectionable features of biblical teaching without having to reject it wholesale. Ultimately, the method does not face up to the difficulties encountered in Scripture; it merely provides a convenient strategy for escaping from them by permitting the reader to privilege some parts of the Hebrew Bible over others. The unfortunate effect of this preferential weighting of the biblical teaching is that it violates the integrity of the Bible as a whole, and relegates some parts of Scripture to a position of secondary importance. In view of these difficulties, some have wondered whether a canonical approach to Scripture might be preferable, and it is to this possibility that we must now turn.

The Canonical Approach

One of the main exponents of the canonical approach to Scripture was Brevard Childs who, in numerous publications, argued that the Bible could only properly be appreciated theologically and ethically when account was taken of the full range of the biblical witness. Childs' arguments were first outlined in detail in 1970 in a volume entitled *Biblical Theology in Crisis*[27], the first part of which (13–87) was concerned to trace the rise and fall of the Biblical Theology Movement, which had been a major feature of post-war biblical studies in the United States[28]. By the early 1960s the movement had all but collapsed, and one of the reasons for its demise, according to Childs, "was its failure to take the Biblical text seriously in its canonical form"[29]. On the basis of his analysis of the shortcomings of the movement, Childs offered his

---

[27] Some of the issues raised in the 1970 volume had already been anticipated in an article published by Childs in 1964 (432–49), and they were subsequently developed in detail in several full-length studies (see, especially, his 1979 volume, detailed reviews of which appeared in *JSOT* 16 [1980] and *HBT* 2 [1980], with responses by Childs, and the volumes which appeared in 1984, 1985, 1992, and 2004a). For detailed discussions of Childs' general approach, see the studies by Brett (1991) and Noble (1995), and for Childs' own reflections on recent scholarly contributions to the "canon" debate, see Childs 2006:33–53.

[28] For a briefer account of the movement, see Barr 1976:104–106. Some scholars have questioned whether there ever was a "movement" as such (cf. Smart 1979:9–17), while others have argued that the movement was not specifically American but was international (Terrien 1981:143 n.3). One of the main influences on the movement was George Ernest Wright; see, in particular, his volumes published in 1950 and 1952.

[29] Childs 1970:102. Barr claims that Childs conspicuously fails to present any evidence to support his contention that it was lack of attention to the canon that was the cause of the movement's demise; hence, Barr claims that Childs' outline of the Biblical Theology Movement in the first four chapters of his book appears completely unrelated to the rest of the volume, so that his proposal for a canonical reading of Scripture, when it appears, "comes like a rabbit out of a hat" (Barr 1983:134).

own proposals for constructing a biblically based theology, the primary feature of which would involve a "disciplined theological reflection of the Bible in the context of the canon"[30]. Previous scholarly approaches, according to Childs, had been too atomistic and analytical, and had not been sufficiently concerned with the unity and totality of Scripture. Biblical scholars had placed too much emphasis on the origins of the text and too little on its reception, or—to put it another way—there had been too much of a move backwards to the original sources and not enough of a move forwards to an understanding of the text in its final, canonical form. Adherents of the historical-critical approach had dissipated their energies on speculative reconstructions that served only to detract attention from the texts themselves, and they had ignored the function of the final shape of the canonical texts within the community of faith[31]. Childs did not deny the validity of the historical-critical approach, but he was relentless in pointing out its deficiencies, for he believed that it had not "provided the scholarly Biblical research of the sort the church sorely needs"[32].

In this regard, Childs felt it important to rehabilitate an exegetical tradition that had always existed in the church but had been largely ignored or abandoned with the rise of the historical-critical approach. That tradition

---

[30] Childs 1970:122. For better or worse, the term "canon criticism" (or "canonical criticism") is now widely used to describe a number of disparate approaches to the Hebrew Bible which have in common a focus on the canon (see Sanders 1972: ix–xx; 1980:173–97). Childs himself did not wish this term to be applied to his own approach, since it implied that he was proposing a new critical methodology designed merely to supplement the traditional disciplines of historical criticism (such as form-, source-, or redaction-criticism; 1979:82). Barton, commenting on Childs' approach, observes that "any criticism of it which assumes that it is merely a minor addition to existing methods will be bound to miss the mark" (1984:90–91). The expression favoured by Childs himself was "canonical approach" or "holistic approach", the latter term appearing, among other places, as the title of the final chapter of his 1992 volume (719–27).

[31] Carroll predicted that Childs' approach would probably help "to orchestrate the growing discontent among theologically minded scholars and students of the Bible who feel that the historical critical method does not do justice to the religious dimension or the hermeneutical richness of the Bible" (1980–1:75). In fact, such discontent with the historical-critical approach pre-dates Childs, and can be discerned as early as the late 1940s (see Barton 1999:39–43).

[32] Childs 1970:122. To claim, as some have done, that Childs' approach involved "the repudiation of the critical method" (cf., e.g., Hayes and Prussner 1985:270) and "the denigration of past scholarship" (Barr 1999:393) is both unfair and untrue (cf. Provan 1998:206–7); Childs' point was simply that the historical-critical method alone was inadequate for studying the Bible as the Scripture of the church (1970:141–2). Indeed, in his 1979 volume Childs goes out of his way to express appreciation for the scholarly research produced by historical critics, and in his commentary on the book of Exodus considerable attention is devoted to earlier stages of the text, though he concedes that "the study of the prehistory has its proper function within exegesis only in illuminating the final text" (1974: xv). Barr's contention that Childs' 1979 volume represents an attempt "to demolish what are believed to be the structures of traditional scholarship and replace them with something different" (1983:155), and that the said volume demonstrates "increased hostility to any and all exegesis that seeks in any way to penetrate back to an earlier stage" (1999:393) is well wide of the mark, and represents a gross misunderstanding of Childs' basic position.

had endeavoured to relate various parts of the Bible to one another and
to work consistently from the context of the whole canon. Such a tradition
could be traced back to the early Church Fathers, such as Irenaeus, Tertullian,
Augustine and Jerome, who had all worked in conscious awareness of the
canonical dimensions of the text, and had struggled to find ways of dealing
theologically with the Hebrew Bible and New Testament as part of the canon
of Scripture[33]. In the period of the Reformation, Luther had similarly tried
to come to terms with the relation between the two Testaments, and Calvin's
exposition of the Psalms was admired by Childs because he brought "the whole
spectrum of Biblical teaching to bear on a particular verse"[34]. Childs was at
pains to emphasize that the canonical approach which he advocated was not
a return to a pre-critical period of Bible study; nevertheless, he believed that
the writings of the early Church Fathers and the great classics of the Reformed
and Lutheran post-Reformation tradition provided a welcome antidote to the
one-sided emphasis of much contemporary biblical scholarship, preoccupied
as it was with the development of the biblical literature and the separating of
the "original" material from the "secondary".

Given Childs' emphasis on the centrality of the canon for biblical exegesis,
it will come as no surprise that he was highly critical of the kind of selective
approach to the biblical text associated with adherents of the "canon within
the canon" strategy, for such a procedure, in his opinion, merely encouraged
readers to seek a warrant for a particular viewpoint, or justification for a
particular action, by referring to a specific verse or passage within Scripture[35].
Childs believed that to focus too narrowly on selected texts could lead to a
distortion of the moral and theological witness of the Bible, for such texts had
not been tested against the totality of the biblical material. Since the meaning
or significance of a particular passage might change when viewed in its wider

---

[33] Childs went to great lengths to defend the methods of the early Church Fathers and,
indeed, of practitioners of the pre-critical approach in general: "When our seminary-
trained pastors find Augustine incomprehensible, Luther verbose, and Calvin dull, then
obviously the problem lies with the reader and his theological education and not with the
old masters" (1970:147). In the Preface to his 1992 volume, Childs tellingly remarks that
the great volumes of the early Church Fathers and Reformers "look down invitingly" from
his library shelves (xvi), and in his commentary on Isaiah he comments that "the voices of
the great Christian interpreters—Chrysostom, Augustine, Thomas, Luther, Calvin—remain
an enduring guide for truthfully hearing the evangelical witness of Isaiah in a manner
seldom encountered since the Enlightenment" (2001:5).

[34] Childs 1970:145. Childs contrasts Calvin's treatment of the Psalms with the type of
approach adopted by many modern commentators, "who avoid scrupulously any reference
to the New Testament while providing every conceivable Babylonian parallel" (1970:144).

[35] Childs was adamant that any attempt to abstract elements from Scripture in order to
"distinguish the kernel from its husk ... runs directly in the face of the canon's function"
(1985:14). Carroll argues that Childs' notion of canonical shaping seems to be dictated
by the primacy of the Torah, which Childs considers as central and determinative for the
interpretation of the rest of the Hebrew Bible; thus, ironically, Childs implicitly uses the
principle of the "canon within the canon" while at the same time being critical of such an
approach (Carroll 1980–1:75–6).

canonical context, Scripture must be read as an integrated and coherent whole, and the emphasis must be on the total impression gained when the variety of viewpoints expressed in the Bible are taken into account. It was therefore incumbent upon the reader to "hear the full range of notes within all of Scripture" (1970:163), just as it was incumbent upon the exegete "to sketch the *full range* of the Biblical witnesses within the canonical context that have bearing on the subject at issue"[36].

In order to appreciate how the canonical approach might work in practice, we may briefly examine Childs' discussion of the book of Amos (1979:395–410; cf. Croatto 1987: 55–6). Childs observes that most of the book consists largely of denunciations by the prophet against Israel and the nations (1:3–2:16), and against the rich and powerful who exploit and oppress the weak and impoverished (5:10–13; 6:4–7). At the end of the book, however, there is a "sudden shift from a message of total judgment for Israel to one of promise" (1979: 405), and instead of announcing the complete destruction of the northern kingdom (cf. 7:7–9; 8:1–3; 9:1–4), attention now focuses on a message of hope and future prosperity that will accompany the restoration of the Davidic dynasty (9:11–15). Commentators usually assume that the oracle contained in Am. 9:11–15 does not represent the "genuine" words of the prophet Amos but is, rather, a later addition to the book supplied by subsequent editors. Yet, the book of Amos as we have it today is a single text, and Childs insists that it must be read as such if we are properly to grasp the import of its message. No matter that the closing verses do not represent the words of the historical Amos; the point is that the final oracle of salvation modifies the message of the rest of the book and alters the significance of the previous oracles of judgment. God now emerges as redeemer as well as judge, and the divine punishment is proclaimed to be neither inevitable nor irrevocable. Viewed in terms of the book's final canonical shape, the message of judgment is transformed into one of hope and promise for all future generations, and the "original" words of Amos are seen in a broader framework which transcends the perspective of the prophet himself. The later embellishments, therefore, are not to be dismissed as distorting accretions which can conveniently be put to one side; rather, they are an essential aid to understanding the proper construal of the book's message. In effect, the final composition of the book serves as a check and control over any assessment of its meaning, and provides a reminder that its basic message is found not in any individual passage but in the complimen-

---

[36] Childs 1970:132 (his italics). A similar point was made by Birch and Rasmussen, who were equally insistent that it was the canon that should establish a platform from which proper exegesis of Scripture should be launched : "A passage seen by itself might appear quite different in meaning and significance when seen alongside a much wider range of related biblical material" (1989:176). Birch and Rasmussen provide a specific example of how the broader canonical context may alter our understanding of a particular passage (176–9).

tarity established by the book as a whole[37]. Of course, the significance of its
message may change again when it is seen in the broader context of the Book
of the Twelve (cf. Conrad 2003; Nogalski 1993:61–74; Barton 1996:59–73),
and even further permutations of its meaning will result when it is seen in
the context of the entire canon of Scripture. The goal of the interpreter,
therefore, should not be to recover the "original" message of Amos himself, or
the original setting of his oracles, but to discern how, in the final composition
of the book, "the message of Amos was appropriated and formed to serve as
authoritative scripture within the community of faith" (Childs 1979:400).

Although Childs was primarily concerned with the issue of biblical theology,
he recognized that the canonical approach which he advocated could have
far-reaching consequences for the construction of a biblical ethic. In particular,
he believed that the principle of canonicity may serve as a useful interpretative
tool for dealing with the ethically problematic passages of Scripture. When
these passages were allowed to resonate with their wider canonical context they
could be seen in a different perspective, for how we view the Bible as a whole
could have significant implications for how we view its individual units. The
so-called "offensive" passages of the Hebrew Bible were problematic only when
viewed in isolation; if we considered the message of the Bible in its entirety,
and respected its overarching perspective and overall intention, the ethically
objectionable passages would not prove to be quite such a stumbling-block as
is often supposed.

In his chapter on "ethics" in the volume *Biblical Theology of the Old and New
Testaments,* Childs focuses on the ethical shortcomings of the patriarchs as
recorded in the book of Genesis, and he considers how these "troublesome
stories" might become less problematic when considered in their broader
canonical context[38]. Childs observes that when one reflects on how these
stories were regarded in the rest of the Hebrew Bible—in the biblical narratives, the prophets, and the Psalms—a clear pattern emerges, for everything
that happens to the patriarchs is here viewed as part of God's mighty works
of redemption (e.g., Pss. 105 and 106). It is not their virtue or lack of virtue
that is important in the Hebrew Bible, but the fact that they were recipients of
divine favour and were an integral part of God's purpose of salvation (cf. Hos.
12:2ff.). Reading the patriarchal stories in their broader canonical context,

---

[37] Seitz has shown how Isa. 1–66 similarly benefits from a unified reading, for the text in its
final form conveys a message that might not necessarily be deduced from the individual
parts taken in isolation. Thus, the words of comfort in Deutero-Isaiah (chs. 40–55) counter-
balance the pronouncements of judgment in the previous chapters (1–39), and chs. 56–66
offer profound theological perspectives to the post-exilic community on the basis of the
prophetic critique of social justice in the eighth-century Isaiah (1988:105–26). See, also,
Clements 1982:117–29; 1985:95–113.

[38] Childs 1992: 679–80. Childs was here responding to the challenge posed by Bainton
(1930:39–49), who wondered how the Hebrew Bible could be regarded by contemporary
readers as in any way authoritative in the light of the gross immoralities of the patriarchs.

therefore, had a moderating effect on their content, and took the edge off some of their more objectionable features.

Another example of the way in which the canonical approach may serve to neutralize the force of offending passages in the Bible may be found in Childs' discussion of the biblical legislation concerning slavery in his commentary on the book of Exodus. He notes that in some instances the immediate context may modify the effect of a particularly offensive passage. For example, Exod. 21:20–21 states that if a master beats his slave and the slave were to die, the master would be duly punished; however, if the slave survived for a day or two after the beating, the master is exonerated from blame, for it is assumed that he would not deliberately destroy his own "property" (v.21). The law of Exod. 21:26–27, on the other hand, suggests that if a master caused injury to his slave (for example, by incurring the loss of an eye or a tooth), then the slave was to be released forthwith, presumably on humanitarian grounds. Childs claims that this latter law "casts into a different light the earlier, traditional slave law (vv.20f.)", for in this case it is not because the master caused damage to his "property" that the slave is freed, but "because he is an oppressed human being" (Childs 1974:473).

At other times, the ethically problematic aspect of the slave laws could only be mitigated by looking at a much broader canonical context. Childs cites as an example the inconsistency between the way in which male and female slaves are treated in biblical legislation. The law which stipulates that the Hebrew slave should be released after six years' service states that if the male slave had entered servitude single then he would leave single, and if he entered married he would leave married; however, if the master had provided him with a wife during his period of servitude, then the woman was not permitted to leave with her husband, but had to remain in captivity. Childs, clearly troubled by the inequality presupposed by this law, notes that it eventually fell into desuetude, since it was out of kilter with other statements encountered in the Hebrew Bible, which presuppose a more egalitarian view of the sexes: "The sense of cruel inconsistency between this stipulation and the concept of marriage found in Gen. 2.24—not to speak of Matt. 19.6—would finally destroy this law within Israel, but only after [a] considerable passage of time" (1974:468).

Other scholars have similarly found the canonical approach to be helpful when dealing with the slave laws in the Hebrew Bible. They argue, for example, that such passages as Exod. 21:2–11, 20–21, 26–27 should be viewed in the light of Amos' polemic against slavery (Am. 2:6; 8:6), or Nehemiah's outrage at the enslavement of fellow Israelites (Neh. 5:5, 8), or the depiction of all humans as having been created in the "image and likeness of God" (Gen.1:26–7), the latter passage, in particular, having clear implications for the concept of equal rights (cf. McConville 2006:259–81; Wright 2006:282–90; Goldingay 1990:56). The bringing together of texts from various parts of the canon helps us to appreciate the fuller implications of the Bible's teaching concerning slavery, and leads us to ponder on the spirit rather than on the letter of the law. Indeed, it was on the basis of the broader, canonical vision of the Bible concerning the dignity of human beings that the Church eventually opposed the institution of slavery, though both the Hebrew Bible and the New Testament accepted its existence without demur. The Church, in effect, was able to take a step back and see that the institution was not in harmony with the broader view of love, justice and equality found in Scripture[39].

Scholars sympathetic to the canonical approach have argued that other ethically troublesome passages may similarly be rendered less problematic when viewed in a broader, canonical perspective. Thus, for example, texts which emphasize the subordinate position of women appear less offensive when subjected to "the criticism and balance of the other witnesses" (Childs 1970:200), such as the portrayal of the ideal wife in the book of Proverbs, which depicts her assuming a role of considerable authority and influence (Prov. 31:10–31; Childs 1985:186; cf. Cosgrove 2002:143–8). Texts which appear to incite hatred and intolerance towards the enemy are mitigated by those which command love of one's neighbour (Lev. 19:18), and passages which reflect an unfavourable attitude towards foreign nations (Deut. 23:3–6, 20) are tempered by those which exhibit a concern for the needs of the stranger and resident alien (Exod. 22:21; 23:9). In a similar fashion, passages which depict the wrath of God (cf. Exod. 32:9–11: Num.11:10, 33) must be seen in the light of his ample manifestations of love and grace (cf. 2 Chr. 7:3, 6); texts which portray him as a vengeful and bloodthirsty deity (cf. Deut. 7:1–2) must be set alongside those that depict him as patient, long-suffering and slow to anger (cf. Exod. 34:6); passages which cast him as fickle and capricious (cf. 2 Sam. 24:16; Jer. 18:8) must be understood in the context of those which depict the basic consistency of his purpose and the unchangeableness of his character (cf. 1 Sam. 15:29; Mal. 3:6). By viewing different texts alongside one another, emphasis is placed on the totality of Scripture and on the interaction between various parts of the canon, and this serves to mitigate some of the objectionable passages of the Hebrew Bible, for, in the last resort, it is not isolated passages that make the ethics of the Bible distinctive and normative, but the way in which different biblical passages are seen to cohere and interrelate.

---

[39] Cf. Bright 1967: 49–51; Birch 1991:43; Swartley 1983:60–62. Bauckham observes that while the Hebrew Bible does not abolish the institution of slavery, it "treats it as an abnormality to be minimized as far as possible" (1989:108). A similar point is made by Wright who, in his discussion of the biblical slave laws, notes that there are "aspects of Old Testament thought and practice in this area which virtually "neutralized" slavery as an institution and were the seeds of its radical rejection in much later Christian thinking" (1983:179). Among the texts referred to by Wright are Exod. 12:43–44, which allowed the slave to be circumcised and to partake of the Passover; Deut. 16:11–14, which permitted them to join in the feasting and rejoicing of the great festivals; and Exod. 20:10, which enabled slaves, both male and female, to be included in the weekly Sabbath rest.

The Advantages of the Canonical Approach

At first sight, this strategy of dealing with the morally difficult texts of Scripture appears to be very attractive, for in one fell swoop it manages to smooth over the aggressiveness of certain biblical passages and to defuse some of their more inflammatory statements. Moreover, readers are not burdened with the responsibility of having to choose between the competing voices of Scripture, accepting some while rejecting others, for the canonical approach invites them to discover a basic coherence in the Hebrew Bible despite the plurality of its witnesses. Furthermore, by reading Scripture in the light of its dominant emphases, and taking cognizance of its broader perspective, readers are prevented from limiting or distorting its moral witness, and they are provided with a kind of control by which to appraise some of its more dubious ethical statements. They cannot twist the biblical message to mean what they want it to mean, or blow some bits out of proportion to fit some preconceived position of their own, for they are required to pay careful and disciplined attention to the canonical context as a whole, and it is *this* context which must be regarded as authoritative for the meaning of the text (cf. Wright 1995:22). Not surprisingly, therefore, the canonical approach to the interpretation of the Bible has been regarded by many as eminently plausible, for it is argued that by taking into account the whole range of material presented in Scripture, and discerning its "general drift", readers are more likely to arrive at sensible, balanced conclusions as they interpret the biblical texts (Barton 1983:123).

Having briefly reviewed the advantages of the canonical approach, we may now turn to examine how this strategy might be applied to the chapters recounting the possession of the land of Canaan by the Israelites as described in Josh. 6–11.

The Canonical Approach and the "Holy War" Traditions

Childs' discussion of the ethical problems involved in the conquest traditions of the Hebrew Bible occurs in the context of his analysis of the prohibition against killing encountered in the Decalogue (Exod. 20:13; Childs 1985:74–79). Childs concedes at the outset that the sixth commandment poses seemingly insurmountable problems for the construction of a coherent theology of the Hebrew Bible, for the prohibition against killing ill accords with the divine instruction to annihilate the Canaanites (Deut. 7:1–2; 13:15). Childs does not claim that the canonical approach will remove the moral difficulties posed by the existence of such texts in Scripture, but he does argue that when these passages are viewed in their broader canonical context they can be seen in a more nuanced light. Considered in the perspective of the canon as a whole, the clear message conveyed is that the violence and brutality that accompanied Israel's conquest of Canaan belonged entirely to Israel's past, and were on no account to be repeated in the future[40]. The prophets never exhorted the Israelites to wage a "holy war" against their enemies; rather, they envisaged the future age as one of universal peace which God himself would inaugurate (Isa. 2:1–4; 11:1–9). Viewed from a canonical perspective, the conquest of Canaan was assigned a time-bound role in the divine economy; it was an integral part of God's purpose for Israel, but it was, nevertheless, a "once and for all" event.

Furthermore, Childs maintains that such passages as Josh. 6–11 must be viewed in the light of other texts, such as 2 Chr. 28:8ff., which illustrate God's displeasure with the folly and cruelty of war, and Prov. 1:11ff., which emphasize the sheer madness of resorting to violence, which inevitably results in death for all involved. The intolerance exhibited towards the legitimate inhabitants of Canaan in such passages as Deut. 7:1–2; 13:15 must be counterbalanced by the compassionate and solicitous attitude shown towards the widow, orphan and alien in the same book (cf. van Houten 1991:68–108), and despite the divine commands to annihilate the Canaanites, war does not always bear the stamp of approval in the Hebrew Bible[41]. Thus, for example, David was denied by God the privilege of building the temple because his hands were stained with blood (1 Kgs 5:3), and the inhumane acts perpetrated during warfare frequently elicit a divine rebuke (cf. Am. 1:3–2:3; Hab. 2:6–17; cf. Kaiser 1983:177). Just as the gross immoralities of the patriarchs may be seen in a more favourable light when viewed against the background of such texts as Pss. 105 and 106 (Childs 1992:679–80), so the annihilation of the Canaanites may be seen in a different light when counterbalanced by the references to peace and harmony in such passages as Jer. 29:7, 11; Ps. 35:27. The message of the canonical approach is therefore quite simple: discussion of the "holy war" traditions in the Hebrew Bible should not be limited to passages that deal directly with that subject; rather, such texts should always be seen in their larger canonical framework, and although this will not necessarily resolve the problems caused by the existence of such passages in Scripture, their offensive nature will—at least to some extent—be mitigated[42].

[40] Childs 1985:78–79; cf. 1992:92. A similar point is made by Wright, who claims that the conquest of Canaan was a "unique and limited historical event [which] was never meant to become a model for how all future generations were to behave toward their contemporary enemies" (2008:90).
[41] Niditch argues that there are six different ideologies of war represented in the Hebrew Bible, ranging from those which glorify war to others which reflect a more pacifist attitude. Her volume attempts to understand "who in Israel might have espoused which ideology and when in the history of the biblical tradition" (1993:5).
[42] Christopher Wright has argued that the conquest narrative is problematic partly because it has been read in isolation, rather than in the wider framework of the Bible as a whole: "We need to see the conquest narrative in the framework of the Old Testament story, in the framework of God's sovereign justice, and in the framework of God's whole plan of salvation" (2008:87).

The Drawbacks of the Canonical Approach

Childs' work on the role of the canon in biblical interpretation has provoked much lively and intense debate among scholars, and it has generated a great deal of comment, both sympathetic and antagonistic[43]. On the one hand, many agree that it is inherently reasonable to suppose that each text must find its meaning in its wider context, and they concede that the canonical approach encourages a more balanced interpretation of Scripture, and may provide a welcome corrective to one's own predetermined prejudices and predispositions. On the other hand, others see the canonical strategy as essentially flawed, and regard it as a crude attempt to return to the pre-critical era of biblical interpretation. Having noted the advantages of the canonical approach, and the way it has been applied to the "holy war" traditions of the Hebrew Bible, we must now turn to focus on some of its more problematic features. Three

---

[43] Among those in general sympathy with Childs' canonical reading of Scripture, mention may be made of Rendtorff 1993; Birch 1991:43–6; Birch and Rasmussen 1989:171–80; Janzen 1994; and Seitz 1988:105–26; 2006:58–110. Writing on the ethics of the Hebrew Bible, Kaiser notes that "the time is long overdue for a holistic approach to the subject" (1983:24; cf. 142–3), and Seitz argues that Childs' approach "offers the most compelling, comprehensive account of biblical interpretation and theology presently on offer" (2006:63). On the other hand, one of the main opponents of the canonical approach has been James Barr, whose prickly antipathy to Childs' writings has often unfortunately bordered on the personal. His relentless tirade against Childs in his volume *The Concept of Biblical Theology* (1999:387–438) has been criticized by scholars for its tone as well as its content, and his negative appraisal appears at times to be both unfair and intemperate. Seitz calls it "one of the more embarrassing chapters in modern biblical studies for its devolution into highly personal, *ad hominem* evaluation" (2006:69–70 n.35), and Brueggemann, while expressing his appreciation of Barr's volume, wishes "that its generosity were not here and there sabotaged by emotive dismissals that gives the lie to his attempted 'objectivity'" (2000:71). In fact, the long-running battle between Barr and Childs might constitute an interesting volume in its own right. In his earlier publications, Barr appears to have given the approach advocated by Childs a cautious welcome (e.g. 1974:273–4; 1980a: 45–47, 144–45 n. 3), expressing much sympathy with his emphasis on the final form of the text, and regarding it as making up for a "defect in the critical approach as it has generally been practised" (Barr 1980a:46). In these publications, Barr evidently did not feel that the traditional historical-critical approach was in any way being threatened, and he was happy to concede (presumably with no pun intended!) that Childs "remains entirely a child of the critical movement" (1980b:15). However, Barr felt that Childs, in his later writings, appeared to be absolutizing his canonical approach and regarding it as *the* single, all-sufficient method for studying the Bible (cf. Barr 2000:110–12). This was no doubt why Barr was able to write far more approvingly of Sanders' canonical-critical approach, for, unlike Childs, Sanders regarded his method as an addition to existing methodologies rather than as "an absolute revolution which will sweep them all away" (Barr 1983:156). For his part, Childs claimed that his position had been misrepresented by Barr, and insisted that his "canonical analysis reflects the critical tools of the 20th century" (1980:204). Barton's contention that Barr's 1983 volume represents "the definitive demolition of canon criticism in its present form" (1984:225) seems, in retrospect, somewhat premature (the observation was omitted in the later 1996 edition of Barton's book), and it is probably nearer the truth to say that the jury is still deliberating, and that a final verdict on Childs' canonical approach has yet to be passed.

issues, in particular, call for comment. The first concerns the practicality of the approach; the second revolves around the concept of "canon"; and the third raises issues concerning the diversity of the biblical witness.

(a) Is it practical?

It is clear from the above discussion that one of the hallmarks of the canonical approach is its emphasis on comprehensiveness. The strategy involves bringing the full spectrum of the biblical witness into focus and insists that the entire canon must shape our ethical response to the issues of the day. Such a strategy, as we have seen, has some obvious advantages, not the least of which is that it provides a welcome corrective to the excessive fragmentation of the biblical text into countless sources, which was the inevitable result of previous scholarly obsession with the minutiae of literary, historical and philological problems. But while Childs' insistence that the entire canon should provide a frame of reference for ethical interpretation seems, in principle, perfectly sound and commendable, in practice it is flawed by some serious difficulties.

The first—and perhaps most obvious—concerns the practicality of the method. The logic of Childs' approach is that the Bible in its entirety must be considered as a single text in order for the lines of communication between the various passages to be properly appreciated. But this begs a number of questions. How are ordinary readers expected to take cognizance of the totality of the biblical witness?[44] How can they do justice to the complexity and diversity of the moral voices within Scripture, and take account of all the dialectical conversations going on at the same time within the corpus of the Bible? For the canonical approach insists that the witness of both Testaments "in their canonical integrity" be taken into account (Childs 1992:80), since "the whole is more than the sum of its two parts" (Childs 1970:109), and it is both Testaments together that constitute the Scripture of the church[45]. But even this, Childs would claim, is merely the starting-point of one's ethical reflection,

---

[44] As Clines points out, the Bible with which most people in contemporary society are familiar is a "fragmented Bible": "[Our culture] thinks it knows the Bible, but it knows the Bible mainly as a book of quotes. It knows its purple passages and its most dramatic moments. But it does not know its longueurs; it does not know its rhythms and its shape. It does not know it as a whole, and therefore it does not know its variety, for its variety is only a function of its unity" (1997:53).

[45] Childs concedes that there are few models available to guide us in our ethical reflection on both Testaments, and notes that in modern scholarly debates there seems little concern with how one should move exegetically to include the whole Bible. He does commend K.H. Miskotte's provocative volume, *When the Gods are Silent,* since it seeks to present a theological reflection on the Hebrew Bible in conversation with both Judaism and the New Testament, though he concedes that the volume is virtually unknown in the Anglo-American world "in part from the book's difficult style, and in part from the unfortunate theological deafness of its readers" (1992:707).

for the reader must then proceed to consider how a particular passage has been interpreted within the traditions of the synagogue and church. To appreciate fully the teaching of the Hebrew Bible on a particular issue "requires all the knowledge and wisdom of the entire theological enterprise, including the New Testament, systematic theology, ethics and church history"[46].

Now such a rigorous and systematic study will surely be beyond the reach of most readers of Scripture. Indeed, even Childs himself concedes that at first the task of relating the diverse witnesses of both Testaments is bound to seem "quite overwhelming" (1992:558), and in his volume *Old Testament Theology in a Canonical Context* he recognizes that to confine attention to the theological import of the Hebrew Bible is problematic enough without having to come to grips with "the sheer mass of material and the overwhelming complexity of issues which arise when the New Testament is also included"[47]. Seitz comments with regard to the canonical approach that "rarely is it said that it seeks to do too much and is disqualified by virtue of its ambition" (2006:62). Although Seitz himself defends the canonical approach against such criticism, it is precisely the ambitious nature of the strategy that is one of its main stumbling-blocks, for it is questionable whether people have either the time or the inclination for the kind of sustained and disciplined reflection on Scripture which the canonical approach seems to demand[48].

Defenders of the canonical approach will no doubt brush such objections aside, arguing that the strategy is true to peoples' experience of reading Scripture, and is perfectly in accord with the way they read literary texts in general. After all, it is at the canonical level that people come to the text of Scripture; they read it in its final, completed form and they are not, by and large, interested in the complex tradition-history of the text, or in scholarly speculations regarding the origins of a particular passage (Dunn 1987:166–7, 172–3). As Brenneman has observed, people read the biblical narratives as they are and not as historical critics would prefer them to be read (1997:132). Moreover, the canonical approach is said to chime in well with modern literary theories which emphasize that literary works should be understood on their own terms, in the form in which they stand before us on the printed page; previous stages or editions are regarded as an irrelevant distraction which would merely hinder the reader from focusing on the patterns and contours

---

[46] Childs 1985:192. Childs' commentary on the book of Exodus (1974) suggests how such an approach might proceed in practice, for in each section he places the text in its New Testament context and investigates how it has been interpreted by theologians of the patristic period and by medieval Jewish commentators.

[47] Childs 1985:17. Even Barth (whom Childs so admired) insisted that a biblical theology "can never consist in more than a series of attempted approximations" and "cannot consist in an attempt to introduce the totality of the biblical witness" (*CD* i/2:483–4).

[48] With regard to Childs' approach, Barton notes that there are "very considerable difficulties in applying the method in practice" (1984:87), and he wonders whether there was a way of modifying the approach, "giving it a narrower and less ambitious scope" (1984:100).

established by the final form of the text. Thus (it is argued) how we read the Bible is not unlike how we might read any piece of literature and, indeed, how the Bible *has* been read by some of our most eminent literary critics[49].

However, to claim that the canonical approach merely invites readers to read the Bible as they would any other piece of literature seems highly misleading, for the fact is that they do not normally read the Bible in the same way that they might read a novel by Dickens or a play by Shakespeare. We read novels or plays as coherent, self-contained entities, whereas we usually read the Bible in short units, focusing on a particular passage or chapter, and we seldom insist that our reading be guided by the totality of the biblical canon. The argument that the canonical approach is completely in tune with the way readers read the Bible is therefore highly questionable[50]. Moreover, the canonical approach is also out of sync with the way in which the Bible actually functions in the church. While the Bible is admittedly read in church in its final, canonical form, there is little attempt in Christian worship at the kind of pan-canonical comprehensiveness demanded by the method advocated by Childs. Unlike the synagogue, where the entire Torah is read methodically in sequence from beginning to end, and where other passages are read in conjunction with various festivals, the church provides lectionaries with prescribed readings for the congregation which aim to represent a *selection* of texts from various parts of the Bible. Even sermons are usually based on a particular verse or verses, and although attention might occasionally be paid to their immediate context, it is rare indeed for the entire canonical context to be taken into account. Thus, in worship, preaching and in the private devotion of the individual, the "canon" as such plays a fairly minimal role[51].

Before leaving the issue of practicality, it is perhaps worth noting that some scholars are of the view that the canonical approach involves a degree of circularity in its argumentation. The strategy maintains that how we view the Bible as a whole has implications for how we interpret individual texts, and how we interpret individual texts has implications for how we view the Bible as a whole. Cynics might claim that the canonical approach is, for this very reason, something of a non-starter, for if we must grasp the whole before we can understand the parts then, arguably, we will never understand anything.

---

[49] See, for example, Frye 1982; Kermode 1979; Kermode and Alter (eds) 1987. Both Barr (1983:77, 158–9) and Barton (1984:141–54) have noted affinities between the canonical approach and movements in secular literary criticism, though Childs himself would certainly not wish his approach to be viewed as a purely literary pursuit (1979:74).

[50] For a different view, however, see Barton (1999:48), who argues that a canonical reading is what "ordinary Christian believers instinctively engage in whenever they open a Bible". Barton even views the canonical approach as "essentially an attempt to formulate carefully and programmatically the attitude towards the biblical text that most believers share".

[51] Barr comments that "doubtless 99% of active church-goers have never heard the word 'canon'" (1999:450). It might be added that some of the terms used by adherents of the canonical approach, such as "canonical integrity" (Childs:1992:80), or "canonical intentionality" (Childs 1979:79), will mean even less to most church-goers.

As Barton notes, we would "need to have read every part of the Old Testament with understanding before we can begin to read any part of it, and this is self-contradictory"[52]. Warnke makes the point even more emphatically:

> The problem here is that if one begins to understand the individual parts of a text in light of an assumption as to the meaning of its whole, it is not clear how these parts, so understood, can lead one to revise one's understanding of the whole. Conversely, if one projects a meaning of the whole on the basis of an interpretation of the way in which individual parts cohere with one another, how can the understanding of the whole, so projected, lead one to change one's understanding of the parts? Why, in other words, is the hermeneutic circle not simply a vicious one in which one's understanding of the individual parts of a text confirms one's assumption as to the meaning of the whole and vice versa? (1987:84).

In other words, taken to its logical conclusion, the canonical approach is not only impractical, but impossible.

(b) The Concept of "Canon"

The basic premise of Childs' canonical approach is that the "canon of the Christian church is the most appropriate context from which to do Biblical Theology" (1970:99). The final, canonical level of the text is therefore accorded a certain primacy over other levels, and it is this level, according to Childs, that should form the sole, authoritative context for biblical interpretation. However, Childs' continued insistence on the "normative status of the final form of the text" (1979:75) has been questioned by a number of scholars. Why, they ask, should priority be granted to this particular stage in the development of the tradition? Why should the final form of the tradition be absolutized in this way? Why should the canon be regarded as any more normative and authoritative than the pre-canonical stages of the text's development? In this regard, Douglas A. Knight has argued forcefully that every stage in the history of the biblical tradition has as much right to its own integrity as the final canonical form. His words are worth quoting in full:

> The structure of faith precedes the rise of scripture, and this underscores the theological importance of the early stages. One must follow the process from origin to end, from first traditions to final texts, from initial religious

---

[52] Barton concedes, however, that this may be pressing the idea of canonical reading too far, for all reading of literature has some circularity inherent in it, as readers constantly make connections between various parts of the text (1984:82).

responses to last theological statements. Truth should be identified programmatically with neither the genesis nor the telos. The process throughout is
dynamic, marked by imagination, reflection, vitality, routine, experimen-
tation, dissent, and diversity. The task is to grasp this fully, with balance and
without prejudice toward one stage or the other. This dynamic quality of
biblical literature, not simply its final static form, accounts for the extraor-
dinary effect it has had on two millennia of world history[53].

The inspiration which supposedly led to the formation of the canon was
presumably qualitatively no different from that of the original authors of the
biblical text or its later redactors[54], and once we recognize that there may be
different levels of canonical authority then it becomes increasingly difficult to
assign authority only to the canonical phase[55].

Of course, in Childs' favour, it could be argued that decades of scholarly
obsession with the text's pre-history has had the unfortunate effect of elevating
the significance of the text's "original meaning" out of all proportion, and
that his canonical approach provides a welcome corrective to the excessive
emphasis on the earliest level in the history of the tradition. But while one
may agree with Childs that the earlier or "original" text should not in any way
be regarded as superior to the later, it is by no means clear why the later, just
because it is "final", should be regarded as superior to the earlier. In his desire
to focus on the canonical stage, Childs has simply moved from one extreme to
the other: instead of granting supreme authority to the earliest or "original"
words, he has elected to absolutize the final form of the tradition.

Moreover, to claim, as Childs does, that the canon of the Christian church
should be regarded as normative immediately begs the question: which canon?
If the canon were a generally agreed corpus of literature which had clear-cut
divisions, then the issue might be relatively straightforward: what was included
in it would be regarded as authoritative, and what was excluded would not.
But the fact is that the various branches of the Church have never been in
complete agreement as to which books belong to the Bible. The Protestant

---

[53] Knight 1980:146; cf. 1977:4–8. Noble similarly questions the logic of prioritizing the final
form of the text: "Childs himself accepts, in significant measure, the standard critical
reconstructions of the traditions behind the text (particularly as regards literary sources);
but when the same reconstructions also show that the dominant influences in the
formation of these traditions, and hence in the shaping of the final text, were such factors
as political infighting, poor historiographical methodology, misunderstandings of the
material, or sheer antiquarianism, it is far from clear why priority should still be accorded
to the canonical form" (1995:48).

[54] Seitz observes that one of the perceived weaknesses of Childs' approach is that it is often
viewed as "giving a kind of moral authority to later institutionalizing instincts instead of the
'genius of the original inspiration'" (2006:62).

[55] Dunn has argued that there are several levels of "canonical" authority, including the
tradition-history level, the final author or final composition level, the canonical level, and
the ecclesiastical level (1987:141–74).

Church has traditionally accepted only the books found in the Hebrew canon (albeit in a different order), while the Roman Catholic Church includes in its Bible certain books found in the Septuagint but which do not appear in the Hebrew Bible. The canons of the Greek Orthodox Church and the Ethiopian Orthodox Church are different again, as, of course, is the Jewish canon[56]. Thus it is all very well to proclaim the canon of Scripture as normative and authoritative—but which canon do we mean? For his part, Childs favours the Masoretic text of the Hebrew Scriptures, since this is the one form of the Hebrew Bible that Jews and Christians have in common (1979:100–101); but his attempts to justify a Christian adherence to the Hebrew rather than the Greek canon on biblical grounds seem rather strained, given that for most New Testament authors it was the Septuagint that constituted the canon of Jewish Scriptures (Dunn 1987:152; Gerstenberger 2002:14; Sanders 1980:187; Barton 1984:100; Noble 1995:43).

Now it could be argued that the question of "which canon?" does not substantially weaken Childs' case, for his main point is that the meaning of a given text has its proper significance in a canonical context, and it is probable that the significance of a particular passage would not change appreciably if the limits of the canon were differently defined. For example, if one were to omit Esther from the canon of the Hebrew Bible and substitute 1 Maccabees, or (with regard to the New Testament) if one were to omit James and include the *Didache*, very little of any substance would change, for the "general drift" of Scripture is not determined by the inclusion or omission of relatively marginal books. What seems more critical for Childs' argument, however, is not whether this or that canon is regarded as binding, but whether *any* canon should be deemed to be normative and authoritative (cf. Dunn 1987:141). Why should this particular collection of books (irrespective of precisely which are included or excluded) have any more influence and authority than any other collection? Of course, Christians today have been conditioned to believe that the canon is firmly closed, and that they must abide by decisions concerning its extent handed down from the distant past. However, recent scholars have argued in favour of a far more flexible notion of canonicity. The canon (they contend) is merely an artificial construct imposed by the dominant theologians of the Christian Church in the third or fourth century C.E. Why should we turn the community of the canonizing period into the ultimate arbiters of Scripture?[57]

---

[56] The Roman Catholic Church accepts, in addition to the Hebrew canon, the books of Tobit, Judith, Wisdom, Ben Sira, and 1 and 2 Maccabees. The Greek Orthodox Church uses the Septuagint, which includes this longer canon and, in addition, 1 and 2 Esdras, the Prayer of Manasseh, Psalm 151, 3 Maccabees and (in some versions) the Odes of Solomon, the Psalms of Solomon and 4 Maccabees. The Ethiopian Orthodox Church also includes 1 Enoch and Jubilees. See Goldingay 1990:138.

[57] Barr criticizes Childs' approach partly because the very notion of a "canon" is extrinsic to the biblical text. It is, he claims, "a derivative, a secondary or tertiary, concept, of great interest but not of the highest theological importance. It is unlikely in face of the biblical

Why accept the freezing of tradition in one particular form at one particular period and regard this as determinative for all later generations? Should not the canon be open to subsequent qualification and correction in the light of later developments in the theological traditions of Judaism and Christianity? Could not those traditions themselves be the bearers of new revelations which might perhaps transcend and even occasionally reverse the postulates of the biblical text? Indeed, should not the community of faith abandon the constraints and constrictions imposed by what Childs himself called this "restrictive outer boundary" (1979:544) and contemplate the inclusion of texts not presently in Scripture? In other words, why cannot the canon as we recognize it be regarded as the record "*not only of a destination but a record of the journey as well*"?[58]

Needless to say, such arguments cut little ice with Childs, who insists that a normative role cannot be assigned either to the pre-history of the text or to later post-canonical traditions, for it is only the text in its final canonical form that "bears witness to the full history of revelation" (1979:75–6). But, surely, God's revelation extends beyond the canon itself into the post-canonical tradition of interpretation that continues up to the present (cf. Birch 1980:123). As David Brown remarks, "it seems odd to postulate a God without revelatory impact upon the history of the Church when that history is not significantly different in fallibility and conditionedness from the history of the biblical community itself" (1999:1). We today are part of a community of faith who are continually being shaped by and giving shape to the traditions as we respond to the challenges of new historical situations. What is unclear in Childs' argument is why God's providential guidance of the community's interpretation should cease at the end of the biblical period, especially since Childs himself recognizes that "the God of Israel is a *living God who continues to make his will known for his people*" (1992:677; my italics).

(c) The Diversity of the Biblical Witness

The difficulty with reading the Bible canonically is further exacerbated by the fact that its ethical prescriptions are often in conflict with one another. Childs'

---

evidence that it can be made into the cornerstone of any convincing biblical theology" (1983:63-4). Barton observes a curious paradox in Childs' thinking at this point. On the one hand, Childs insists that we must read the Bible in its canonical context because that is how the Church decided it should be read by fixing the limits of the canon; yet, at the same time, Childs argues that our interpretation of the Bible should *not* be guided by the exegetical tradition of the Church, which was given to such practices as allegorization (of which Childs would not approve). Thus, on Childs' view, "it is in principle possible that the very same generation of Christians who fixed the main outlines of the canon is also a hopelessly unreliable guide to the correct way of reading that canon" (1984:97).

[58] Birch and Rasmussen 1989:174 (their italics); cf. Birch 1980:122. A similar point, using similar imagery, is made by Croatto, who observes that "the canon is not the beginning of a tradition ... nor is it its end. It is a moment in a continuous journey" (1987:48).

approach presupposes that there is "a remarkable convergence within the variety of the Old Testament witness" (1992:684), and that it is at least possible, in principle, to outline a "biblical view" concerning such issues as wealth, poverty, justice etc. Childs continually emphasizes that readers of Scripture need to contemplate "the oneness of the biblical witness" (1992:719), and recognize that "there is a unity within the divine will and a continuity within the tradition" (1992:676)[59]. Of course, Childs does not deny that there are occasional tensions and differences between biblical texts, and that various passages evince shifting emphases and interests; nevertheless, he maintains that, taken as a whole, the Bible expresses a relatively uniform world-view and can therefore be regarded as a coherent guide to ethical living.

Such an assurance will no doubt be warmly welcomed by those who look to Scripture as a basis for faith and practice, but who might be alarmed by the seeming inconsistencies within the biblical tradition, for the canonical approach has the reassuring effect of smoothing over the contradictions and making the path straight for contemporary readers who do not want to be ruffled by any unexplained irregularities in Scripture. The Bible, they are solemnly assured, is not a random jumble of isolated precepts without any discernible underlying rationale; rather, it presupposes at least a measure of unity and homogeneity and—despite its rich diversity—evinces a broadly coherent ethical vision[60]. Once the truths expressed in all the various passages are synthesized in the right way, the central message of the Bible will emerge and will provide the community of faith with a firm foundation upon which its beliefs can be based. The canonical approach, therefore, tries to achieve the difficult balancing act of recognizing the rich diversity of ethical principles in the Bible on the one hand, while upholding the essential unity of biblical thought on the other.

The problem with this approach, however, is that it often gives a misleading impression that the biblical texts share a commonality of ethical viewpoints whereas, in fact, they display considerable variation in their moral perspective. As soon as we begin to look at the entire panoply of Scripture, we immediately become aware as never before of the dissonance and contradictions within the Bible, and the wide range of options and perspectives which it affords. The canon, as it now stands, canonizes diversity, and the fact is that there is more diversification in the Bible than adherents of the canonical approach

---

[59] Ironically, just two pages earlier, Childs criticizes Kaiser's attempt to "discover in the Old Testament universal principles of ethical behaviour and moral values which reflect the consistent will of God both for Israel and the world" precisely because "historical changes within the Old Testament itself as well as the great diversity in content resist such an imposed pattern of ethical unity" (1992:674).

[60] The striving for unity which tends to characterize adherents of the canonical approach is well expressed by Barton who notes that, although we know that the various books of the Bible do not have a single author, "the meaning they have as a canon is the meaning they *would* have had if they *had* had a single author" (1984:102).

are generally willing to contemplate. David Pleins has argued that even on such critical issues as "social justice", the biblical tradition does not present us with one simple, unified vision; on the contrary, what we have in the Bible are many different views and divergent perspectives[61]. Consequently, the canonical approach—far from helping the modern reader to reach satisfying ethical conclusions—could well turn out to be a recipe for moral confusion.

Of course, it is in the interests of the canonical method to downplay (though not to deny) the dissonances and contradictions within Scripture, and although Childs himself is aware that his own approach may easily degenerate into a facile harmonization of conflicting viewpoints, there can be no doubt that the impulse of the method which he advocates is towards synthesis[62]. For better or worse, it raises an expectation that the various traditions of the Bible will cohere and that the different voices will come together to form a reasonably harmonious choir. In order to do this, it attempts to reconfigure the multiple witnesses of Scripture into some sort of coherent message, and thereby gives the impression that the Bible represents a unified ethical vision, albeit perhaps with differences in emphasis.

The problem with this strategy, however, is that it attempts to systematize the unsystematizable[63]. Individual traditions are often suppressed in the interest of maintaining a coherent whole, and the plurality of perspectives is dissolved in an attempt to achieve a harmony where patently no harmony exists[64]. Moreover, by subordinating the original meaning of a passage to the canonical context, the specificity of individual passages is obscured, and the overall effect of Childs' programme is to "deny the text its own say" (Brueggemann 1997:92).

---

[61] In this regard, Pleins criticizes liberation theologians for failing to recognize the conflictual character of the biblical texts concerning such issues as social justice, wealth and poverty. They write about poverty and injustice as if all the biblical genres deal uniformly with the subject and speak with one voice, whereas there are varying perspectives on these issues in the Hebrew Bible, owing to the fact that the prophets, historians, legislators and wise men of ancient Israel held different and often radically conflicting approaches to the social and ethical issues of the day. Pleins argues that such divergent outlooks—sometimes even within the same genre—"disrupts our search for an adequate approach to the use of the whole of Scripture in the context of a contemporary discussion of social ethics" (2001:522).

[62] Childs, for example, while observing that the Hebrew Bible's understanding of God is very diverse, argues that "there are clearly some unifying themes, some characteristic patterns, and some strong elements of unity which resist atomizing the whole into unrelated fragments" (1992:354).

[63] Pleins argues that we should learn from the fact that rabbinic interpretation over the centuries has been reluctant to subscribe to the Christian attempt to compose a "biblical theology", as if one general, overarching perspective could be produced from the variety of material available. He suggests that the conflictual character of the legal debates which characterize the Mishna and Talmud is far truer to the biblical documents than is the Christian penchant for systematic theology (2001:21).

[64] Birch and Rasmussen (1989:176) claim that the danger of the canonical approach is that it runs the risk of discovering tensions and contradictions within the biblical material; but, surely, the risk is far more likely to be in the opposite direction of imposing a strained unity on the variegated deposit of material within the Bible.

Adherents of the canonical approach would no doubt claim that the tensions and contradictions within the biblical text have been grossly exaggerated and that, despite the variety and diversity within the Bible, certain common themes and approaches *can* be discerned. Taken as a whole (they argue) Scripture establishes some moral values as commendable and others as unacceptable, and it is clear from the "general drift" of the Bible which is which. The basic presupposition underlying such an argument is that the various texts of the Bible share certain common underlying perspectives, and that there is a general consensus in the Bible concerning such issues as war and peace, justice and oppression, wealth and poverty etc. But on what grounds do we decide what constitutes the Bible's central interpretative position on such issues? On what basis are we to determine which particular traditions comprise what Childs calls the "inner dynamic of Biblical thought" (Childs 1970:133)? The fact is that adherents of the canonical approach have singularly failed to lay down any objective criteria to enable readers to gain a sense of the Bible's priorities, and consequently it is usually the subjective judgment of the individual that determines which traditions are most truly expressive of the Bible's witness as a whole. The canonical approach ostensibly aims to gauge the dominant voice of Scripture, but the dominant voice is often defined in terms of the voice we want to hear[65]. It is, to say the least, curious that the traditions which Childs regards as "bearers of the essential testimony" (1992:334) of the Bible are invariably ones which we ourselves would be happy to endorse. It is we who decide what the "general thrust" of Scripture is, and the temptation is to ignore the diversity within the Bible in an attempt to make it conform to our own agendas and our own expectations about what the Bible *ought* to say[66]. What is taken to be the main thrust of the Hebrew Bible is often merely a reflection of the values, prejudices and presuppositions of the individual reader. As Cyril Rodd has observed, "the "thrust" is as much that of the reader as of the writings. . .[and] the fact that the principles discovered are always such as are acceptable today should immediately suggest that something is wrong" (2001:322–3).

The fact is that the task of discovering the "general drift" of Scripture is not as easy as adherents of the canonical approach would like to believe, nor is it always clear which moral principles are compatible and which are

---

[65] Cf. Barton, who comments: "If it is essentially the Christian or Jewish community that defines the limits of the Old Testament canon, does this not mean that the interpreter is under some constraint, not just to read the particular *form* of the Old Testament his community accepts, but also to read it *in the manner* his community regards as normative?" (1984:95).

[66] That it is our own agenda that is the determinative factor in deciding what constitutes the "general drift" of Scripture is implied in Christopher Wright's description of the canonical strategy: "A *canonical* approach would be to look at the ethical teaching of the major sections of the Old Testament to enquire what they have to offer us as usable material *that we can theologically synthesize into our own Christian ethical agenda*" (1995:117; my italics).

incompatible with biblical thought. The case of warfare in the Hebrew Bible provides an interesting case in point, for to argue that the main thrust of Scripture is represented by prophecies of peace and harmony, such as those found in the prophetic literature, overlooks the fact that many of these prophecies are, in fact, infused with the language of war. Thus, for example, in Isa. 11:1–9 the messianic ruler who will come to inaugurate an era of universal peace will "strike the earth with the rod of his mouth" and will "kill the wicked" with the breath of his lips (Isa. 11:4*b*). Similarly, Zechariah looks forward to an age of peace in the land of Judah when old men and women would sit watching children play in the streets (Zech. 8:4–5), but other passages in the book imply that the peace envisaged will only come about when Israel's enemies have been quelled by Yahweh, who is depicted as marching out as a warrior against them (cf. Zech. 9:1–8, 14–15; Rodd 2001:193–5). The offending texts are often conveniently ignored because readers have been predisposed to find in the Hebrew Bible a message of unqualified peace and harmony.

Nowhere is this better illustrated than in the way biblical scholars have dealt with two contrasting passages of Scripture, namely, Isa. 2:2–4 and Joel 3:9–12. Isaiah's oracle describes a reign of peace resulting from the nations voluntarily dismantling their weapons and transforming them into agricultural implements:

"They shall beat their swords into ploughshares
  and their spears into pruning hooks" (Isa. 2:4).

The passage in Joel, on the other hand, represents a deliberate reworking of Isaiah's vision to inspire universal war:

"Beat your ploughshares into swords
  and your pruning hooks into spears" (Joel 3:10).

Here, therefore, is a case of two canonical prophets apparently contradicting each other within the sacred canon of Scripture. As a result, the so-called "ploughshares" passages could legitimately be appealed to by peacemakers and warmongers alike, for the Isaianic passage provides a satisfying biblical warrant for those who favour peace, while the passage in Joel provides an equally potent warrant for those who favour war. Brenneman provides a detailed and helpful discussion of the two passages, and concludes that it is Isaiah's construal of the peaceful dominion of Yahweh, rather than Joel's violent portrayal, that comes closest to a truly biblical hermeneutic[67]. One suspects, however, that

---

[67] Brenneman 1997:142. Far from lamenting the existence of these conflicting prophetic utterances within the same canon of Scripture, Brenneman regards them as laudable and necessary, for the passages reflecting peace and harmony constitute a counter-reading to the Bible's militant traditions, and thus "form a self-correcting mechanism that finally disciplines Scripture's own violent content" (1997:8).

his conclusions concerning the "general drift" of Scripture are based on his instinct as to what the Bible *should* be teaching, rather than on a balanced judgment predicated on the relative prominence of pronouncements of peace and war in the Hebrew Bible[68].

Conclusion

In this chapter we have considered two very different approaches for dealing with the ethically problematic passages of Scripture, both of which have some obvious advantages, but both of which are also marred by certain flaws.

The "canon within the canon" strategy is bound to be viewed by many as an attractive option, not least because it represents a common-sense approach to the teaching of the Bible. It is simply a fact that people do not regard all portions of Scripture as of equal significance and status, and they instinctively feel that some elements in the Bible are central while others are more marginal. Consequently, they fully accept that the Hebrew Bible is not intended to provide a guide to normative behaviour in all its particulars. There will be aspects of its teaching which virtually everyone would reject (the putting to death of adulterers, homosexuals, and recalcitrant sons, to name but a few), while there will be other aspects that virtually everyone would accept (care for the poor and underprivileged, justice in the legal system etc.). Moreover, there is a certain inevitability about the approach, for the variety of material in the Hebrew Bible is so rich and diverse that we cannot possibly retrieve it in its entirety and follow its teaching in a completely systematic and coherent way. Common sense dictates that we are bound to be selective in our approach, and that some aspects will almost certainly take precedence over others.

The weakness of the "canon within the canon" approach, however, is that it lacks any objective, independent criteria to help us in our choosing, for it is by no means clear on what basis we should decide which values are acceptable and which are unacceptable. Will we reject all patterns of behaviour that do not happen to coincide with our own high-minded ideals? On what grounds should we esteem the Israelite concepts of justice and community but reject the violence and power-structures which were just as endemic to their culture? Why should some ethical principles be regarded as exemplary and others as dubious? In the absence of adequate criteria to justify our selectivity, the process of choosing inevitably becomes arbitrary and subjective, and each reader is, in effect, invited to construct his or her own hierarchy of moral values on the basis of the biblical testimony. The strategy seems to say: search

---

[68] Writing with regard to the Hebrew Bible, Knierim observes that "a survey of the total evidence shows, perhaps contrary to well-meaning opinion, that war is much more documented as justified than it is criticized" (1995:103).

out among the stipulations of the Hebrew Bible until you find ones whose moral teaching suits you. But then why turn to the Bible at all if we only use it to support and buttress beliefs we have already accepted anyway? The complacently seductive invitation to "choose what you want and discard the rest", however tempting, must be viewed with considerable reserve.

In many ways, the canonical approach advocated by Childs may be viewed as remedying some of the defects which we have observed in the "canon within the canon" strategy. By insisting that the testimony of all the biblical witnesses in their complexity and diversity be taken into account, this approach guards against absolutizing any one viewpoint, and prevents an arbitrary selection of texts based on the prejudices and predispositions of the individual reader. Any effort to make the Bible conform to our own narrowly constructed agendas is stopped in its tracks, and any attempt to endow a limited portion of Scripture with absolute moral authority is immediately forestalled. The canonical approach tries to ensure that the "biblical ethic" is not predicated on this or that text taken in isolation but is based, rather, on the "general drift" of Scripture read as a unified work; no single verse, or passage, or book, can by itself be determinative for ethical decision-making unless and until it has been "tested" against the broader witness of the Bible as a whole. For many concerned with biblical ethics, this seems eminently preferable to the "canon within the canon" approach, for those who attend to the entire range of canonical witnesses are surely on firmer ground than those who base their moral convictions on a limited sample of canonical evidence.

Furthermore, the canonical approach may have much to contribute to ways of reading and understanding the Bible in general. Studies on the book of Isaiah, for example, have demonstrated how a fresh appreciation of the material can emerge when isolated passages are viewed in the context of the book as a whole. The canonical approach serves as a salutary reminder that texts can prove mutually illuminating, and that inter-textual dialogue can often help the reader to penetrate the deeper significance of a particular passage and appreciate its fuller implications. Just as in a picture every detail contributes something to its total effect as a work of art, so each passage in the Bible contributes something distinctive to the total impression of the whole. By insisting that we overcome our myopia and peer beyond the immediate text to survey the biblical landscape in its entirety, we are made aware of the dynamic inter-relation between various passages of Scripture, and between the Hebrew Bible and the New Testament.

But, as was the case with the "canon within the canon" approach, this strategy is also beset by certain difficulties. The first concerns the very practicality of the method, for it is by no means easy for readers of Scripture to engage with the full range of material at their disposal. Moreover, the fact that we have a relatively large and diverse body of texts makes the task of evaluating the whole of Scripture extremely difficult. Secondly, the very notion of the "canon" has proved problematic. Are we to be concerned with the Jewish canon of the Hebrew Bible or (as Childs insists) the Christian canon of the Old and New Testament, and if the latter, do we opt for the longer canon of the Catholic Church or the narrower canon of the Protestant tradition? While this problem is by no means insurmountable for Childs' thesis, the issue of "canon" does raise important questions that call for some kind of resolution. For example, why privilege the "canon" which, after all, is merely a dogmatic construct imposed upon the Bible from without? Why grant priority to this particular stage in the development of the tradition? Childs is concerned to allow each witness within the final form of the canon "its own integrity" (1992:551), but why not respect the integrity of the individual traditions in the prehistory of the text? Why should the final form of the process of trans-mission be absoutized and regarded as more authoritative and normative than the discernable preliminary stages prior to the completion of these books? Thirdly, the diversity of the biblical witness presents adherents of the canonical approach with a further difficulty, for the task of discerning the "main thrust" or the "general drift" of Scripture is by no means as straightforward as is often supposed. The danger of trying to present a pan-canonical approach is that tensions are suppressed and individual voices in the text are muffled, and the temptation is to try to unite the divergent witnesses of Scripture and make them coalesce into a harmonious whole.

The way in which the two contrasting approaches discussed in this chapter have dealt with the "holy war" traditions of the Hebrew Bible has proved most illuminating. Of the two strategies considered, the "canon within the canon" approach undoubtedly provides the most convenient way of relieving Christians of the embarrassment caused by the existence of such passages as Josh. 6–11 within Scripture. The strategy recognizes, with a refreshing frankness, that Scripture is not always morally edifying and it invites us, in effect, to skip over those parts which offend our moral sensibilities and focus, instead, on those which we are likely to find valuable as a source of ethical guidance in our lives. With regard to such morally difficult passages as Josh. 6–11, the "canon within the canon" approach may be regarded as something of a "damage limitation" exercise: it downplays the significance of the offensive texts in the Hebrew Bible by trying to limit discussion to its more favourable aspects. The solution suggested by Childs' canonical approach, on the other hand, is rather more subtle, for it maintains that by taking cognizance of the diversity of viewpoints in the Bible we will be able to relativize the more problematic ones. The strategy recognizes that some parts of Scripture fall way short of the high ideals espoused in other parts, but that when the Hebrew Bible is viewed in its entirety it is clear that the ethically objectionable perspec-tives are not without counter moral witness. By viewing the biblical testimony in its entirety, we are insulated from some of its more outlandish aspects, for it is the impression of the Bible as a whole that moulds our disposition, influences our perspective, and guides our actions.

To what extent the canonical strategy succeeds in practice, however, is debatable. The fact is that the tactic of highlighting the passages of peace associated with the eschatological age does not negate the force of the biblical endorsements of violence, any more than reading the patriarchal stories in the context of the canon helps to mitigate some of their more unsavoury aspects. There remains much that is "wild and untamed" (Brueggemann) about the ethical witness of the Hebrew Bible which neither the "canon within the canon" nor the canonical approach, despite their valiant efforts, can fully domesticate.

Chapter 5

The Paradigmatic Approach

The so-called "paradigmatic approach" has proved to be one of the most popular strategies deployed by biblical scholars to make the biblical provisions relevant to issues of contemporary concern and, to a lesser extent, it has been viewed as a useful hermeneutical tool to counter the ethically problematic passages of Scripture. Adherents of this strategy maintain that the morality of the Hebrew Bible is embedded in certain foundational principles, and it should not be supposed for a moment that its ethical and religious directives must determine our beliefs and practices to the last detail. Rather, the biblical material provides us with broad, general principles that guide us in our ethical decision-making, and it establishes a standard to which we can appeal in order to justify the correctness of a position taken or to test the propriety of an action performed or contemplated. In effect, the approach affords a basic orientation to life and leads us to discover "the sort of attitudes and conduct God expects from his people" (Lalleman 2004:xiv).

One of the main exponents of this approach has been Christopher J.H. Wright who, in numerous publications over the years, has argued very eloquently in favour of a "paradigmatic handling of the Old Testament for ethics"[1]. Wright has sought to explain the strategy by referring to the use of the term "paradigm" by grammarians. In grammatical terms, a paradigm is a verb or noun which is used as a model or example of the way in which countless other words in a language may be formed, and the "paradigmatic" approach to the ethics of the Hebrew Bible maintains that the laws and narratives

---

[1] Wright 2004:64. The paradigmatic approach is the methodological key to most of the essays contained in Wright's 1995 volume, *Walking in the Ways of the Lord*, though he had already made extensive use of the concept in his earlier study, *Living as the People of God* (1983). Although Wright was by no means the first to use the term "paradigm" in connection with biblical ethics, it is largely as a result of his publications that the strategy has proved to be popular and influential among biblical scholars. Lalleman, for example, is of the view that the "paradigmatic approach seems to provide a good perspective from which we can look at the whole of the Old Testament for its ethical relevance" (2004:50), while Goldingay agrees that the search for underlying principles is "a useful means to discover what are the equivalent statements for today" (1990:54). Rogerson expresses some sympathy with Wright's approach, concluding that the Hebrew Bible best contributes to Christian ethics by "challenging modern society to imitate its principles in ways appropriate to today's world" (2004:36). The term "paradigm" is used in the sub-title of Janzen's volume on the ethics of the Hebrew Bible, though his understanding of the term is slightly different from that of Wright (Janzen 1994:26–28; cf. Lalleman 2004:52–53).

The Immoral Bible

which emerged from ancient Israel should be regarded only as a "model" or "example" of the type of conduct deemed appropriate or inappropriate[2]. To transpose the provisions of the Hebrew Bible to the modern world and apply them as they stand would severely limit their applicability, and would be rather like "taking the paradigms of a grammar book as the only words one could use in that particular language" (Wright 1983:43). The point of the grammatical paradigm is that it has to be applied to other words, and the point of the ethical material contained in the Hebrew Bible is that it has to be applied to circumstances other than those to which they were originally addressed. Thus the fact that many biblical laws and customs cannot be viewed as normative or prescriptive as they stand need not be regarded as problematic, for it is not the laws or customs *per se* that are to be applied but the essential principles that can be drawn from them.

The Advantages of the Paradigmatic Approach

Adherents of this approach have little difficulty in demonstrating its attractiveness as a method of dealing with the ethics of the Hebrew Bible. In the first place, it is argued that the strategy is not only useful but entirely necessary if we are to extract from the biblical text a meaning that is relevant and applicable to the modern age. Since we cannot simply lift all the laws and institutions of the Hebrew Bible out of their historical context and apply them as they stand to contemporary conditions, the search for "underlying principles" is regarded as the only logical way of relating the demands of Scripture to contemporary life. Indeed, it is argued that if the approach is not adopted there is a sense in which the ethical relevance of the Hebrew Bible would be very restricted, for its use would be confined to those matters about which the ancient Israelites themselves happen to have expressed concern[3]. Applying the paradigmatic approach enables the social and cultural aspects of Israel's life to issue forth in new and perpetually relevant ethical principles which can be adapted to fit the contemporary situation.

A few examples will suffice to illustrate how the paradigmatic approach might function in practice. The law instructing the Israelites to refrain from reaping the edges of the field, or from gathering gleanings of their harvest (Lev. 19:9–10; Deut. 24:19–21), may appear irrelevant as it stands, but the

---

[2] Wright defines the term "paradigm" as "a particular, specific, concrete case that has wider relevance or application beyond its own particularity" (2004:65). For an explanation of the "paradigmatic approach" as applied to the ethics of the Hebrew Bible, see Wright 1983:40–45; 1995:57–66.

[3] As Wright observes, if the biblical material is not applied paradigmatically, the moral pronouncements of the Hebrew Bible would be "ethically gagged and bound" (1995:95), and "would have a very limited shelf-life indeed" (2004:105 n.3).

principle underlying the injunction—that of sharing with the poor and caring for the vulnerable—is as relevant today as ever (Bauckham 1989:12; Lalleman 2004:50–51). In a similar vein, the law of the Jubilee year (Lev. 25:8–55), which decreed that all property which had been forfeited to the creditor must periodically be restored to its original owner, clearly has no relevance in the modern world; yet, the principle underlying the law—the importance of restoring dignity and independence to those afflicted by poverty, and the need to show compassion to people who have become poor, homeless and debt-ridden—has universal significance and import (cf. Rogerson 2004:27, 65–6). The laws prohibiting lending at interest (Exod. 22:25; Lev. 25:36–37; Deut. 23:19–20; cf. Ezek. 22:12), while probably justified in an ancient agrarian society, where poor landowners were forced to borrow from the wealthy and were charged exorbitant interest rates for the privilege[4], are hardly acceptable as they stand in our own post-industrial economy; yet, the principle which underlies the law—that the poor should be protected from exploitation by the wealthy—carries abiding moral force.

In each of the above cases, what is regarded as important is not the law *per se* but the principle which it enshrines, and the challenge facing readers of the Hebrew Bible is to discover that principle and to consider how it may be applied in the most appropriate way to the kinds of situations in which they are likely to find themselves. In fact, in the case of the law prohibiting lending at interest, it is only when the actual injunction is reversed—and lending at interest is permitted and encouraged—that the poor and destitute can be helped, and the purpose of the law can truly be fulfilled[5]. In this case, as in many others, the rationale underlying the law and the justification for its. promulgation is considered to carry more weight than the letter of the law itself. The above examples illustrate how the paradigmatic approach respects both the nature and spirit of the text, and it is argued that only by adopting such a strategy can the moral teaching of Scripture prove a fruitful source of guidance for our own ethical thoughts and actions.

Furthermore, by applying the paradigmatic approach, readers of Scripture may be afforded guidance on issues of contemporary concern that are not specifically mentioned in the Bible, and while the biblical text may not provide

---

[4] It is generally agreed that such loans were needed primarily to purchase the annual necessities of agricultural life (such as seed corn) rather than for commercial investment. Although there is no definite information in the Hebrew Bible regarding the rate of interest charged in ancient Israel, it is known that in Babylon during the first dynasty it was about 20–25% on money and about 33% on grain (cf. Driver and Miles 1952:176). Leemans (1950:32–3) notes that this rate of interest was not unduly high, since in a land as agriculturally productive as Babylonia, the farmer would have had a good return on his crop.

[5] Cosgrove regards the biblical law concerning lending at interest as a particularly good example of a case where the application of the letter of the law in contemporary society would violate justice, and where it is reasonable to go according to the intent of the law rather than according to its letter (2002:34–37).

explicit answers to our modern ethical dilemmas, it may at least prove to be helpful in suggesting the parameters of morally permissible behaviour. For example, the Bible does not offer direct guidance on such controversial issues as abortion[6], genetic engineering or euthanasia, but the biblical principles regarding the sanctity of human life (cf. Gen. 1:27; 9:5–6), and the laws that enjoin care for the weak, defenceless and vulnerable in society (Deut. 15:7–11; 24:12–13; cf. Ps. 82:2–4), may help us to develop an ethical position when contemplating such issues[7]. Thus, even when confronted with problems that have no precedent in the Bible, this approach enables us to "sound out" the biblical material for values that might inform our ethical decision-making, and it opens up the possibility to probe the Hebrew Bible for ethical insights in new and creative ways. As Wright observes, the strategy "sets limits to our behaviour without telling us in specific terms what we must do in every situation" (1995:116; cf. Lalleman 2004:47).

The paradigmatic approach also raises the intriguing possibility that the commands of the Hebrew Bible may not always have been understood literally even by the people of ancient Israel themselves (cf. Goldingay 1990:54–55). It has been argued, for example, that many of the injunctions contained in the Pentateuch were not hard and fast statutes intended to be applied to the letter in the formal courts; rather, they were viewed as general instructions concerning the type of acceptable behaviour expected of the people of Israel. In a detailed discussion of the lawbooks contained in the Hebrew Bible, Dale Patrick has argued that they were intended "not for judicial application but for instruction in the values, principles, concepts, and procedures of the unwritten divine Law" (1985:198). The apodictic commandments found in the Decalogues, and scattered throughout much of the Pentateuch, "are more like moral precepts than legal prescriptions", and their aim seems to have been to "elicit conformity to the fundamental norms of the social order" (Patrick 1985:198). One of the arguments adduced in favour of this view is the fact that the legislation contained in the Hebrew Bible does not constitute a comprehensive or exhaustive set of rules that might have been referred to for regular consultation by judicial authorities[8]; rather, such rules as are recorded appear to have been intended to encourage judges to make their own judgment "in the spirit of the law and according to its underlying principles and customary procedures" (Patrick 1985:199). Moreover, the fact that some of the provisions

---

[6] Rogerson (2004:90) suggests that abortion was not commonly practised, if at all, in ancient Israel, lest a male child (regarded as highly desirable in that culture) be lost. Abortion was, however, practised (and punished) elsewhere in the ancient Near East, as is evident from the laws of Assyria and Babylon (cf. *ANET* 185; Driver and Miles 1952:367).

[7] Rogerson (2004:98) sees no reason why such passages as Ps. 82:2–4, when applied to our present world, should not include the unborn among the weak and defenceless.

[8] As Patrick observes, one can think of numerous cases of death or injury not covered by the laws of Exod. 21:12–14, 18–36, and many examples of theft and damage to property not mentioned in Exod. 22:1–15 (1985:199).

of the law appear not to have been implemented in practice[9], and that the lawbooks contain some provisions that are clearly idealistic or utopian[10], seems to confirm that they were not designed for practical application in judicial cases but were intended merely to embody some basic principles of social justice. According to this view, therefore, the "laws" were developed merely as guidelines for judges and the people at large, and they served, in effect, as the "conscience of the community" (Patrick 1985:200) by leading the people to embrace the values and principles expected by their God. Such an interpretation of the nature of Israel's laws is regarded as highly significant by adherents of the paradigmatic approach (Bauckham 1989:20–40; cf. Wright 1995:104), for it suggests that the search for underlying principles is not an anachronistic imposition upon the material in the Hebrew Bible, but is a genuine reflection of the way in which its laws were understood by the people of ancient Israel themselves. Even in their original formulation, therefore, they were intended not so much as statutes to be obeyed but as illustrations designed to educate people in the intention of the law, "so that they will learn by analogy how to behave in cases the Law does not mention" (Bauckham 1989:25).

Finally, the attractiveness of the paradigmatic approach lies in the fact that principles are, by their very nature, often more useful than specific commands, for principles tend to be flexible, adaptable and open-ended, whereas laws, by contrast, are often characterized by their rigidity and intractability. The principle of "an eye for an eye" enunciated in the law of Exod. 21:23–25, for example, has very limited applicability if enforced to the letter (as it is in societies which demand the death penalty for murder), and the notion of exact retribution which it implies, if carried to its logical conclusion, is hardly one which would commend itself to modern sensibilities (since we would not burgle a burglar or rape a rapist)[11]; on the other hand, if we search out the purpose underlying the law, then it becomes much more useful, for it may be understood to enunciate the entirely reasonable principle of proportionality, whereby the more serious the crime, the more severe the punishment[12]. Thus while most people would regard the literal application of the "lex talionis" as crude and barbaric, the more general notion that the punishment should be commensurate with the offence is one which is likely to meet with widespread

[9] A case in point may be the death penalty imposed for adultery (cf. Lev. 20:10). As McKeating has observed, although there are many references to adultery in the Hebrew Bible, there is no record of this punishment ever having been implemented (1979:57–72). Cf. Goldingay 1995:92.

[10] An example of a law commonly regarded as utopian is that relating to the Jubilee year (Lev. 25:8–55). For the view that this was no more than an idealistic proposal which was never actually enforced in Israel, see Weber 1952:71–2; Ginzberg 1932:368.

[11] One is reminded of the saying attributed to Gandhi: "An eye for an eye leaves the whole world blind".

[12] It is unlikely that the principle of "lex talionis" was applied literally even in ancient Israel (except in the case of offences which merited the death penalty), for there are very few penalties involving bodily mutilation in biblical law (cf. Patrick 1985:76–77).

approval. Moreover, in an age that is increasingly suspicious of all forms of authoritarian control, the notion that the text of Scripture is intended to be illuminative rather than prescriptive (cf. Spohn 1995:124), and that it speaks to the moral life at the level of basic values and principles rather than laws and regulations, is bound to be one which people in the twenty-first century will find most appealing.

The Ethically Problematic Passages of the Hebrew Bible

By and large, adherents of the paradigmatic approach have tended to focus on the biblical material that can command some measure of approval and support rather than the more dubious pronouncements that are likely to offend our moral sensibilities. Consequently, the strategy has primarily been used as a hermeneutical device to make the Bible relevant to contemporary issues rather than to overcome the ethically problematic passages of Scripture. Nevertheless, the search for underlying principles has proved helpful in many cases where the application of the letter of the law might violate our sense of natural justice. It is argued that passages such as those which appear to justify slavery, war crimes, and capital punishment are problematic only if we adopt an overly literal and restrictive approach to the biblical text; once we learn to root out their objectives and underlying principles, even some of the morally offensive portions of Scripture may be seen to function as a valuable guide for human conduct. As R.H. Kennett long ago observed, once the Hebrew Bible is viewed in its proper perspective, "it will commonly be found that things which to unintelligent literal interpretation are an occasion of stumbling embody a principle which should be for our spiritual and moral wealth" (1925:394). Thus, for example, the laws of the Hebrew Bible concerning slavery (Exod. 21:2–11; Deut. 15:12–18) may ostensibly seem to be shameful and reprehensible, but they are not so objectionable once they are understood as provisions designed to uphold the dignity and worth of all human beings, whatever their social status. The concept of Israel's special election, often seen as providing religious justification for elitist claims of racial superiority over other groups and nations[13], becomes far less problematic once it is understood that the principle underlying God's action was to bring a blessing to the nations of the earth, and to reveal to them his redemptive purpose (cf. Gen. 18:17–18; 22:17–18; 26:4–5).

In his discussion of the use of the paradigm by grammarians, Wright observes that its object is to teach us not only how to apply a verb but how

---

[13] Cf. Plaskow 1990:96–107; Clines 1995:199–201; 1997:100–101. Knierim argues that Israel's exclusive election by God "represents an insurmountable crisis for the Old Testament's claim to Yahweh's universal justice" (1995:451).

not to apply it. Knowing the paradigm enables us to critique bad grammar as well as to write good grammar. In a similar way, the paradigmatic approach to the ethics of the Hebrew Bible can help us not only in "positive ethical articulation" but also in "negative ethical critique" (2004:66). There are many cases in the Hebrew Bible where a literal interpretation of the law may appear to us to be unduly harsh or even absurd, but if we go behind the letter of the law, and consider its justification and rationale, its severity may—at least to some extent—be mitigated. Richard Bauckham notes, as an example, the case of the rebellious son in Deut. 21:18–21. According to this law, a persistently recalcitrant son must be brought before the elders of the community and, if found guilty, was to be stoned to death. Such a penalty, repellent though it appears to contemporary readers, must be understood in the context of ancient Israelite culture, where parents had a social function which went far beyond their role in contemporary society. Heads of families often acted both as a local council and a local court; thus, respect due to parents in ancient Israel was in part the respect due to the agents of law enforcement and government in that society. The incorrigible behaviour of the son in the law of Deut. 21:18–21 would thus have been deemed a threat not only to the well-being of the family but to the welfare of the community as a whole. The fact that the death penalty was imposed merely underlines the seriousness with which the offence was viewed, and although we today would regard such a punishment as utterly reprehensible, the principle undergirding the law may still be relevant, for it represents a challenge to the widespread contempt for the old and vulnerable which characterizes our own youth-centred culture, and it may be construed as supporting a degree of strictness and severity in the law's response to serious juvenile criminality (Bauckham 1989:31–33; cf. Wright 1983:167–8).

The Drawbacks of the Paradigmatic Approach

The paradigmatic approach has not, however, been without its detractors. One of the criticisms frequently levelled against the approach is that it tends to produce skewed readings of the biblical text in which the principles discerned are no more than a mirror of the interpreter's own preconceived value judgments. It was precisely for this reason that Karl Barth polemicized vigorously against any strategy which involved extracting "principles" from the biblical material, for such an approach merely encouraged interpreters to indulge their own wishes, whims, and desires, while disingenuously claiming for them a biblical sanction. Barth warned in no uncertain terms that those who approached the biblical text merely to extract ethical principles "must realize that they are taking a disastrous freedom with the Bible, and if they appeal to the Bible they must be reminded that they are appealing to a Bible that they have first adjusted to their own convenience" (CD ii/2:681). In a

similar vein, critics of the paradigmatic approach claim that its adherents come
to the Bible with their own ethical agenda, and tend to make the text conform
to their own moral expectations so that, by a happy coincidence, what is found
is what is sought[14]. In this respect, the criticism levelled against the paradigmatic approach is not unlike that noted in the previous chapter with regard
to the canonical approach: its adherents tend to construe the significance of
the text in suspiciously convenient ways, so that the truths extrapolated from
the biblical material are invariably those we want to hear[15]. Indeed, the cynic
may well come to the conclusion that, whenever this approach is applied, no
passage of Scripture, whatever it says, ever witnesses to anything other than
what happens to chime in with the interpreter's prior personal convictions.

It was in order to pre-empt such criticisms that Wright insisted that the
paradigmatic approach was a much more subtle and sophisticated process
than simply scanning the Bible in search of principles which could readily be
applied to modern society. In order to discern the contemporary relevance of
a particular law, it was essential to consider how it related to, and functioned
within, the overall social system of ancient Israel, much as Wayne Meeks
(1987) sought to illuminate the ethics of the New Testament by viewing it in
the context of the social, economic and political context of early Christianity
(Wright 1995:115). Wright maintains that, in order to determine the original
objective of any specific law, a range of pertinent questions must be asked: In
ancient Israelite society, whose interests was this law trying to protect? Whose
power was it seeking to restrict? What kind of behaviour was it designed to
encourage or discourage? What kind of values was it trying to promote or
undermine? When such questions are addressed to the biblical material, we
gain a far more nuanced understanding of the purpose of Israel's laws and this,
in turn, enables us to achieve a much more targeted application of them to
our own ethical concerns[16]. Once we appreciate the primary objectives of the

---

[14] The point is well made by Deidun: "Experience surely teaches us (if common sense failed
to do so) that interpreters who turn to biblical texts in search of "relevance" will surely find
what they are looking for, but only after imposing on the texts their own notions of what
counts as relevant" (1998:4).

[15] Wright wonders why Christians, "including those fully committed to biblical authority,
differ over the moral interpretation of the biblical evidence on many issues" (1995:65).
The answer, of course, is perfectly obvious: the principles they derive from the text are
invariably going to be those that conform to their own values and expectations. Thus, for
example, some will derive from the opening chapters of Genesis the principle of equality
of the sexes on the basis of Gen. 1:27, while others will derive the principle of the subordination of women on the basis of Gen. 2:18–25. For a discussion of these chapters which
brings out the egalitarian dimensions of the text, as opposed to traditional patriarchal and
misogynist interpretations, see Trible 1978:72–143.

[16] For example, the gradation of penalties applied by the ancient Israelites shows a clear
priority of human life over property, and this order of priorities may provide a challenge
to the sometimes distorted values of our modern judicial systems: "It is certainly possible
to set the scale of moral values reflected in Israel's penalties over against those of our own
society and then to observe the shortcomings and suggest reforms in order to bring our

biblical laws and understand the moral principles that governed their promulgation, they can be reformulated and reapplied to our own contemporary society[17]. By observing how the Israelites addressed various issues within their own culture and within their own historical context, we may be guided in the way in which we should address the ethical challenges that face us in our very different culture and context[18]. The application of such a procedure provides us not merely with highly generalized principles "but with much more sharply articulated objectives derived from the paradigm of the society God called Israel to be" (Wright 1995:116). Indeed, "the more closely and sharply we can perceive and articulate the very particularity of Israel, the more confident we can be in making choices ... that are legitimate within the contours and limits of the paradigm God has given us" (Wright 1995:116).

Since the paradigmatic approach, by definition, involves reading more into the text than is actually there, one can certainly sympathize with Wright's attempt to identify some substantive criteria for judging the validity of the proposed appropriation of a particular passage. Indeed, it is arguable that, of all the scholars who have adopted the paradigmatic approach, none has been more mindful than Wright of the need to ensure that the text is not being manipulated to reflect the interpreter's own concerns and interests. Referring to the work of Michael Schluter and Roy Clements (1990), Wright lists some of the potential pitfalls that are sometimes adduced by those who question the validity of the paradigmatic approach:

How does one determine the "right" principle when different interpreters derive different principles from the same text or texts?... How do we organize or prioritize our derived principles if they come into conflict with each other? How can we avoid our selection of derived principles being nothing more than a subjective statement of our own biases tangentially linked to the biblical text? (1995:107–8).

Wright's answer to such questions is to insist that the principles derived from the Hebrew Bible must be true to the nature of Israel as reflected in

own system of law and justice more in line with biblical priorities" (Wright 1995:105). This may be regarded as a fairly typical example of the way Wright considers that the objective of the biblical law can be achieved in our own very different situation, and how we can bring our own social objectives to point in the same direction.

[17] Wright 1995:114–16. A similar procedure is advocated by Goldingay, who argues that, in interpreting the biblical laws, "we need to move behind the concrete command to the principles that underlie it, not so as to stop there but so as to turn these principles back into concrete commands applicable to our own situations" (1995:92).

[18] Wright suggests that a similar process occurs when we use the example of Jesus paradigmatically in our ethical decisions, for we seek to move from what we know Jesus did to what we might reasonably presume he would do in our changed situation (Wright 1983:44; 2004:73). This suggests, however, a highly subjective process by which the "principle" is perceived intuitively rather than by a laborious process of critical analysis,

the biblical material. We derive our basic principles by analyzing the way in which the ancient Israelites derived theirs. As we saw in the case of the rebellious son, this involves understanding a particular law (or institution) in its original context in ancient Israelite society, and trying to discern its primary objective within that society, so that it can be reformulated and reapplied in terms of modern conditions. Only thus can we ensure that there is a real and tangible connection between the text examined and the principle to which it is supposed to bear witness, and only thus can we ensure that the paradigmatic approach does not simply open the floodgates to a range of fanciful, speculative and artificial interpretations of the biblical text.

While Wright is certainly to be applauded for trying to ensure that the principles we derive from the biblical text are valid and legitimate, the method which he proposes seems rather contrived and convoluted. For example, the law prohibiting lending at interest, discussed above, ostensibly seems simple enough, and the principle that can be generalized from the law—the need to curtail greed and to refrain from taking advantage of the vulnerable in society—appears relatively straightforward. However, once it is proposed that the law be understood against the background of Israel's social, economic and political institutions, its significance suddenly becomes much more intricate and complicated, for the injunction must now be seen "in relation to Israel's system of land tenure and economic objectives, which in turn are bound up with the importance and role of the extended families, which in turn relate to other features of Israel's judicial and social life" (Wright 1995:108). The magnitude of the task involved in setting the law in its original context should not be underestimated, for what is required is far more than a passing knowledge of ancient Israel's life and culture; on the contrary, "a *comprehensive* understanding of the *total* Israelite social system" (Wright 1995:173; my italics) is desired if we are properly to appreciate any single feature of it. Now whether ordinary readers of the Hebrew Bible are going to be sufficiently *au fait* with ancient Israel's life and institutions to appreciate the full significance of the principle underlying each of the biblical laws must be regarded as most doubtful. It should, perhaps, be added that Wright's insistence that each text be examined in the context of Israel's own life and experience presupposes that we know far more about ancient Israelite society than most contemporary biblical scholars will allow. Moreover, the paradigmatic approach involves a considerable feat of the imagination on the part of the reader, for we are required to go back to the "hard given reality of the text of the Bible itself and *imaginatively* to live with Israel in their world ("inhabiting the text"), before returning to the equally hard given reality of our own world, to discover *imaginatively* how that paradigm challenges our ethical response there" (2004:70; my italics). The repeated use of "imaginatively" in this sentence is highly significant, for it begs the question as to how far this approach is really grounded in the text and how far in the imagination of the interpreter. Are the points of contact between the text and the principle derived from it imaginative or imaginary? Despite Wright's arguments, it seems doubtful whether the method which he advocates can ever be regarded as a foolproof way to ensure that the principle derived from the biblical text is valid and legitimate.

At this point a further complication arises, for even if it could be demonstrated beyond any doubt that the principles discovered have been legitimately appropriated from the text, it is questionable whether such derived principles can have any normative significance[19]. In theory, it would be possible for a hundred interpreters to draw out as many principles from the same text and, if that were to happen, whose "principle" should be regarded as normative? As Richard B. Hays has remarked, the ethical principles of the Bible are either normative at the level of their own claims or they are invalid. In fact, Hays makes an important point when he maintains that the biblical texts should only be granted authority "*in the mode in which they speak*" (1996:294; his italics). Presumably this means that the interpreter should respect not only the content of the text but also its form. Wright claims to respect both the form and content of the biblical material (1995:15), but this is precisely what the paradigmatic approach does *not* do. Rules are rules and must not be confused with principles or paradigms[20]. The fact is that if we do not respect the form of the biblical material, the paradigmatic approach may be used as a means of avoiding the implications of the text and providing a convenient escape route from some of its more uncomfortable demands. As an example of such casuistry, Hays refers to Jesus' command in the Gospels to sell all one's possessions and give the proceeds to the poor (Lk. 12:33). Adherents of the paradigmatic approach would no doubt claim that such a command should not, of course, be interpreted literally (since that would be most inconvenient for the well-heeled citizens of Western society); it merely enunciates a general principle to give generously to those in need[21]. But how is the command in

---

[19] Even Goldingay, who is by no means averse to deriving principles from the biblical text, maintains that only the biblical text itself, not the hypothetical principles derived from it, can be regarded as normative (1990:55). Wright (1995:95) criticizes this view, since it implies that either we have an authoritative text which we cannot apply directly, or we have derivative principles which can be applied but which have no intrinsic moral authority. Of course, this is a completely false dichotomy, for there are plenty of authoritative texts in the Hebrew Bible that can be applied directly without needing to look for any "principles" that might underlie them.

[20] A clear example of a "principle" in the Bible is Jesus' words in the Sermon on the Mount: "If anyone forces you to go one mile, go also the second mile" (Mt. 5:41). Clearly, this statement would hardly be interpreted literally (either by ourselves or by Jesus' contemporaries); rather, it is recognized that it merely states a principle (reflected in the popular adage of "going the extra mile"), viz., the need to serve others beyond conventional requirements or expectations.

[21] Hays expresses his utter exasperation with such interpretations in no uncertain terms: "Christian preachers, at least since the time of Clement of Alexandria, have preached hundreds of thousands of disastrous sermons that say, in effect, "Now the text says x, but of course it couldn't really mean that, so we must see the underlying principle to

the Gospel qualitatively any different from the commands in the Hebrew Bible prohibiting murder and theft? Why are we bound by the letter of the law in one case but only by the spirit of the law in the other? The paradigmatic approach can all too easily degenerate into an intellectually dishonest way of escaping the implications of the law's demands, and it can be a means of evading the obvious meaning of the text when that meaning proves too inconvenient (cf. Goldingay 1990:55; Cosgrove 2002:192).

Two further points may briefly be made concerning the paradigmatic approach. Firstly, its adherents appear to labour under the mistaken belief that all the biblical material must somehow be relevant, and if it is not obviously and directly relevant then, by some exegetical sleight-of-hand, it must be made relevant and applicable to contemporary issues[22]. What they do not appear to realize, however, is that the Hebrew Bible contains material which has different degrees of relevance. Failure to recognize this has all too often meant that the biblical evidence has been contorted to accommodate utterly alien issues (such as those concerning abortion or euthanasia) and this, in turn, has inevitably led to the imposition of anachronistic elements which distort the true understanding of the biblical text. If some laws and institutions have only a limited significance (or no significance at all) for contemporary society, then so be it; we should simply accept that such is the case, and not seek some convoluted method to try to "make" them applicable and relevant.

Secondly, a question must be raised concerning the utility of such a strategy, for the principles derived from the text are often so vague and self-evident that nobody would seriously want to quibble with them. The result, as often as not, is such a level of generalization that one is left wondering why the strategy needs to be deployed at all[23]. By and large, the principles derived merely

which it points, which is y". Let there be a moratorium on such preaching!" (1996:294). Nevertheless, Hays endorses the paradigmatic approach to Scripture, provided that there are adequate controls in place to ensure that the principles derived from the text are valid and legitimate. Although he makes no reference to the work of Wright, his own approach (viz., placing our own community's life imaginatively within the world articulated by the text) is broadly similar.

[22] That there seems to be an unacknowledged assumption among adherents of the paradigmatic approach that the entire Bible must have something authoritative and relevant to say is implied by Wright, who argues that when this strategy is properly applied "*no text* is dismissed just because 'it does not apply to us'" (1983:64; my italics).

[23] For example, Rogerson, in his discussion of the law of the goring ox in Exod. 21:28–32, claims that the letter of the law (which states that the owner of an ox known to be a gorer should be put to death) clearly no longer holds, but its underlying principle (that lives should not be put at risk by dangerous animals) is still relevant (2004:17). While the principle derived by Rogerson from the law seems perfectly valid, one is inevitably left wondering whether it is not merely stating the obvious. After all, do we really need the law of the goring ox and the "principle" derived from it to remind us that owners of dangerous animals have a responsibility to keep them under strict control? The point is well made by Cyril Rodd: "How many Christians, I wonder, based their decision that pit bull terriers needed to be legally controlled on the Old Testament law, or even thought of that law when they watched on their television screens children who had been savaged by dogs?"

confirm the moral consensus shared by all thoughtful and sensitive people, religious and non-religious alike, and they usually serve only to corroborate the ethical beliefs and values which we had probably already accepted anyway. After all, to claim on the basis of particular laws that exploiting the vulnerable is wrong, and that one should give generously to the poor, is only marginally more controversial than saying we should all be in favour of motherhood and apple pie. The principles derived from the text would probably be acceptable to all right-minded people, but it is doubtful whether they would regard them as particularly useful or even as particularly interesting.

The Paradigmatic Approach and the "Holy War" Traditions

Given the profound significance that Wright attaches to the concept of "land" in his construction of the ethics of the Hebrew Bible (1983:46–102; 1995:181–212), it is somewhat surprising that the conquest of Canaan receives scant attention, at least in his earlier publications. As if to make amends for this omission, he seeks in his later writings to tackle the subject head-on, and although he modestly makes no claims to solving the problem, he does attempt to grapple with it in the light of perspectives derived from the Bible itself (2004:472–80; 2008:73–108).

In this regard, it is crucial for Wright's argument that not only is the ethics of the Hebrew Bible to be understood paradigmatically, but that Israel herself is viewed in Scripture as a "paradigm" (1983:40–45; 1995:147–78). The crucial text in this connection is Exod. 19:3–6, especially v. 6: "You shall be for me a priestly kingdom and a holy nation". The terms "priestly kingdom" and "holy nation" are regarded as highly significant, for Wright claims that they encapsulate the role and mission which God intended for the people of Israel. As a "priestly kingdom", it was their duty to represent God to the nations by revealing to them his moral demands and his redemptive purpose. Thus, just as it was through the priest that the people of Israel came to know God, so it was through Israel that other nations would come to know him. Israel had been chosen, redeemed and brought into a covenant relationship with God in order to "showcase" his ideals for humanity, and in this sense Israel was God's "role model" or "paradigm" of what a nation ought ideally to be (Deut. 4:6–8; cf. Wright 2004:73–74; Lalleman 2004:36). The task given to Israel was that of "living as the people of God" (to quote the title of one of Wright's earlier volumes) in the midst of the nations, and manifesting his character and will in their own lives. There was a real sense, therefore, in which "the medium

(2001:308). It is interesting to observe that Paul derives from the law which prohibits an ox from being muzzled when it is treading the grain (Deut. 25:4) the general principle that missionaries should be provided for financially (1 Cor. 9:8–12), which rather supports the view that virtually any principle can be extracted from a biblical text if you try hard enough!

were themselves part of the message" (1983:40; 1995:30). But the people were not only to serve as a model or example for others to follow; it was through them that God would bring other nations into a covenant relationship with himself. Hence, Israel's very existence had a "missionary relevance". This was already prefigured in God's promise to Abraham that his descendants would be a "blessing to the nations" (Gen. 12:1–3), and it was a theme taken up by Deutero-Isaiah, who pronounced that Israel was to be a "light to the nations" (Isa. 42:6; 49:6). However, Israel's missionary purpose could only successfully be fulfilled if she became a "holy nation", that is, a people set apart from other nations as distinctive and different, and this distinctiveness was to affect every aspect of their national life, including their religious, social, economic and political affairs. In many observable ways, the social system of the ancient Israelites was, consciously and deliberately, different from, and sometimes completely opposed to, the norms generally accepted by their neighbours, so much so that the emergence of Israel "introduced a new paradigm of beliefs and values into the ancient Near Eastern world"[24].

It is against this understanding of the role and significance of Israel as a nation that Wright understands the account of the conquest of Canaan. If Israel was, indeed, to serve as a "model" or "paradigm" for other nations, her distinctiveness had to be preserved at all costs, as is made clear in Lev. 18:3: "You shall not do as they do in the land of Egypt where you lived, and you shall not do as they do in the land of Canaan, to which I am bringing you" (cf. Exod. 23:23–24; Deut. 6:14; 7:5–6; 29:16–18). Now it is clear that Israel's distinctiveness would be seriously compromised if the people were to settle alongside the Canaanites in the land, for the latter are known to have practised child sacrifice, idolatry and cultic prostitution (Deut. 12:29–31; 18:9–14; 23:17–18), evils that could easily have led the people of Israel astray (Wright 1983:175). The fact that Canaanite culture was "degraded" (Wright 2008:106) is regarded as significant, for this puts the conquest narrative within a moral framework that distinguished it from ethnocentric genocide or from violence inflicted in an arbitrary, random or malevolent way[25]. The conquest of Canaan

---

[24] Wright 1995:59. Among the distinctive features which set Israel apart from her neighbours, Wright notes the valuing of human life above property in the scale of offences and in the forms of punishment; the absence of imprisonment as a legal penalty; the almost total absence of forms of bodily mutilation as punishment (common in other law codes); strict limits on corporal punishment; and particular legislative concern for the protection of the weak and vulnerable, including unparalleled legal rights for slaves (1995:63).

[25] Wright 2004:475–6; 2008:93–94. Wright objects to the use of the word "genocide" to describe the Israelite conquest of Canaan since, in modern parlance, the word implies an element of "vicious self-interest usually based on myths of racial superiority" (2008:92). Yet, Wright appears to have no qualms about stating that the Egyptians at the time of the exodus were "guilty of gross violation of normal family life through a policy of state-sponsored genocide" (1995:219). Since the *OED* defines the word as the "annihilation of a race", its use in this context seems amply justified.

was therefore "an act of warranted judgment" (2008:107) on a people whose religion had become debased and whose life had become corrupt.

Wright concedes that the biblical account of the conquest of Canaan might be regarded as undermining his concept of Israel as a "paradigm", for if Israel was, indeed, to be a model or example for others, how could their brutal annihilation of the Canaanites possibly be regarded as in any way exemplary? Moreover, if Israel's missionary challenge was to bring a blessing to the nations, how could this be squared with the suffering they inflicted upon the native inhabitants of the promised land? Wright asks, quite properly, "Does the conquest narrative not stand in an impossibly deconstructive relationship with the promise of blessing?" (2004:472). To which the only reasonable answer, surely, is a resounding "Yes!". But, of course, Wright does not yield to such awkward questions so easily, and while conceding that the account of the occupation of Canaan in Josh. 6–11 is a "grim narrative of judgment and destruction" (2008:98), and that nothing can remove the feeling of revulsion generated by these chapters, he insists that they must be seen as "part of the total Bible story, which is the story of salvation and ultimately a story of universal blessing" (2008:98). Seen in this broader perspective, and in the light of God's long-term goal for humankind, "even the historical defeat of the Canaanites by Israel will ultimately be seen to be *part of an overall history of salvation* for which the nations themselves will praise God"[26].

Now this attempt to overcome the ethical problem caused by Israel's annihilation of the Canaanites is seriously flawed. In the first place, the very notion of Israel as a "paradigm" must surely be questioned, for in what sense can the actions of the Israelites as recorded in the Hebrew Bible possibly be regarded as a "model" or "example" for others to follow? Given that the people of Israel practised polygamy, permitted slavery, and were not averse to annihilating an entire population, how can we possibly accept Wright's contention that there was a sense in which "everything connected with them was exemplary in principle"? (2004:156). Of course, Wright himself is aware of the potential difficulties inherent in the notion of Israel as a "paradigm", for the nation could just as well be regarded as a model of a xenophobic and homophobic regime, or as a model of a society which promoted slavery and patriarchal domination within the family. Thus Wright is compelled to argue that a paradigm is not so much to be imitated as applied. But this only raises a further difficulty, for

[26] Wright 2008:106 (his italics). A similar approach was advocated half a century earlier by his namesake, George Ernest Wright, who came to the conclusion that the conquest of Canaan was part of the divine plan, since God had "a purpose of universal redemption in the midst of and for a sinful world" (Wright and Fuller 1957:108). One is reminded of Kierkegaard's notion of the "teleological suspension of the ethical" (1983:66), namely, that there are occasions when, for the ultimate supreme good, normal moral judgment must be temporarily suspended (cf. Barr 1993:219). In this case (so the argument goes), given that Israel was to bring salvation to the nations, the annihilation of the Canaanites, though unfortunate, may be deemed necessary for the greater good.

it inevitably begs the question as to who is to decide which aspects of Israel's existence are paradigmatic and which are not, and on what basis are such decisions to be made? Indeed, there seems to be a fundamental inconsistency in Wright's argument, for he insists that the law was given to Israel in order to mould and shape her behaviour so that the nation could serve as a "paradigm" for others; yet, it is that very law that condones slavery, promotes the subordination of women, and demands the annihilation of the Canaanites.

Furthermore, Wright's emphasis on the significance of Israel's missionary role must also be called in question, for this is a feature which appears to figure far more prominently in his own writings than in the Hebrew Bible itself[27]. In claiming that Israel was to be a "light to the nations" (Isa. 42:6; 49:6), it must be remembered that it is the Suffering Servant who fulfils this role, and scholars are by no means unanimous that the Suffering Servant is to be identified with Israel[28]. Moreover, to seek to justify Israel's annihilation of the Canaanites on the basis that her vocation was to become a vehicle of blessing to other nations (cf. Gen. 12:1–3; 18:18; 22:18; 26:4; 28:14) rather overlooks the fact that there are many passages which suggest that Israel was anything but a blessing to the nations with which she came into contact (cf. Clines 1995: 208–9). Indeed, such nations could be forgiven for asking: if these are blessings, who needs curses (cf. Clines 1995:208–9)? It is interesting to note that Wright himself at one point concedes that the notion of Israel's "missionary purpose" is neither common nor widespread in the Hebrew Bible, and he is forced to conclude (rather lamely) that this must have been a feature of their calling that Israel tended to forget! (1995:130). But even if we allow that Israel had a missionary purpose, and that that purpose could only be fulfilled if they were to remain uncontaminated by Canaanite influence, it is by no means clear why the Canaanites had to be completely annihilated in order to remove all temptation. Why could they not have been exiled from the land, as many of the Jews were later to be exiled to Babylon? The fact is that in seeking to eliminate one ethical problem Wright merely creates another, for he is forced to concede that, with regard to the destruction of the Canaanites, the end, in effect, justifies the means. Needless to say, such an argument is highly problematic from the ethical point of view, for even if the indigenous population of Canaan was particularly wicked and depraved (an assumption by no means shared by all biblical scholars), it is doubtful whether this would warrant the destruction

---

[27] Goldingay claims that it is "doubtful whether in Isaiah 40–55 or anywhere else (except Isa. 66:19?) it is wise to speak of Israel's being called to a 'mission' to the nations", and he suggests that this is merely a construct imposed on the Bible from without (2000:182).

[28] The question of the identity of the Suffering Servant has received a bewildering variety of answers. While it is quite possible that the Servant represents Israel (or a remnant within Israel), it is equally possible that the prophet had a particular individual in mind, and among the various contenders suggested are Moses, Cyrus, Jeremiah, and even Deutero-Isaiah himself. For a detailed discussion of the various possibilities, see North 1948:28–116.

of an entire population[29]. By emphasizing the wickedness and depravity of the Canaanites, Wright simply accepts uncritically the ideology of the biblical writers, and fails to see that this was a common ploy (still widely used today) of vilifying and demonizing the enemy in order to justify their destruction.

It is thus difficult to see how the paradigmatic approach can be used to resolve the ethical problem caused by the narrative of the conquest of Canaan in Josh. 6–11. On the contrary, as J.J. Collins has observed, one of the troubling aspects of the story in Joshua is precisely the way it has been used analogically over the centuries as a legitimating paradigm of violent conquest—by white colonists in North America[30], by right-wing Zionists and their conservative Christian supporters in modern Israel[31], and by the Boers in South Africa (Collins 2005:62–63; cf. Goldingay 1995:66). As Collins has perceptively remarked: "Attractive though it may be to proclaim the Bible as the Word of God when it advocates justice and freedom and to point to modern analogies, we must remember that it is the same Bible that commands the slaughter of the Canaanites and Amalekites and that it lends itself all too readily to analogical application in those cases too" (2005:74).

Conclusion

The attraction of the paradigmatic approach for those concerned to explicate the ethics of the Hebrew Bible is perfectly understandable, for it is a strategy that aims to be true to the spirit of the biblical text while at the same time making it relevant and applicable to the modern world. Even passages which may at first sight appear obsolete or irrelevant are regarded as potentially valuable, for they may contain principles which transcend their culture-bound limitations and which speak all the more tellingly to the needs of contemporary society. In this way, the strategy may be said to overcome what Wright calls the "hermeneutical despair of cultural relativity" (1995:173), for it suggests that it is possible to transfer ethical values out of one culture and into another.

---

[29] As A.G. Hunter has observed, when we find ourselves excusing mass slaughter in the name of morality then something is very seriously wrong (2003:100–101).

[30] R.A. Warrior, a member of the Osage Nation of American Indians, provides a Native American liberation reading of the conquest narrative in which the Native Americans are identified with the Canaanites, "the people who already lived in the promised land" (2006:237). The conquest stories merely provided the Puritans and other European settlers in North America with a biblical text which appeared to justify the destruction of the indigenous population; cf. Aichele 1995:284–6.

[31] Greenberg notes that this movement legitimates itself by appeal to Jewish sources, especially the tradition of the conquest and the dispossession of the native inhabitants of the land. He emphasizes, however, that the Hebrew Bible knows of no general injunction of lasting validity to settle in the land and expel its inhabitants, and consequently the contention of contemporary militant nationalistic religious movements that land seizures are scripturally grounded is both specious and unfounded (1995:461–71).

Moreover, the problem of the specificity and historical conditionality of the ethical demands of the Hebrew Bible is conveniently resolved by means of this approach, for by rooting out the underlying principles of a text we may be able to generalize or universalize its meaning and make it relevant and applicable to various situations in today's world. Viewed in this way, the ethical teaching of the Hebrew Bible may be used in a flexible manner to resolve problems and issues which have no precedent as such in Scripture, and readers are invited to search the biblical material for signposts pointing them to destinations which were not, perhaps, located on the original map. Moreover, it is claimed that the paradigmatic approach may help to resolve some of the ethically problematic passages of the Hebrew Bible, for it is argued that it is precisely when this strategy is not applied, and biblical texts are interpreted literally, that the Bible has been used (or, rather, misused) to justify such evils as slavery, racial discrimination and ethnic cleansing.

But the paradigmatic approach, however appealing it might ostensibly appear, inevitably raises some uncomfortable questions. How do we know that the derivative moral principles that we cull from Scripture are legitimate within the contours of the paradigm? How do we distinguish between what is an acceptable extension and application of a text and what is not? How do we prevent our derived principles from being merely a subjective statement of our own particular predilections? Will not different people be inclined to draw different—and perhaps even conflicting—principles from the same texts and make the Bible say what they want it to say? The danger of the paradigmatic approach to Scripture is that it invites readers to indulge in a "hermeneutics of desire" (Ostriker 1997:165), and permits them to draw from the text whatever lesson or message they please. Once the Hebrew Bible is dragged from its literal and historical moorings, it can be made to mean many things, and this particular strategy courts the risk of imposing an arbitrary meaning on the biblical text and throwing open the gates to every conceivable vagary of interpretation.

It was in order to avoid this danger that Wright sought to establish certain controls to ensure that the derived principles arose naturally from the text and were not imposed upon it from without in an arbitrary, artificial way. But the method which he advocated was seen to be unduly complicated, and raised as many problems as it resolved. Indeed, even Wright himself concedes that the approach which he favours is "immensely demanding", though he hastens to sweeten the pill by assuring us that it "sharpens one's whole use of the wide range of scriptural texts" (1995:66). Certainly, when applied to the accounts of the conquest of Canaan, the strategy is found wanting, and Wright's contention that "what God did in, for and through Israel was ultimately for the benefit of the nations" (1995:112) sounds rather hollow when viewed in the context of the conquest of the land of Canaan.

The criticisms levelled against the paradigmatic approach should not, of course, be taken to imply that the Hebrew Bible is devoid of any general principles. The so-called "love command" of Lev. 19:18, 34, for example, is an obvious case of a principle which stands on a par with anything encountered in the New Testament. But the danger of the paradigmatic approach is that it may reduce the ethical teaching of the Hebrew Bible to mere platitudes and vague generalizations with which nobody would wish to disagree. To disregard the plain meaning of the text and discover another more edifying meaning in order to make the Hebrew Bible relevant and palatable seems a strangely disingenuous way of interpreting Scripture, and it is difficult to avoid the conclusion that by deploying such a strategy we are merely making excuses for not facing up to what the text actually says.

Chapter 6

The Reader–Response Approach

One of the most important aspects of biblical scholarship during the past few decades has been a focus on the literary approach to the Bible, and many scholars have adopted the methodologies of comparative literature in an attempt to understand the biblical text. This trend has been chronicled many times and need not detain us here[1]. Our concern in this chapter, rather, is to pursue one particular approach suggested by secular literary critics which might prove helpful when considering the ethically problematic passages of Scripture. That approach is known as "reader–response criticism". This term is used to refer to a diverse assortment of methodologies and practices, and the spectrum of reader–response critics is so broad that it is questionable whether they should all be categorized under one neat heading[2]. Indeed, if we were to ask reader–response critics the ostensibly simple question, "Who *is* the reader?", it is likely that we would be provided with a confusingly large number of different answers, for over the years the discipline has developed a rich panoply of different types of "reader". These have been defined and classified in various ways, and include, for example, the "implied reader" (Iser, Booth), the "model reader" (Eco), the "ideal reader" (Culler), the "informed reader" (Fish) and the "actual reader" (Jauss), to name but a few[3].

The type of reader which will be of primary concern to us, however, will be the one designated by Judith Fetterley as the "resisting reader"[4]. Resisting readers feel that they have a duty to converse and interact with the text, and believe that literary compositions should be read in an openly critical, rather than in a passively receptive, way. Instead of tacitly accepting the standards of

---

[1] See Barton 1984; McKnight 1988; Thiselton 1992:515–55; Davies 2003a:20–37; Brett 1993:13–31; Aichele 1995:20–69.

[2] Many different approaches are represented in the volumes edited by Suleiman and Crosman (1980) and Tompkins (1980), both of which contain excellent annotated bibliographies. Suleiman (1980:3–45) subdivides reader-oriented (or, as she prefers to call it, "audience oriented") criticism into six major categories: rhetorical; semiotic and structuralist; phenomenological; subjective and psychoanalytic; sociological and historical; and hermeneutic.

[3] Other definitions include the "real reader", the "intended reader", the "hypothetical reader", the "authorial reader", the "competent reader", and the "average reader". See Fowler 1985:5–23; 1991:26.

[4] Fetterley's study of the "resisting reader" (1978), now commonly regarded as a classic of feminist reader–response criticism, was concerned to examine the problem encountered by the female reader reading male-oriented works of American literary fiction.

judgment established in the text and capitulating uncritically to its demands, they are prepared to challenge its assumptions, to question its insights, and (if necessary) to discredit its claims. They may want to resist texts that appear to be oppressive or tyrannical and reject demands that they feel should not (and perhaps cannot) be fulfilled. They may want to argue that the tradition underlying a particular text is ethically questionable and that to accept it as it stands is both morally and intellectually indefensible. In brief, they may want to read "against the grain" of the text and call its content into account in their own court of ethical judgment.

According to this approach, then, reading is not an exercise for passive spectators, for it involves a variety of activities, including reflection, judgment, appraisal, assessment, evaluation, and these activities, in turn, inevitably lead to approval or disapproval, acclaim or criticism, acceptance or rejection. The text opens itself up to a kind of dialogue between two interlocutors, and readers are challenged to contribute to the conversation with their own questions and reactions. Whereas readers have traditionally been content to ask, simply, "What does the text *say*?", the resisting reader will go a step further and ask, "What does the text say *to me*?" and, even more importantly, "What do *I* say *to it*?" (Jauss 1982:146–7). The reaction of the reader is regarded as of paramount importance, for the aim of reader–response criticism is to revitalize our engagement with the text and make us more conscious of our own response to what we are reading.

Wayne Booth, one of the most influential and engaging critics of secular literature, recounts how he became alerted to the importance of the effect of literature on those who read it by the reaction of one of his black colleagues at the University of Chicago, Paul Moses, who (much to the astonishment of his fellow teachers) expressed his unwillingness to teach *Huckleberry Finn* to a cohort of first-year students because of the deleterious effect its contents might have on the impressionable minds that might read it:

> It's hard for me to say this, but I have to say it anyway. I simply can't teach *Huckleberry Finn* again. The way Mark Twain portrays Jim is so offensive to me that I get angry in class, and I can't get all those liberal white kids to understand why I am angry. What's more, I don't think it's right to subject students, black or white, to the many distorted views of race on which that book is based. No, it's not the word "nigger" I'm objecting to, it's the whole range of assumptions about slavery and its consequences, and about how whites should deal with liberated slaves, and how liberated slaves should behave or will behave toward whites, good ones and bad ones. That book is just bad education, and the fact that it's so cleverly written makes it even more troublesome to me (Booth 1988:3; cf. 2006:225).

The words of Paul Moses (as recounted by Booth) underline one of the most important tenets of reader–response criticism, namely, that all literature should be held ethically accountable, if only because of the profound influence, for good or ill, that it may exercise upon its readers. The American critic Stanley Fish, one of the leading figures in the reader–response movement, argued that all readers should be encouraged to reflect upon the impact that a literary work had had upon them, for the literary text was not so much an object to be analyzed as an effect to be experienced. Consequently, the fundamental question that should be asked of any text was not "What does this text *mean*?" but "What does this text *do*?" (Fish 1972:387–8). What kind of values does it advocate? Is it doing anyone any harm? What effect does it have upon its readers? Does it promote hatred and violence? Does it encourage racism, misogyny, colonialism, xenophobia or homophobia? Does it contribute to the general well-being of society or does it have a negative, detrimental effect, perhaps by reinforcing the language of oppression and domination? It was not enough for literary critics to understand the text or even to evaluate its content; it was their responsibility to consider the impact which any given text had on the individual who reads it.

Reader–response Criticism and the Hebrew Bible

Now the reader–response approach, and especially the notion of the "resisting reader", may provide a valuable resource for dealing with the ethically problematic passages of Scripture, for it is arguable that such passages are unsettling only because readers have been conditioned to remain slavishly respectful to the text's claims and to respond to its demands with uncritical obeisance[5]. Readers of the Hebrew Bible have traditionally felt themselves to be passive recipients of the text, obliged to submit to its authority and to acquiesce in its value judgments. The type of approach deployed by secular reader–response critics, however, serves to remind us that we have a duty to enter into dialogue with the text and to consider the extent to which the views adumbrated by the biblical authors agree or conflict with our own. As we read Scripture, we must respond as thinking individuals and feel free to draw our own conclusions regarding the validity or otherwise of its claims. Our task is to engage in a vigorous debate with the Hebrew Bible, resisting statements that appear to be morally objectionable, and taking a critical stance against what we may regard as the excesses of the biblical text. Unlike the "canon within the canon" approach, which has the effect of ignoring the ethically problematic passages of the Hebrew Bible (and thus downgrading them to a position of secondary importance), this strategy recognizes the canonical status of

[5] For reader–response approaches to the Bible, see Detweiler 1985; Croatto 1987; McKnight 1988, 1989; Clines 1990, 1995; and for a discussion of the way in which feminist biblical critics have appropriated the insights of reader–response criticism, see Davies 2003b.

these texts but invites the reader to wrestle with them and to question their presuppositions and ideologies.

Among scholars of the Hebrew Bible, David Clines has been in the vanguard of those who have argued that "understanding" the biblical text should not be the only (or even primary) goal of interpretation; rather, biblical scholars should be engaged in the business of critique, and should be prepared to evaluate the text's claims and assumptions. Clines concedes that such an approach may well cause a certain unease in scholarly circles, for biblical exegetes have generally been reticent to engage in what may be termed "ethical criticism" (Booth 1988:3–22); their interest, rather, has traditionally been that of the theologian, sociologist or anthropologist, and consequently they have conceived their task as being to describe, as dispassionately as possible, the customs, beliefs and practices of the ancient Israelites. What they have singularly failed to do, according to Clines, is to enter the domain of the moral philosopher and critically appraise the biblical statements. They have been quite prepared to question the historical accuracy or reliability of the biblical traditions, but have shied away from questioning the validity of its moral norms and underlying assumptions. They have usually proceeded from an examination of the text to an explanation of its meaning without pausing for a moment to pass judgment on its content. As a result, the task of evaluation has all but been evacuated from the realm of biblical criticism. In typical flamboyant style, Clines chides his fellow academics who have been content merely to describe the ethical values of the Hebrew Bible, and who have been unwilling to emerge from the safe haven of descriptive discourse to engage openly in the tasks of evaluation and critique:

> Not one academic biblical scholar in a hundred will tell you that their primary task is to *critique* the Bible. For some reason, we have convinced ourselves that our business is simply to *understand*, to *interpret*. Here we have some difficult texts from the ancient world, we say, rightly enough. Do you want to know what they *mean*? Then come to us, we are the experts, we *understand* them, we shall tell you how to *interpret* them. But don't ask us for *evaluation*, for *critique*. Oh no, we are objective scholars, and we prefer to keep hidden our personal preferences and our ethical and religious views about the subject matter of our study[6].

For Clines, such evaluation entails reading "against the grain" of the text or, in his terms, "reading from left to right". Hebrew convention, of course, demands that we read "from right to left", and Clines regards this expression

---

[6] Clines 1997:23 (his italics); cf. 1993:84–87; 1995:18–21. Prior expresses similar dissatisfaction with prevailing scholarly assessments of biblical texts, and argues that interpreters have generally preferred "the security of silence to risking the opprobrium of speaking out" (1997:294).

as a metaphor for the way in which the biblical authors would have wanted us to read the text, and how biblical commentators over the generations (with very few exceptions) *have* read the text. They have traditionally succumbed to its ideology, allowing themselves to be persuaded that it is obvious, natural and commonsensical. In the process, they have suppressed their critical instincts and screened out questions of value, thus leaving "half their proper task unattempted"[7]. Clines concedes that there is nothing inherently wrong with adopting the ideology of the text, provided we realize that that is what we are doing, and provided we do not object when we see other, less forgiving, readers reading "from left to right" by opposing the text's claims and questioning its ideology.

As Clines observes, there is no shortage of material in the Hebrew Bible that demands such ethical critique, for it contains numerous passages that should make us angry and provoke in all, apart from the emotionally anaesthetized, a sense of moral outrage. Such texts include Amos 6:4–7, which threatens with exile (!) the rich whose only "crime" appears to have been their penchant for luxurious living[8]; Psalm 24, which uses war imagery to describe the deity's activities (1995:175–6); and Psalm 2, which claims that the Israelite king will shatter the nations of the earth, though their only "crime" was their desire for freedom from bondage (1995:244–75). For Clines, it is not enough to understand and explain such texts, for the responsible interpreter must be prepared to repudiate, deplore and (if necessary) reject their claims. Biblical interpreters must consider themselves ethically accountable, for failure to critique the Hebrew Bible may be construed as tacit approval of the values it promotes, and a resolute refusal to engage in ethical judgment merely compounds the moral dubiety of the text by perpetuating its claims and lending it the interpreter's own moral authority.

---

[7] Clines 1995:21. In his discussion of Psalm 2, Clines states that "too many readers are in bondage either to the text or to the approved interpretations of the text—or to both" (1995:274). Earlier in the chapter he makes the same point, but in more exaggerated terms: "I stand to be corrected, but I believe that every interpretation of and commentary on this psalm ever written adopts the viewpoint of the text, and, moreover, assumes that the readers addressed by the scholarly commentator share the ideology of the text and its author" (244).

[8] Clines is so incensed at the injustice of such punishment (and even more so at the failure of commentators to criticize or even notice such injustice) that he gives free rein to his annoyance: "Is there some sin in having expensive ivory inlays on your bedframe?... No doubt meat of any kind was something of a delicacy in ancient Israel, and these people are eating meat of choice animals prepared for the table; but is that wrong?... And as for singing idle songs, who among the readers of Amos can cast a stone? Has karaoke suddenly become a sin, as well as a social disease? Drinking wine out of bowls instead of cups does admittedly sound greedy, and anointing yourself with the finest (and presumably most expensive) oil rather than bargain basement value-for-money oil is certainly self-indulgent. But how serious is self-indulgence? Is it a crime? Is it a sin that deserves a sentence of deportation? Does being wealthy and conspicuously consuming renewable natural resources (wine, oil, mutton and elephant tusks) put you in line for exile, by any reasonable standards?" (1995:78–80).

It should be emphasized at this point that reader–response criticism is concerned to critique not only the text itself but various readings of the text[9]. This process of "commenting on the commentators" has been labelled by Clines as "metacommentary", a term he explains as follows: "When we write commentary, we read what commentators say. When we write metacommentary, we notice what commentators do" (1995:76). In a provocative chapter entitled "Metacommentating Amos", he observes that what biblical commentators have done, almost without exception, is to adopt Amos' views regarding the social and economic ills of ancient Israel. The ideology of the text has cast its magic spell over them to such an extent that they have been seduced into a readerly identification with the prophet's outlook. Instead of taking a step back from the text and critically questioning its assumptions, they have merged into empathetic harmony with the text's ideology and have all but accepted it as their own. Such is the complicity between the text and its readers that they have automatically conferred unquestioned moral authority upon the prophet and accepted without further thought his own version of the truth. Amos claims to be a man of God, and so commentators assume that what he says must be right and true. Thus, when the prophet threatens with exile the self-indulgent who lie on beds of ivory and eat of the choicest meats (Am. 6:4–7), his social analysis is accepted without demur, and the threat of deportation is regarded as just and fair. Similarly, when Amos castigates the foreign nations for their antisocial activities, and threatens them with destruction and ruin (Am. 1:3–2:3), "high-minded commentators who would not harm a fly themselves suddenly join the hanging and flogging brigade and think no punishment too severe" (1995:91). The irony, of course, is that such interpreters often pride themselves on providing an interpretation that is neutral, dispassionate and value-free whereas, in fact, they have been taken in by the text's ideology, lulled into a state of passive acceptance, and seduced into accepting as valid and legitimate a set of values which, in their more guarded moments, they might reject, or at least question.

Not unnaturally, the reader–response approach will be regarded with considerable reserve by some biblical scholars, for to critique the biblical text may be construed as exhibiting a lack of deference towards the canon of Scripture, while criticizing one's fellow scholars may be viewed as an unseemly ruffling of feathers within the academy. Before considering such reservations, however, it will be convenient to consider how this approach might be helpful in discussing the "holy war" traditions of the Hebrew Bible.

[9] Feminist biblical critics have carried out this exercise to particularly good effect. Phyllis Trible, for example, in her discussion of Gen. 2–3, has argued that (predominantly male) interpreters have exhibited more misogynistic tendencies than the biblical text itself, which actually bears witness to a remarkable equality between the sexes in the original creation of humankind (1978:72–143; cf. Davies 2003b:99–103).

Reader–response Criticism and the "Holy War" Traditions

Now the biblical passages describing the annihilation of the Canaanites in
Josh. 6–11 must surely feature prominently in the list of biblical texts that
modern readers of Scripture would wish to question or reject, for the depiction
of God encountered in these chapters is seriously defective, and the actions
attributed to his people are clearly morally offensive. At this point, it might
be appropriate to remind ourselves of the sheer horror of the account of the
conquest of Canaan as depicted in Josh. 6–11, and the reasons afforded by
Deuteronomy to justify the total annihilation of the indigenous population.
The chapters in Joshua depict Israel as engaging in a "holy war" which involved
the extermination of men, women, children and animals, and the wanton
destruction of the cities in which they lived. In the space of twelve verses in
Josh. 10 (vv. 28–39), the Israelites are said to have attacked six cities, in each
case destroying every living person within them and leaving no survivors. The
full impact of Joshua's massacre of this region of Canaan (the hill country, the
Negeb, the lowland, and the slopes) is succinctly summarized in v. 40: "He left
no one remaining, but utterly destroyed all that breathed, as the LORD God of
Israel had commanded". The reasons given in Deuteronomy for destroying the
Canaanites (and other inhabitants of the land listed in Deut. 7:1) are twofold.
Firstly, it is implied that only by a programme of complete annihilation could
Israel be protected from the malign influence of the native inhabitants, whose
wickedness apparently knew no bounds (Deut. 7:3–4; 9:4; 20:17–18); secondly,
it was only thus that God could honour his promise to give the gift of land to
Abraham's descendants (Deut. 9:5; cf. Gen. 17:3–8).

Now the need for an ethical critique of Scripture is surely no more apparent
than in these texts, since they inevitably raise some particularly troubling
questions in the minds of all right-minded readers of the Bible[10]. For what
type of God is it who demands (and receives) human sacrifice in exchange
for victory[11]? What sort of deity is it who appears to approve of such wanton
and meaningless destruction? How can such a supposedly benign God act with
such malevolence? Does not the divine command to annihilate the Canaanites
suggest that he is "a chauvinistic, nationalistic and militaristic xenophobe"
(Prior 1997:13)? And does not his instruction to "utterly destroy" the native
inhabitants of Canaan (Deut. 7:1–2) suggest a deity given to fanaticism, bigotry
and intolerance? And what are we to make of the actions of the Israelites
themselves? Should we not express our abhorrence at the gratuitous brutality

[10] This has been forcefully argued by Michael Prior, who comments: "When a people is
dispossessed, dispersed and humiliated by others, one's moral sensitivities are enlivened.
When such activities are carried out, not only with alleged divine support, but at the alleged
express command of God, one's moral self recoils in horror. Any association of God with
the destruction of people must be subjected to an ethical analysis" (1997:13).
[11] For the idea of the "ban" as a form of sacrifice to the deity, see Niditch 1993:29–37.

which they inflicted upon their victims? Would we want to defend their occupation of the "promised land", given that it involved genocide on such a mass scale, and would clearly be regarded today as a breach of international law and as a flagrant disregard of basic human rights (cf. Moyise 2004:99)? Indeed, does not the entire account of the excessive violence and cruelty inflicted upon the indigenous population of Canaan contradict the fundamental values of the biblical tradition, with its emphasis on the importance of preserving human life, its care for the oppressed and vulnerable in society (cf. Exod. 22:21–24), and its dire warnings against the shedding of blood (cf. Gen. 9:5)? And as for the justification provided in Deuteronomy for this act of genocide, are we really prepared to accept that the extermination of an entire population is the price that must be paid if the divine promise to the patriarchs was to be fulfilled? Even if the Canaanites were as decadent and immoral as the biblical tradition suggests (which is by no means certain), did the people really deserve to be decimated for their wickedness? The answer given to such questions may not satisfy, but at least reader–response criticism ensures that such questions are being asked.

The problem is, of course, that such questions seldom *are* asked in the standard biblical commentaries[12]. Even when the biblical text describes the decimation of an entire population by divine command, most commentators tend to bury their heads in the sand and pretend that no problem exists or, if they do concede that there is a problem, they appear unwilling to subject the text to serious and sustained ethical critique[13]. Indeed, if we apply Clines' "metacommentary" to the scholarly writings on the "holy war" traditions in the Hebrew Bible, what we usually find is that commentators have simply accepted at face value the ideology inscribed in the biblical text. For example, the reason the Canaanites deserved to be annihilated, according to Deut. 9:4–5; 18:9–14, was because they had profaned the land with their idolatry and abomination. Now a moment's thought should have alerted exegetes to the fact that this could not have been the *real* reason why the Canaanites had to be exterminated, for if they were annihilated simply on account of their wickedness, why was there need to destroy their animals as well? It is perfectly obvious that the real reason the Canaanites were decimated was because they happened to be living in the land in which the Israelites wanted to settle (or, rather, the land in

[12] The point is well made by Prior, who notes that the ethnocentric, xenophobic and militaristic character of the Hebrew Bible "is treated in conventional biblical scholarship as if it were above any questioning on moral grounds, even by criteria derived from other parts of the Bible. Most commentators are uninfluenced by considerations of human rights, when these conflict with a naïve reading of the sacred text, and appear to be unperturbed by its advocacy of plunder, murder and the exploitation of indigenous peoples, all under the guise of fidelity to the eternal validity of the Sinaitic covenant" (1997:291).

[13] In a random sample of commentaries on the book of Joshua, commentators seemed far more concerned to identify the cities destroyed by the invading Israelites than in addressing the ethical aspects of the invasion.

which God wanted the Israelites to settle)[14]. As James Barr has remarked, "the people of Jericho are consecrated to destruction for only one reason, namely that they are people living in Jericho" (1993:216–7). But this very obvious fact seems to have escaped many biblical commentators, who appear quite content to accept as axiomatic the judgment of the biblical authors regarding the corrupt nature and immoral practices of the Canaanites[15]. Thus, we are told by reputable scholars that the "ban" was only imposed upon nations that were "morally irredeemable" (Gordon 1986:147), and since the Canaanites were, in the words of George Ernest Wright, "one of the weakest, most decadent, and most immoral cultures of the civilized world at the time" (Wright and Fuller 1957:108), it is clear that they were "ripe for judgment" (Eichrodt I 1961:140). Far from engaging in an ethical critique of the biblical text, scholars practically vie with one another to defend the values which it adumbrates. W.F. Albright, for example, not only accepted the view of the biblical text that the Canaanites were wicked, but argued that this debased and degenerate culture needed to be replaced by one that was morally superior: "From the impartial standpoint of a philosopher of history, it often seems necessary that a people of markedly inferior type should vanish before a people of superior potentialities, since there is a point beyond which racial mixture cannot go without disaster"[16]. Indeed, he even went on to claim that it was fortunate for the faith of Israel that the annihilation of the indigenous population took place, for the Israelite "decimation of the Canaanites prevented the complete fusion of the two kindred folk which would almost inevitably have depressed Yahwistic standards to a point where recovery was impossible"[17]. So there we have it! Ethnic cleansing was a legitimate means of ensuring the religious and cultic

[14] This is why Deut. 20:10–18 states that if a city lies outside the land to be given by God as Israel's inheritance, the Israelites were to accept an offering of peace and subject the inhabitants to forced labour; only if the cities were within the land in which the Israelites were to settle were all the inhabitants to be killed.

[15] Kaiser is one of many biblical scholars who accepts unquestioningly the ideology of the biblical text: "When a people starts to burn their children in honor of their gods (Lev. 18:21), practice sodomy, bestiality, and all sorts of loathsome vices (Lev. 18:23, 24; 20:3), the land itself begins to 'vomit' them out as the body heaves under the load of internal poisons (Lev. 18:25, 27–30)" (1983:268). Whitelam (1996:57) quotes the words of the Bishop of Salisbury in 1903, which betray a similar (albeit much earlier) uncritical acceptance of the biblical witness: "Nothing, I think, that has been discovered makes us feel any regret at the suppression of Canaanite civilization by Israelite civilization ... the Bible has not misrepresented at all the abomination of Canaanite culture which was superseded by the Israelite culture" (cited by Said 1992:79).

[16] Albright 1940:214. Whitelam claims that "the assumption of much of biblical scholarship is that 'Israelite' culture succeeds, replaces, and surpasses 'Canaanite' culture" (1996:52).

[17] Albright 1940:214. Whitelam (1996:6) maintains that two very different schools of thought, represented by Albright and Bright on the one hand and Alt and Noth on the other, shared the assumption that Israel was superior to the indigenous population of Canaan. Since Bright's *History* has proved so popular in British and American universities and seminaries, the notion of Israel's uniqueness and the superiority of her culture over that of Canaan has been absorbed unquestioningly by countless students over more than three decades.

purity of Israel[18]. The Canaanites were to be decimated because the Israelites lacked sufficient faith or strength of character to resist their malign influence. Apparently, the brutal annihilation of an entire population was all part of Israel's moral agenda. Even John Bright, while conceding that the conquest was a "bloody and brutal business", found himself desperately searching for some crumbs of comfort in the conquest narrative by emphasizing that "the *ḥērem* was applied only in the case of certain Canaanite cities that resisted" (1972:138–9), as though that made everything alright.

Of course, once scholars had managed to persuade themselves that the Canaanites were a morally degenerate nation, it became much easier to excuse the admittedly extreme measures that were taken to get rid of them. Thus, W.S. Bruce, for example, defended the "wars of extermination" against the indigenous peoples, claiming that the Israelites were merely "the instrument of the righteous Lord against those who had polluted His land with unspeakable defilement"[19]. G. E. Wright concluded that Israel was God's "agent of destruction against a sinful civilization", and in God's moral order "such flagrant wickedness must be destroyed" (Wright and Fuller 1957:108). But the most remarkable attempt to justify the extermination of the indigenous population came from W.F. Albright who, writing of the "ban", penned these astonishing words:

> Strictly speaking this Semitic custom was no worse, from the humanitarian point of view, than the reciprocal massacres of Protestants and Catholics in the seventeenth century … or than the massacre of Armenians by Turks and of Kirghiz by Russians during the First World War, or than the recent slaughter of non-combatants in Spain by both sides. It is questionable whether a strictly detached observer would consider it as bad as the starvation of helpless Germany after the armistice in 1918 or the bombing of Rotterdam in 1940. In those days [i.e., in the days of ancient Israel] warfare was total, just as it is again becoming after the lapse of over three millennia[20].

---

[18] Cf. Collins 2005:62. A different reason is provided in Deut. 25:17–19 for exterminating the Amalekites from the land, namely, that they had shown a lack of compassion in attacking the Israelites during the wilderness wandering. As Hunter has observed, commentators have generally failed to appreciate that this is a classic case of portraying the victims as aggressors in order to justify their elimination (2003:99).

[19] Bruce 1909:287. As Niditch observed (1993:6), he even managed a condescending swipe at the Jewish people, claiming that "even the Jews have felt as if the command to destroy the Canaanites compromised the gracious character of Jehovah" (1909:283), the implication being that Christians would believe that as a matter of course, but the fact that even the Jews felt this way must make it all the more deplorable.

[20] Albright 1940:213. Whitelam comments that this justification of the slaughter of the Canaanites by one of the great icons of twentieth-century biblical scholarship represents "an outpouring of undisguised racism which is staggering" (1996:84). The original edition of Albright's work was published in 1940, with the third edition appearing in 1957. As Whitelam notes, it is surprising that even in the later edition, by which time the full horrors of the Holocaust had been exposed, Albright felt no need to revise his opinion

What becomes clear from applying a "metacommentary" to the conquest traditions recorded in Josh. 6–11 is that the great majority of commentators— both Christian and Jewish—align themselves with the dominant voice in the text and identify with the people of Israel as they read the biblical account[21]. Needless to say, that is precisely what the biblical writers would have wanted them to do, and it is a tribute to their success that they have been able to manipulate scholars into accepting their point of view, for the job of purveyors of ideology in every age has been to persuade people to see the world as *they* see it and not as it is in itself.

But suppose we were to refuse to be co-opted into accepting the ideology of the text? Suppose we were to read "against the grain" of these chapters and apply to them a "hermeneutic of suspicion"?[22] Suppose we were to read the conquest narratives from the perspective of the Canaanites as opposed to that of the Israelites?[23] If this were to happen, the entire story would, of course, be read in quite a different light. We would be raising questions regarding the legitimacy of Israel's occupation of the land, and wondering why the rights of the indigenous population had been so lightly dismissed[24]. We might even feel a sense of guilt that the native inhabitants' point of view had been neglected, and that the Canaanites had effectively been "explicitly excluded from the world of moral concern"[25].

When we come to ask the question posed by Stanley Fish, "What does this text *do*?", the immediate answer is that it has led biblical scholars (perhaps subconsciously) to regard the viewpoint reflected in the Hebrew Bible as "normative", thus making them, in effect, co-conspirators of the text's subversiveness. On

that a "superior" race had the right to exterminate an "inferior" one. Whitelam appears to have been the first to draw attention to the unfortunate statements of Albright and Wright quoted in the above paragraphs; the words of these two eminent biblical scholars have often featured in subsequent discussions of the ethics of "holy war"; see, e.g., Hunter 2003:101; Collins 2005:64.

[21] This is particularly evident in the comment by G.E. Wright to the effect that "it was a great thing for Israel that she got her land" and "it was likewise a great thing for the Canaanites in the long run" (Wright and Fuller 1957:108). As Whitelam notes, it is "astounding that he should believe that it was to the benefit of the indigenous people that they were wiped out and their land appropriated by Israelites or Arameans" (1996:94).

[22] The "hermeneutic of suspicion" has been applied very effectively to the Hebrew Bible by feminist biblical critics, most notably Esther Fuchs (2000); on the practice of "reading against the grain" of the text, see Moyise 2004:94–106; Davies 2003b:91–94.

[23] One of the merits of recent post-colonial studies of the Hebrew Bible is that its practitioners identify not with the Israelites but with the indigenous people whose land was taken away from them. See Prior 1997; Sugirtharajah 1998.

[24] As they are, for example, by Aharoni, who argued that the people of Israel were "the first and only people" to make the land of Canaan "its natural homeland" (1982:90). As Whitelam observes, no justification is given for this view, and no explanation is provided as to why it is Israel alone that can claim the territory as its "natural homeland" (1996:54).

[25] Walzer 1985:142; cf. Collins 2005:64. As Whitelam has demonstrated, this neglect has had far-reaching political consequences, for its effect has been to deny any continuity or legitimacy to Palestinian history and to convince the guild of biblical scholars that only the history of Israel should be the proper and legitimate object of study (1996:58).

a broader level, the answer to Fish's question is much more serious, for what the text has "done" is to justify colonialism and exploitation, and to bring untold suffering to countless communities resulting, in some cases, in their virtual annihilation as a people (cf. Prior 1997:14). This is precisely why ethical critique should be an important element in the armoury of biblical scholars. What is missing from biblical scholarship is what Schüssler Fiorenza has called "*a hermeneutics of ethical and theological evaluation*" (1999:51; her italics). The challenge of reader–response criticism to the guild of biblical scholars is therefore quite clear and uncompromising: they must free themselves from that most debilitating of all inhibitions—the fear of expressing their repugnance of a biblical text. Such a clarion call to conscience may not quicken the pulse of the majority of biblical exegetes who may, perhaps, entertain serious reservations concerning the entire reader–response enterprise. It will now be necessary to consider what those reservations might be and whether they can be overcome.

The Drawbacks of the Reader–response Approach

Many will no doubt feel instinctively uneasy about applying a "hermeneutic of suspicion" to the biblical text, and may well harbour serious misgivings about the propriety of adopting a reader–response approach to the Hebrew Bible, for such a strategy seems to compromise the very essence of Scripture, reducing the transcendent, inspired word of God to the level of the human, the mundane and the ephemeral. Certainly, biblical scholars of a conservative disposition might argue that the Bible, because of its canonical status, should enjoy what J. J. Collins has termed a "presumption of transcendent value" (2005:25), which should render it immune to criticism and correction. The words and actions of God, however questionable in our own eyes, must not be subjected to critical scrutiny and judged by human standards[26]. It is not a "hermeneutic of suspicion" that the Bible demands but a "hermeneutic of consent", and the text of Scripture should be treated with reverential deference, not soiled with ideological probings. The role of the reader, according to this view, is to submit to the authority of Scripture, not to question

---

[26] Kaiser, for example, begins with the presumption that God is completely good, just and beyond reproach, and any divine actions or words that seem to conflict with these expectations are rationalized as good, just (in the circumstances) and necessary: "What God is in his character and what he wills in his revelation, defines what is right; conversely it is right, good, acceptable and satisfying to all because of his known character and will" (1983:3). On this basis, Kaiser is forced to concede that the Hebrew Bible upholds the justice and righteousness of God even in the command to eradicate the Canaanites (267), and he comes to the rather naïve conclusion that "God's character and the acts he requires are fully consistent with everything that both testaments would lead us to expect in our God" (269).

or criticize it, and the task of the exegete is to affirm the values embodied in the biblical text, not to repudiate or reject them.

Moreover, while there may well be some unsavoury aspects to the biblical text, these (it is argued) should not be explained away by whatever strategy happens to be in vogue among the guild of biblical scholars. After all, it may be that in another decade or so the reader–response approach will be airily dismissed as a passing fad, and a different methodology will have captured our allegiance[27]. Those who adopt the reader–response approach, it is argued, are simply in thrall to one of the transient trends of biblical scholarship, and it is by no means clear why the Bible should be left at the mercy of one of the "here today, gone tomorrow" fashions of the literary establishment.

Other scholars may feel wary of the reader–response approach, not because of any loyalty to established dogma concerning the status of the biblical text, but because they have been schooled in the dominant methodologies of historical criticism, and feel that it is simply not their task to evaluate the text or pass moral judgment on its content. Indeed, biblical scholars have often made a virtue of suppressing their ethical judgments in the firm belief that academic integrity demands that the Bible should be read with a studied neutrality. Moral adjudication, on the other hand, is necessarily subjective, reflecting the individual's personal preferences and prejudices[28], and it is easy to see how reader–response criticism can be used simply as a way to legitimate our particular ideology and predisposition. Besides, if we read the Hebrew Bible simply in order to take issue with its more unsavoury aspects, while appealing to its more positive, life-enhancing statements to confirm and corroborate values we already hold anyway, why bother reading the Bible at all? Does not reading the Bible end up in little more than an exercise in self-reflection, so that we are using Scripture (in the words of Norman Holland) merely to "replicate ourselves" (1976:342)?

Can a Reader–response Approach to the Hebrew Bible be Justified?

Scholars who feel inhibited from applying to Scripture a "hermeneutic of suspicion" because of their reverence for the Bible as a sacred text, or because

---

[27] In the words of W. R. Inge, quoted by Dennis Nineham, "he who marries the spirit of the age will soon find himself a widower" (Nineham 1976:109, 227).

[28] Indeed, practitioners of the reader–response approach make no pretence to disguise the subjectivity of their judgments. As Clines has remarked, "'ethical' can only mean 'ethical to me and people who think like me', and if I don't make judgments according to my own standards, according to whose standards shall I be making them, and in what sense could those judgments be *mine?*". Since there are "no absolutes, no universal standards", there are no objective grounds for preferring one view over another (1995:109).

of their doubts concerning the reader–response approach in general, may find some reassurance in the fact that the biblical authors themselves frequently exercise a critical role, questioning past beliefs and querying past judgments. Far from accepting passively the values that they had imbibed, their strategy was to probe, question, modify and even reject some of their inherited traditions. What is often overlooked is that the Hebrew Bible not only reflects the ethical and theological assumptions of its time, but frequently questions and challenges those assumptions. As Brueggemann has observed, the biblical text is "pervasively disputatious" (1997:317), and the religion of Israel was always a "probing, questioning, insisting, disjunctive faith" (318). When Abraham fears that God will slay the innocent along with the guilty of Sodom, he has the temerity to demand that God live up to the best standard according to which human justice was administered (Gen. 18:22–33; cf. Rodd 1971–2:137–9). Job similarly confronts God with the accusation that the punishment he had received was totally disproportionate to any wrongdoing which he may have committed (Job 9:13–24; 16:6–17). The Psalmists often question the essential justice of God, especially when they see wickedness unrequited or, worse still, evil seemingly rewarded with temporal prosperity (cf. Pss. 10:1–12; 73:12–14). The book of Ecclesiastes questions the breezy optimism of the sapiential tradition, and provides a radical critique of the intrinsic connection between act and consequence, and the concomitant idea of divine retribution (Eccles. 2:14–16; 3:19; 9:1–3). During the time of Malachi, the populace in general was apparently questioning the effectiveness of God as the sustainer of the moral order, believing that "all who do evil are good in the sight of the LORD", and wondering, as a result, "where is the God of justice?" (Mal. 2:17)[29]. If the traditions of ancient Israel were to remain normative and meaningful, they had to be critically appraised and had to maintain their value and relevance in the face of critical questioning. The presence in the Hebrew Bible of such "struggle-ridden texts" (Mosala 1989:27) suggests that Scripture does not require or sanction a morality of unquestioning obedience; on the contrary, they imply that God himself could be called to account and reprimanded when he fails to act according to the criteria of basic human justice. What such passages indicate is that the Hebrew Bible comes to us bearing clear traces of its own critique of tradition, and there is a real sense in which the "hermeneutic of suspicion" is deeply rooted within the biblical text itself.

Susan Niditch has argued persuasively that a powerful critique of the violence associated with warfare may be found within the Hebrew Bible, for some of the biblical authors themselves evidently felt distinctly uncomfortable with the

---

[29] Laytner (1990) contends that such protests against God are found in the literature of practically every period of Jewish history, from the Hebrew Bible to rabbinic texts, from medieval liturgical poetry to the Hasidic tale, and from Yiddish folksongs to post-Holocaust poetry and literature.

traditions recounting the cruelties and atrocities of war[30]. Such a critique may be seen, for example, in the way the Chronicler has edited out certain stories, such as David eliminating the lame and blind during his conquest of Jerusalem (2 Sam. 5:6–10), and his arbitrary treatment of prisoners of war recorded in 2 Sam. 8:2 (cf. 1 Chr. 18:2). In 1 Chr. 22:6–11, David is disqualified from building the temple in Jerusalem because he was a warrior who had killed in battle; it was to be Solomon, his son, the man of peace (playing on the etymology of his name) who would be permitted to build the house of God (v.9), not the one sullied by the blood of war. In 2 Chr. 28:8–15, the Chronicler, in recounting the treatment of defeated captives, highlights God's displeasure with the folly and cruelty of war, and commends the merciful clothing and feeding of the prisoners. A similar plea for fair treatment of prisoners of war occurs in 2 Kgs 6:20–23, and a powerful critique of the intolerable aspects of warring behaviour is encountered in the oracles against the foreign nations in Am. 1:3–2:3. In addition to a critique of warfare in general, Niditch argues that there is also an implicit criticism of aspects of the "holy war" tradition in the Hebrew Bible. By regarding the "ban" as a form of sacrifice to the deity, Niditch suggests that the biblical authors were trying to abdicate human responsibility for the killing (1993:136). Hosea's condemnation of Jehu's excess (Hos. 1:4) may be regarded as a "criticism of ban-like activities" (1993:136), and in the holy war carried out against the Midianites, the severity of the "ban" is to some extent mitigated by the injunction that virgin girls were to be spared (Num. 31:17–18)[31]. The evidence at our disposal would seem to suggest that the biblical authors do "worry about the ethics of killing in war and make peace with themselves in various ways"[32].

Now the presence in Scripture of such critical questioning may be regarded as a sanction for our own moral critique of the Hebrew Bible[33]. By reading

---

[30] Niditch 1993:136–7. Prior (1997:229 n.11, 263) points to some passages in the Hebrew Bible which reveal a sense of guilt and remorse at the occupation of a land that originally belonged to others (Josh. 24:13; cf. 1 Macc. 15:33–34). For the general critique of war in antiquity, see Bainton 1961:22–26.

[31] Niditch (1993:137) suggests that the fact that "guilt offerings" were to be presented to God after the war against the Midianites (Num. 31) perhaps suggests an element of compunction regarding the almost complete annihilation of the enemy.

[32] Niditch 1993:21. Rodd denies that there is a critique of war in the Hebrew Bible, but this is based on his misguided assumption that issues such as war were viewed as a normal fact of life in ancient Israel and were not therefore regarded as a problem which needed to be critiqued. Indeed, Rodd insists that since many issues which would be considered by us as ethically highly-charged were regarded by the people of Israel as a matter of course, "it would have been astonishing if any major features of the culture had been challenged" (2001:272). This statement is itself astonishing, given the constant critique of ethical perspectives that is encountered in the Hebrew Bible. Far nearer the mark is the observation by Brueggemann: "On every religious question the matter is under dispute, and we frequently are able to identify the several voices to the adjudication that are sounded in the text" (1997:64).

[33] As Birch and Rasmussen have remarked, "that the biblical communities themselves can be seen judging and reinterpreting and measuring the tradition against their own experience

the Bible in a probing, questioning manner, we may find ourselves acting in harmony with the biblical writers themselves and conducting an exercise of which they would be the first to approve. As Moyise has observed, justification for reading "against the grain" of the text may be found in the fact that the Bible itself provides the tools for critiquing its own content, so that what we are doing is similar to what the biblical authors themselves did (2004:106). Applying the reader–response approach to the text of Scripture is therefore not to introduce an alien principle into biblical interpretation; rather, it is a way of interpreting the Bible in its own terms. Since an ethical critique of Scripture can be justified on inner-biblical grounds, applying a "hermeneutic of suspicion" to the text should not be viewed as a sign of disrespect for the Bible; what is disrespectful is to gloss over its unwholesome aspects, and to assume "that it will say what we would like it to say" (Clines 1995:192).

Furthermore, it could be argued that an ethical critique of the Hebrew Bible is not only possible but unavoidable, for even a cursory reading reveals that it exhibits many different—and even conflicting—moral norms which inevitably require some form of ethical adjudication[34]. In the prophetic and legal material, in the psalms and the wisdom literature, we find a wide variety of approaches to some of the social issues of the day. One could easily point to texts that appear to condone polygamy and capital punishment, and to other texts that seem to oppose such practices. Sometimes the internal contradictions in the biblical material are perfectly obvious and self-evident, but often such incongruities have to be teased out of the text by means of a sophisticated process which involves exposing elements that the text tries to suppress[35]. Feminist biblical critics, for example, have tried to reconstruct the remains of antithetical undercurrents—what Schüssler Fiorenza calls "subversive memory" (1984:19)—within the biblical text which call in question the dominance of patriarchy and the traditional understanding of gender relations[36]. An analysis of the moral teaching of the Hebrew Bible would be comparatively easy if it provided a coherent and consistent system of ethical thought, but the fact is that there are discordant voices within Scripture, and readers are placed in a

---

of God can be read as a support for similar activity on our part" (1989:174). Phyllis Trible defends her process of "depatriarchalizing" the biblical text on the basis that it was a "hermeneutic operating within Scripture itself" (1973:48). Ruether similarly argues that in applying to the text of the Hebrew Bible a "hermeneutic of suspicion", feminist biblical criticism merely "continues the process of Scriptural hermeneutic itself" (1985:122).

[34] As Gunn and Fewell have observed, the Bible "shows us not merely patriarchy, élitism, and nationalism; it shows us the fragility of these ideologies through irony and counter-voices" (1993:204).

[35] Brueggemann compares this process to Freud's understanding of the interpretation of dreams in that it involves looking for what is repressed, hidden, denied or buried beneath the surface (1997:327).

[36] Cosgrove refers to these as "countercultural" witnesses within Scripture, that is, tendencies in the text that go against the dominant normative values and ideology of the society in which it was produced (2002:90–115). See, also, Pardes 1992.

position where they must often choose between competing claims. Thus, the Bible demands that some texts be critiqued in the light of others, and in this way every reader of Scripture becomes, of necessity, his or her own ethical critic.

Finally, the issue of "critique" requires further clarification, for there is a danger that it will be understood in a predominantly negative sense, and that the entire reader–response enterprise will consequently be regarded as a futile exercise. Such a criticism would be entirely justified were we to allow our critique of Scripture to be one-sided, and fail to appreciate the fact that our questioning of the Hebrew Bible should set in train a dialectical process whereby the Bible also questions us, inviting us to reconsider our priorities, to revise our long-cherished beliefs, and perhaps to re-orient our deeply entrenched ethical positions. When ancient text and modern reader are brought into mutual conversation with one another the world we knew (or thought we knew) may be reconfigured, and our conventional ways of thinking may be overturned. Passages in the prophets, for example, might unsettle our views concerning the notions of justice and equality; the flaws we perceive in the social institutions reflected in the Hebrew Bible may lead us to see the defects and deficiencies in our own contemporary society; the shortcomings we detect in the ethical values of the ancient Israelites may encourage us to reflect on the adequacy of our own beliefs and practices. Cross-cultural judgments must go in both directions, so that as we pass judgment on the Bible we must allow the Bible to pass judgment on us. In this way, an encounter with the past is transformed into an encounter with the present, and we will often find that the Bible we thought we had under cross-examination has turned the tables and begun to interrogate us. Such a reading of the Bible can prove to be a most humbling experience, for all too often we have an overweening trust in the rectitude of our own judgment and in the superiority of our own perspective, and such intellectual arrogance often shields us from self-criticism and self-evaluation. Reading the Hebrew Bible as a resisting reader, far from being a negative exercise, may prove to be a transformative experience in which our own fundamental beliefs and values are called in question.

Conclusion

The reader–response approach recognizes that, while there are undoubtedly passages in Scripture that are uplifting and life-enhancing, there are also many passages that are morally offensive and ethically questionable. The strategy insists that, as we contemplate the ethically dubious passages of the Hebrew Bible, we must learn to become what Judith Fetterley has termed "resisting readers". Just as we might readily concede that parts of the Hebrew Bible are scientifically or historically wrong, so we must be prepared to pronounce that parts of it are *morally* wrong. It is not enough simply to excise such passages from Scripture, or to relegate them to some inferior stage of Israel's development, or dismiss them as out of symmetry with the more palatable parts of Israel's faith and ethics. Rather, the morally offensive passages of the Hebrew Bible, such as Josh. 6–11, must be questioned and critiqued in an open, honest and forthright way.

Reader–response criticism, however, invites us to critique not only the biblical text itself, but the way in which it has been understood and interpreted by biblical exegetes. Our examination of the way in which biblical commentators have broached the account of the conquest of Canaan and its justification in the Hebrew Bible revealed that, by and large, scholars tended to align themselves with the dominant voice of the text, and their general approach to the biblical tradition was far more likely to be consensual rather than critical. They tended to adopt the ideology of the text uncritically, and accept the biblical view that the indigenous population of Canaan was basically immoral, corrupt and lacking the ethical impulse of Yahwism. What was particularly striking was the pusillanimous reluctance of many commentators to engage in ethical critique of the relevant passages, even though the texts in question depicted killing, destruction and horrendous suffering on a mass scale. If the ethical issue was addressed at all by commentators, it was usually done in the most perfunctory way; indeed, it was almost a novelty to encounter a commentary that subjected the ethically problematic passages of Josh. 6–11 to serious and sustained moral critique.

The argument of the present chapter, however, is that there must be a place in biblical scholarship—and a respectable and honourable place—for moral critique and ethical appraisal of the biblical tradition. For why should it be regarded as respectable to undertake a critical evaluation of the sources of the Hebrew Bible but not of its morality? Why should the categories of "truth" and "falsehood" be so readily applied to the historical statements of the Hebrew Bible but not to its value judgments? It is vital that "ethical criticism" be placed firmly on the agenda of the university curriculum, and that the biblical exegete be prepared to tackle what may perhaps be the most important task of the biblical interpreter, namely, that of interacting with the text and reflecting consciously and critically upon the validity or otherwise of its claims.

Clearly, ethical criticism has yet to make its full impact on the realm of biblical studies, and it must be conceded that the application of reader–response criticism to the Hebrew Bible is not without its problems. In the first place, the transition from the historical-critical to the literary-critical approach is not one that many biblical scholars will find particularly easy or congenial. The interests of literary theorists seem alien to the traditional interests of biblical scholars, and many will probably balk at the importation of a methodology that seems so new and unfamiliar. Others may resist such an approach out of deference for the Bible, believing that we cannot question the normative value of its statements without impugning its authority as the Scripture of the church.

While we cannot pretend to have effectively eviscerated all criticisms of the reader–response approach to the biblical text, we have attempted to defend the use of this strategy by arguing that a critique of tradition is authorized by the Hebrew Bible itself, and can thus be justified on inner-biblical grounds. Susan Niditch has argued that there is a critique of violence and brutality within the Hebrew Bible itself, and that the biblical writers occasionally felt distinctly uncomfortable with the traditions recounting the cruelties and atrocities of war. There is a sense, therefore, in which Scripture itself provides a warrant for modern readers to probe its values, to question its assumptions, and to dissent from its teachings. By applying the reader–response approach to the biblical material we are merely continuing ancient Israel's own debate regarding the validity of its ethical norms. Such an approach does not derogate from the authority of Scripture; on the contrary, it merely continues a process encountered within the Hebrew Bible itself, for the biblical authors themselves often assumed a critical, dissociating position with regard to the traditions which they inherited.

Moreover, it was argued that the conflicting perspectives on various issues in Scripture inevitably require some form of ethical adjudication by the reader. The Hebrew Bible is replete with assertions and counter-assertions and, faced with what Brueggemann has called the "conflictual, disputatious quality of Old Testament articulation" (1997:73), we are often placed in a position in which we are forced to decide between the competing claims of Scripture. The text of the Hebrew Bible is "internally argumentative" (Levenson 1993:56), and readers must sometimes choose between seemingly irreconcilable options. But whereas the discordant voices of Scripture are often viewed as a problem, it may be that they can serve as a way of resolving a problem, for the dialogue and debate within the Hebrew Bible may provide a useful starting-point for our own approach to the ethically dubious passages of Scripture. The presence of a plurality of contradictory voices within the Hebrew Bible forces us to make our own decisions, and in the process we become, of necessity, our own ethical critics.

We have been at pains to emphasize, however, that reader–response criticism should not be viewed as an unduly negative approach to the Bible, for it is not intended to be a destructive negation of the values embedded in Scripture; rather, it is a strategy that invites us to engage in continual dialogue with the ethical judgments which it enshrines, and, in the process, we may find our own deeply-held and long-cherished views being questioned or adjusted. As Schüssler Fiorenza has remarked, the Bible "invites transformations" (1985:135), and provided we read the biblical text in a spirit of humility and open-mindedness, we may find ourselves being changed in the process.

Chapter 7

Conclusion

In this volume, we have been concerned to examine some of the strategies deployed by biblical scholars over the years to overcome the ethically problematic passages of Scripture. The very existence of such texts within the canon has led some to question the value, importance and authority of the Hebrew Bible, and to wonder why it should be accepted and affirmed as a foundation for faith. After all, how could a book in which polygamy, slavery, xenophobia and homophobia are openly advocated be relied upon as an infallible and inerrant source of ethical guidance for contemporary communities of faith? Modern readers of the Hebrew Bible cannot simply overlook what the Israelites did (or claimed to have done) to the Canaanites, nor can they ignore the appalling litany of murder and violence found within its pages. Clearly, *some* strategy has to be devised in order to counter the ethically problematic passages of Scripture, otherwise the Hebrew Bible, far from providing sound moral guidance, may well turn out to be "an ethical millstone around the neck of the Christian Church" (Davidson 1959: 373).

The first strategy discussed was the so-called "evolutionary approach", which can be traced back to the latter decades of the nineteenth century and the beginning of the twentieth. During this period, evolution and progress had become very much the order of the day, and for many biblical scholars the evolutionary theory provided the most plausible means of explaining away passages of Scripture that might offend the sensitive conscience. The revolution in the historical-critical method during the nineteenth century meant that a development could be discerned in the Bible's ethical understanding, and the morally unpalatable parts of the Hebrew Bible could be put down to the partial gropings and misconceptions of earlier ages. It stood to reason that divine commands that may have appeared immoral or subversive to later, more enlightened, sensibilities would have been inevitable in Israel at a less developed stage in the nation's moral progress. Such an understanding of the way in which the history of Israel developed provided a welcome strategy for dealing with the accounts of violence and brutality recorded in the Hebrew Bible. It was pointed out that most of the endorsements of violent behaviour were set in the context of the early history of Israel, and reflected the vestiges of a primitive religion which was transcended in later Judaism and Christianity. The merciless slaughter of the Canaanites, for example, belonged to an infantile stage in the moral progress of Israel, and was viewed as representing a fairly naïve understanding of God on the part of the people. As these stories were passed down from generation to generation, however, they received a new interpretation that reflected a changed perception of God, brought about largely by the prophetic witness, with its strong denunciations of gratuitous violence and gross abuses of power (cf. Am. 1:3, 6, 11, 13).

By the middle of the twentieth century, however, the flaws in the evolutionary strategy began to emerge with increasing clarity. It came to be recognized, for example, that one of the inevitable consequences of this approach was that it tended to generate an excessively negative view of the Hebrew Bible. Much of its content came to be regarded as outworn and obsolete, and interpretation of the Hebrew Bible was viewed as little more than a preparatory exercise for the study of the New Testament. The laws and customs of ancient Israel had now been superseded by the provisions of the Sermon on the Mount and, as a result, the overwhelming priority in moral authority was accorded to the teaching of Jesus. The evolutionary approach had the unfortunate effect of pitting the Hebrew Bible against the New Testament, and the strategy merely helped to fuel the notion that the God of the former was a God of wrath and vengeance, while the God of the latter was a God of peace and love. Such a polarisation inevitably resulted in a superficial and distorted view of the Bible, and it is, perhaps, little wonder that the evolutionary approach has tended, over the years, to receive something of a "bad press".

There is some evidence to suggest, however, that the tide is now beginning to turn, and while it would be an exaggeration to claim that there is currently a new-found enthusiasm for the evolutionary theory, it does at least appear that the anti-evolution bandwagon has run its course, and studies such as those of Gerd Theissen (1984) suggest that this strategy may yet prove to be too fruitful to be ignored completely. After all, the Hebrew Bible originated over a period probably spanning a millennium, and it would be foolish not to admit that changes in thought, practice and perspective occurred over the centuries. Of course, it is doubtful whether the evolutionary approach can satisfactorily account for the ethically problematic passages of Scripture, since the texts that portray violence and brutality feature in the New Testament as well as in the Hebrew Bible. Yet, as a strategy, the evolutionary approach is far from being a spent force, and while we clearly cannot speak of a uniform development of Israelite religion and moral consciousness, we *can* recognize various stages of growth in the religious and ethical ideas of the Hebrew people.

A different strategy of dealing with the ethically problematic texts of the Hebrew Bible was advocated by the cultural relativists, who argued that the laws and institutions of ancient Israel were relative to their own time and culture, and were conditioned by their historical and socio-cultural location. In this way, some of the darker aspects of Scripture, such as the atrocities associated with the "holy war" traditions, could be exonerated, at least to some extent, by claiming that they merely reflected the social and historical milieu out of which they arose. In the earliest stages of Israel's religion, everything was incorporated into the religious sphere, and warfare was no exception; thus "holy war" was no more than an extension of a cultic act, and the so-called "ban" was merely a sort of sacrifice, albeit a human one and on a mass scale. In this regard, the Hebrew Bible was seen to bear all the hallmarks of its historical conditioning, and the task of the modern interpreter was not to pass judgment on modes of behaviour which they might deem unacceptable, but to try to understand that behaviour within the context of the culture from which it emerged. After all, what might be right in one particular culture at one particular time might not be right in another culture at another time; each culture must be understood in terms of its own values, and each age must be judged by its own standards. Once the Hebrew Bible was properly contextualized, the problem encountered by its ethically problematic passages could easily be resolved, for by emphasizing the historical particularity of the biblical prescriptions they could be excused from some of their more abhorrent aspects.

The problem with the cultural relativists' approach, however, is that it tends to alienate the ancient text from the modern reader, and make it little more than an object of purely antiquarian interest. Moreover, it is a strategy that inevitably limits the Bible's universal appeal and relevance, for, in its most extreme form, it "effectively gags and paralyses the Bible as an authoritative source of normative ethics" (Wright 1995:172). While we may accept that the biblical laws and narratives are human constructs that reflect the culture of a specific time and place, we have argued that it *is* possible to conduct a dialogue between our modern worldview and that of the ancient Israelites. Texts can speak meaningfully to us although they may originate from cultural and institutional settings very different from our own. What we must not do is capitulate to the view that there is an unbridgeable historical abyss that separates the modern interpreter from the biblical writer. As David Tracy has pointed out, all interpretation is "a mediation between past and present" (1981:99), and there is surely sufficient analogy between the biblical situation and our own to make it possible to apply the former to the latter.

Another strategy that attempts to deal with the ethically problematic passages of Scripture is the so-called "canon within the canon" approach. This method involves a critical sifting of the ethical insights of the Hebrew Bible so that we can more easily extract those principles that have universal and abiding value from those that are merely particular and time-conditioned. Adherents of this approach argue that this method is not only perfectly valid but absolutely necessary: since we cannot possibly be familiar with the entire text of Scripture, this strategy conveniently reduces the sheer quantity and variety of biblical material to more manageable proportions. Moreover, it is argued that this approach is true to the way readers normally broach the text of

Scripture. We all—whether consciously or unconsciously—make selective use of the Bible by prioritizing certain passages (such as the Ten Commandments in the Hebrew Bible or the Sermon on the Mount in the New Testament) over others. By encouraging readers to focus only on those passages which they regard as morally and spiritually edifying, the strategy relieves them of the embarrassment caused by the presence in Scripture of other passages which, quite frankly, they wish were not there.

The problem with the "canon within the canon" approach, however, is that it is highly subjective, and can easily be misused to support the vested interests of particular groups. An eclectic selection of texts can be cited in order to uphold our own moral position and to discredit the moral position of others, resulting in highly prejudicial views—whether concerning anti-Semitism, sexual proclivity, gender equality, economic status or whatever—being justified on biblical grounds. Although the approach is ostensibly well-meaning, it can all too quickly lead to mere assertions of personal convictions bolstered by an apologetic assemblage of relevant proof-texts, thus bringing the entire Bible into disrepute.

Moreover, adherents of this strategy must face up to the simple fact that there are no satisfactory criteria by which to distinguish the biblical injunctions that are valid from those which are not. After all, if only some principles in the Bible are to be considered normative, who is to decide which, and on what grounds? Why should some ethical values be regarded as exemplary and others as dubious? Can we simply discard the unsavoury passages of Scripture by an arbitrary selectivity? Surely we cannot appeal to the Bible as authoritative when it suits our purpose, and blandly disregard it when it does not? Does not this tendency to focus too narrowly on isolated texts limit the range of the biblical witness, and result in a distortion of what the Bible as a whole has to say? It is precisely because of such concerns that many scholars have favoured a more holistic approach to the text of Scripture, and have welcomed the "canonical" strategy advocated by Brevard Childs.

Unlike the "canon within the canon" approach, this strategy emphasizes the need for a comprehensive and balanced account of the biblical testimony. The task of the biblical interpreter, according to Childs, was to "reflect theologically on the whole Christian Bible in the light of the diverse biblical witnesses" (1992:705). Adherents of this approach maintain that, in its diversity, the Bible provides a wide range of ethical viewpoints, none of which can claim to be *the* biblical ethic, but all of which, taken together, may suggest an appropriate response in a given set of circumstances. Such a strategy was clearly designed to provide a corrective to the reductionist approach characterized by the "canon within the canon" principle, and it provided the ultimate antidote to selective appeals to favourite proof-texts. Its stress on the wholeness of Scripture meant that moral judgments could no longer be based on specific passages that seemed to confirm a position already reached on other grounds. The approach allowed the Bible in its entirety to inform one's ethical reflection, and it encouraged readers to engage in dialogue with the full range of biblical witnesses, so that they became aware of the inter-relation of Scripture as a whole and the essential links between the two Testaments. In this way, the canonical approach was seen as providing all the checks and balances necessary for serious ethical reflection on the Bible, and it was viewed as a safeguard against the danger of manipulating the text to support one's own preconceived ideas.

Now there is much to be said in favour of Childs' canonical approach to Scripture. In the first place, it provides a welcome corrective to the historical-critical method by which the Bible had become hopelessly fragmented, and its essential unity distorted or neglected. Moreover, the approach has often brought new and insightful features of the text into prominence, and many recent studies have shown that studying the Bible at the canonical level may uncover a wealth of theological and ethical meaning that is often lost when the text is dismembered into its component sources. Furthermore, the canonical strategy serves as a salutary reminder that the ethics of the Hebrew Bible is contextual, and that the moral principles which it contains can easily be distorted if divorced from their wider context. Discussion of the canonical approach has been particularly pertinent to the present study, for Childs himself was aware that one of the benefits of this strategy was that it could alleviate some of the difficulties caused by the ethically problematic passages of Scripture, and while he did not claim that the problems caused by such texts could be resolved, he believed that they could, at least to some extent, be mitigated.

But although the canonical approach has opened up new interpretative possibilities, and has much to contribute to current debates about biblical ethics and ways of interpreting the Bible in general, we have identified a number of problems inherent in this particular strategy. In the first place, questions were raised concerning Childs' emphasis on the final result of the transmission process. In his view, it is the canonical shape of the text that is authoritative, and it is this that should be the focus of our interest and concern. But we are left asking: Why should the canonical form of the text be granted hermeneutical priority? Why should the authority of Scripture reside in the final form of the process (i.e., canonization) rather than in the process itself? Moreover, while Childs is able to tell us *what* we ought to do (viz, read each passage of the Bible in the context of the whole), and *why* we should do it (viz, so that we can view a particular biblical text in its wider perspective), he does not tell us *how* we should do it. How are ordinary readers expected to take cognizance of the totality of Scripture? Indeed, will they be sufficiently *au fait* with the content of the Bible as a whole to be able to do justice to the complexity and diversity of its moral witness? Furthermore, the canonical approach implies that we can discern an "ethos" or "general drift" in the moral worldview of the Hebrew Bible, and that when we consider a particular issue within the context of the entire canon, a kind of ethical consensus can be seen to emerge. The danger of this approach, however, is that it produces a harmonistic levelling out of the diversity and distinctiveness of the various parts of the Hebrew Bible, so that the text of Scripture is made to speak with a single voice.

Our discussion of the "holy war" traditions in the Hebrew Bible served to highlight the deficiencies of the canonical approach to Scripture, for it was observed that the biblical witness to issues such as war and peace is, in fact, highly ambiguous. Appeals to the gentle nature of the Suffering Servant, or to the peace and harmony associated with the coming Messianic kingdom, do little to detract from the overall impression of violence and brutality which one gains from the pages of the Hebrew Bible in general. Michael Prior poses the following provocative question, which could well be aimed at adherents of the canonical approach: "Is it sufficient to attempt to account for the existence within divinely inspired texts of traditions which portray God as a militaristic and xenophobic ethnicist by balancing them with the portrayal of an omnipotent, merciful and universal God which is known through some other traditions of the Old Testament and Christian revelation?" (1997:268–9). To which one must surely reply a resounding "No!" The fact is that the "tumult of warfare and of warriors and their weaponry resounds throughout the books of the Old Testament" (Knierim 1995:103), and we cannot use the canonical strategy as a ploy to pretend that violence is only an incidental or peripheral feature of the Hebrew Bible which can be glossed over by emphasizing the message of peace, love and forgiveness found in other parts of Scripture (cf. Collins 2003:19).

Another strategy that might have proved useful to deal with the ethically problematic passages of Scripture was the so-called "paradigmatic approach", which has been most clearly and elegantly advocated by Christopher Wright. The primary aim of this approach was to make the Bible relevant to contemporary circumstances by drawing attention to the principles which underlie many of the customs and regulations of ancient Israel. In so doing, it succeeded in making the Hebrew Bible adaptable to a wide range of moral problems, and enabled its practitioners to extract a surplus of meaning above and beyond what was explicitly articulated in the text. After all (they argued) precepts and commands tend to be limited to specific situations, but principles, by their very nature, can be applied over a much wider spectrum, and can enable contemporary readers of Scripture to ponder issues (such as abortion or euthanasia) that are not specifically addressed in the Bible. As such, the paradigmatic approach has been viewed by many as a useful hermeneutical tool to enable biblical ethics to address a whole range of contemporary concerns.

Adherents of the paradigmatic approach claimed that the strategy could also prove useful in dealing with the ethically problematic passages of Scripture. For example, the so-called "lex talionis", which demands an "eye for an eye" and a "life for a life" (Exod. 21:23–24) was problematic only if applied literally;

when understood paradigmatically, it could be interpreted merely as encouraging the principle of proportionality, whereby the severity of the punishment must accord with the gravity of the offence. Similarly, the depiction of Yahweh as a God of war, so often viewed as one of the darker aspects of the teaching of the Hebrew Bible, was not quite so offensive if seen as an expression of the idea that every aspect of human life—including the political and military realms— were under his ultimate jurisdiction.

However, this particular subterfuge for explaining away the ethically problematic passages of Scripture is not without its difficulties. One of the problems with this approach is that different people will derive different— and perhaps mutually exclusive—principles from different texts according to the message they want to extract from the Bible. Some will focus on texts that suggest that material prosperity is a sign of God's blessing, while others will point to passages which express antipathy towards the excessive and unjust accumulation of wealth. The text is made to conform to the prior dogmatic assumptions of the interpreter about what is morally acceptable and unacceptable, and the impression gained is that the focus is not so much on the message the biblical writers sought to communicate, but the message the contemporary reader wants to hear. It is little wonder, therefore, that critics of the paradigmatic approach have argued that any principles derived from the biblical text cannot have any normative force.

Since the paradigmatic approach by definition involved extracting a surplus of meaning that lay beyond the explicit articulation of the text, it is hardly surprising that some of its adherents were anxious to warn against a simplistic application of the text to contemporary circumstances. In this regard, Christopher Wright argued that before any principles could be derived from the Hebrew Bible, the biblical text must be viewed in the context of its original setting in the life and culture of ancient Israel; only when the objective of the law in that setting had been firmly established could it be reformulated and reapplied to contemporary circumstances. However, while such a procedure may be perfectly commendable in principle, in practice it encounters formidable difficulties, for it is doubtful whether ordinary readers of the Hebrew Bible will be sufficiently familiar with ancient Israel's life and institutions to appreciate the full significance of the principle underlying the text. Moreover, Wright's insistence that each text must be examined in the context of Israel's own life and experience presupposes that we know far more about ancient Israelite society than most contemporary biblical scholars will allow.

The final strategy examined in this volume was the "reader–response" approach and, in particular, the type of approach associated with what secular literary critics have termed the "resisting reader". Adherents of this strategy maintain that readers of the Bible have a right—and, indeed, a duty—to probe, question, and oppose statements that seem to them to be morally unacceptable. Far from being passive recipients of the text, they are encouraged to become active agents whose duty it is to subject the ethical implications of the Hebrew Bible to critical scrutiny. In the past, scholarly approaches to the biblical text have tended to be empathetic and consensual, rather than suspicious and critical, and readers of the Bible have been more prone to defend and affirm the values of the text rather than to question and critique them. An examination of the way in which biblical scholars have dealt with the "holy war" traditions of the Hebrew Bible suggested that, for the most part, they had simply aligned themselves with the dominant voice of the text, even to the extent of accepting the biblical justification of the "ban", either by invoking the wickedness and depravity of the Canaanites, or by pointing to the long-term advantages of the divine plan of salvation, which could only have been properly executed if Israel successfully inherited the promised land. Instead of examining the underlying assumptions of the biblical writers, scholars have tended to assume a deferentially uncritical attitude to the text of Scripture, and have simply accepted without question the ideology inscribed in the text. The advantage of the reader–response approach, however, is that it serves as a salutary reminder that the biblical writers have their own axes to grind and their own agendas to promote, and contemporary readers need to compensate for this by reading "against the grain" of the text and "reversing the distorting lens" (Moyise 2004:95).

Reading "against the grain" of the conquest tradition as recorded in the book of Joshua means that we refuse to accept that the annihilation of an entire population was the price that had to be paid if God's promise to the patriarchs was to be fulfilled. To remain passive, unperturbed and non-committal in the face of such gratuitous violence is nothing less than an abdication of our responsibility as biblical exegetes. Biblical scholars need to apply to the text of Scripture the kind of moral and ideological critique that scholars such as Wayne Booth (1988; 2006), Terry Eagleton (1978) and J. Hillis Miller (1987) have applied to secular literature. There is certainly no shortage of passages in the Hebrew Bible that call for moral critique, and if biblical scholarship is not to remain self-centred and self-serving, it must articulate clearly the ethical ramifications of such texts, and the concrete implications of the ideology which they promote.

While it is probably true to say that ethical criticism has yet to make its full impact upon the realm of biblical study, it is no less true that an important aspect of the discipline is denied if we refrain from exercising ethical critique. As James Barr has remarked: "[H]ow much would the study of an ancient thinker like Plato have been impoverished if throughout the ages scholars had confined themselves to expounding the text and its internal semantic linkages and had rigorously excluded from their minds the question: 'Is Plato right?'" (Barr 1980a:25). It is a sad indictment of the discipline that ethical criticism has usually been dispatched to the margins of biblical study, since scholars have traditionally had little appetite for engaging in a detailed critique of the values inherent in the biblical text. Some have no doubt been reluctant to engage in ethical criticism of the Bible because they accord the text of Scripture a privileged status which, in their view, should render it immune to criticism and correction; others have been wary of applying such an approach to the biblical text because they believe that it violates academic norms of objectivity. It was argued, however, that scholars who feel inhibited from applying an ethical critique to the text of Scripture may find some reassurance in the fact that such a critique is encountered within the biblical tradition itself. In Abram's debate with God concerning the proposed destruction of Sodom, or in Job's restless questioning of the divine justice, profound questions are raised within the Hebrew Bible concerning the very nature and character of God. The biblical writers recognized that if the traditions of ancient Israel were to remain meaningful, they had to be rigorously appraised, and had to maintain their value and relevance in the face of critical questioning. It is therefore arguable that applying the "reader-response" approach to the biblical text is not to introduce an alien principle into biblical interpretation; on the contrary, the warrant for this strategy is that it is precisely the kind of process that is evident within the biblical tradition itself. It is a strategy that meets the requirements of intellectual honesty and critical rigour, while at the same time being faithful to the concerns of the biblical writers.

It was emphasized, however, that the reader–response strategy must not be viewed as a one-sidedly negative approach to the biblical text, as though it merely entailed a rejection of all the ideas in the Bible of which we do not approve. A critical reading of Scripture should lead us to celebrate the biblical values that are life-enhancing and ennobling, as well as to question those which seem dubious and problematical. Our reading of Scripture should set in train a dialectical process whereby ancient text and modern reader are brought into a mutual conversation, so that as we pass judgment on the Bible we allow the Bible to pass judgment on us. The resisting reading thus becomes a transformative reading in which our own deeply entrenched views are revised, reconsidered and modified. This way of reading the Bible not only revitalizes our engagement with the text, but encourages in us a spirit of humility, open-mindedness and self-reflection, as we come to recognize the provisional nature of our own conclusions, and the need to challenge and transcend our own narrow horizons. Such a reading, however, can only occur when we learn to regard Scripture as a conversation partner, sometimes congenial, sometimes cantankerous, but a partner, nonetheless, in a long-term conversation to which we are all invited to contribute.

Bibliography

Aharoni, Y., *The Archaeology of the Land of Israel* (trans. by A.F. Rainey; London: SCM Press), 1982.

Aichele, G. (ed.), *The Postmodern Bible: The Bible and Culture Collective* (New Haven and London: Yale University Press), 1995.

Albright, W.F., *From the Stone Age to Christianity: Monotheism and the Historical Process* (Baltimore: The Johns Hopkins Press), 1940.

—— *History, Archaeology and Christian Humanism* (New York: McGraw-Hill), 1964.

——*Yahweh and the Gods of Canaan* (London: The Athlone Press), 1968.

Alter, R., and Kermode, F. (eds), *The Literary Guide to the Bible* (London: Fontana Press), 1987.

Arnold, T., *Sermons* (vol. 2, 3ʳᵈ edn; London: Rivingtons), 1844.

Ateek, N.S., *Justice, and Only Justice: A Palestinian Theology of Liberation* (Maryknoll, NY: Orbis Books), 1989.

Bach, A., "Reading Allowed: Feminist Biblical Criticism Approaching the Millennium", *Currents in Research: Biblical Studies* 1:191–215, 1993.

Bailey, L.R., "The Lectionary in Critical Perspective", *Int* 31:139–53, 1977.

Bainton, R.H., "The Immoralities of the Patriarchs according to the Exegesis of the Late Middle Ages and the Reformers", *HTR* 23:39–49, 1930.

—— *Christian Attitudes Toward War and Peace: A Historical Survey and Critical Re-evaluation* (London: Hodder and Stoughton), 1961.

Barnes, J., *Nothing to be Frightened of* (London: Jonathan Cape), 2008.

Barr, J., "The Old Testament and the New Crisis of Biblical Authority", *Int* 25: 24–40, 1971.

—— *The Bible in the Modern World* (London: SCM Press), 1973.

—— "Trends and Prospects in Biblical Theology", *JTS* 25:265–82, 1974.

—— "Biblical Theology", *IDBSup*:104–111, 1976.

—— *Fundamentalism* (London: SCM Press), 1977.

—— *The Scope and Authority of the Bible* (*Explorations in Theology* 7; London: SCM Press), 1980a.

—— Review article of B.S. Childs, *Introduction to the Old Testament as Scripture*, *JSOT* 16:12–23, 1980b.

—— *Holy Scripture: Canon, Authority, Criticism* (Oxford: Clarendon Press), 1983.

—— *Biblical Faith and Natural Theology* (Oxford: Clarendon Press), 1993.

—— *The Concept of Biblical Theology: An Old Testament Perspective* (London: SCM Press), 1999.

—— "Predictions and Surprises: A Response to Walter Brueggemann's Review", *HBT* 22:93–109, 2000.

Barth, K., *The Word of God and the Word of Man* (trans. by D. Horton; London: Hodder and Stoughton), 1928

—— *The Epistle to the Romans* (Oxford: Oxford University Press), 1933.

—— *Church Dogmatics* (13 vols; Edinburgh: T. & T. Clark), 1956–70.

Bartholomew, C.G. *et al.* (eds), *Canon and Biblical Interpretation* (Milton Keynes: Paternoster Press; Grand Rapids, MI: Zondervan), 2006.

Barton, J., "Understanding Old Testament Ethics", *JSOT* 9:44–64, 1978.

—— "Reflections on Cultural Relativism", *Theology* 82:103–109, 191–9, 1979.

—— "Approaches to Ethics in the Old Testament", in J.W. Rogerson (ed.), *Beginning Old Testament Study* (London: SPCK):113–30, 1983.

—— *Reading the Old Testament: Method in Biblical Study* (London: Darton, Longman and Todd; new edn 1996), 1984.

—— *People of the Book? The Authority of the Bible in Christianity* (London: SPCK), 1988.

—— "Wellhausen's *Prolegomena to the History of Israel*: Influences and Effects", in D. Smith-Christopher (ed.) 1995:316–29, 1995.

—— "The Canonical Meaning of the Book of the Twelve", in J. Barton and D.J. Reimer (eds), *After the Exile: Essays in Honour of Rex Mason* (Macon, GA: Mercer University Press):59–73, 1996.

—— *The Spirit and the Letter: Studies in the Biblical Canon* (London: SPCK), 1997.

—— *Ethics and the Old Testament* (London: SCM Press), 1998.

—— "Canon and Old Testament Interpretation", in E.Ball (ed.), *In Search of True Wisdom: Essays in Old Testament Interpretation in Honour of Ronald E. Clements* (JSOTSup 300; Sheffield: Sheffield Academic Press):37–52, 1999.

—— "Imitation of God in the Old Testament", in R.P. Gordon (ed.), *The God of Israel* (Cambridge: University of Cambridge Oriental Publications):34–46, 2007.

Barton, J. (ed.), *The Cambridge Companion to Biblical Interpretation* (Cambridge: Cambridge University Press), 1998.

Bauckham, R., *The Bible in Politics: How to Read the Bible Politically* (London: SPCK), 1989.

Bekkenkamp, J., and Sherwood, Y. (eds), *Sanctified Aggression: Legacies of Biblical and Post Biblical Vocabularies of Violence* (London and New York: T. & T. Clark International), 2003.

Benedict, R., *Patterns of Culture* (London: Routledge), 1935.

Benjamin, W., *Illuminations* (ed. with introduction by H. Arendt; trans. by H. Zohn; London: Cape), 1970.

Bewer, J.A., "The Christian Minister and the Old Testament", *JR* 10:16–21, 1930.

Birch, B.C., "Tradition, Canon and Biblical Theology", *HBT* 2:113–125, 1980.

—— *Let Justice Roll Down: The Old Testament, Ethics, and Christian Life* (Louisville, KY: Westminster John Knox Press), 1991.

Birch, B.C., and Rasmussen, L.L., *Bible and Ethics in the Christian Life* (revised edn; Minneapolis: Augsburg Publishing House), 1989.

Blenkinsopp, J., *Prophecy and Canon: A Contribution to the Study of Jewish Origins* (Notre Dame, Indiana: University of Notre Dame Press), 1977.

Boesak, A.A., *Comfort and Protest: Reflections on the Apocalypse of John of Patmos* (Edinburgh: Saint Andrew Press), 1987.

Booth, W.C. *The Company We Keep: An Ethics of Fiction* (Berkeley: University of California Press), 1988.

—— *The Essential Wayne Booth* (ed. with an introduction by W. Jost; Chicago and London: University of Chicago Press), 2006.

Bowden, J., "Appendix: Ideologies, Text and Tradition", in G. Lüdemann 1996:146–61, 1996.

Brekelmans, C.H.W., *De Ḥerem in het Oude Testament* (Nijmegen: Centrale drukkerij), 1959.

Brenneman, J.E., *Canons in Conflict: Negotiating Texts in True and False Prophecy* (Oxford: Oxford University Press), 1997.

Brenner, A., "On Prophetic Propaganda and the Politics of 'Love': The Case of Jeremiah", in A.Brenner (ed.), *A Feminist Companion to the Latter Prophets* (Sheffield: Sheffield Academic Press):256–74, 1995.

Brett, M.G., *Biblical Criticism in Crisis? The Impact of the Canonical Approach on Old Testament Studies* (Cambridge: Cambridge University Press), 1991.

—— "The Future of Reader Criticisms?", in F. Watson (ed.) 1993:13–31, 1993.

—— *Decolonizing God: The Bible in the Tides of Empire* (Sheffield: Sheffield Phoenix Press), 2008.

Brichto, H.C.,"The Case of the Sōtā and a Reconsideration of Biblical Law", *HUCA* 46:55–70, 1975.

Bright, J., *The Authority of the Old Testament* (London: SCM Press), 1967.

—— *A History of Israel* (2nd edn; London: SCM Press), 1972.

Brown, D., *Tradition and Imagination: Revelation and Change* (Oxford: Oxford University Press), 1999.

Bruce, W.S., *The Ethics of the Old Testament* (Edinburgh: T. & T. Clark), 1909.

Brueggemann, W., *Theology of the Old Testament: Testimony, Dispute, Advocacy* (Minneapolis: Fortress Press), 1997.

—— "James Barr on Old Testament Theology. A Review of *The Concept of Biblical Theology: An Old Testament Perspective*", *HBT* 22:58–74, 2000.

Budd, P.J., "Holiness and Cult", in R.E. Clements (ed.), *The World of Ancient Israel: Sociological, Anthropological and Political Perspectives* (Cambridge: Cambridge University Press):275–98, 1989.

Bultmann, R., *Jesus Christ and Mythology* (New York: Charles Scribner's Sons), 1958.

—— *New Testament and Mythology and other Basic* Writings (edited, selected and translated by S.M. Ogden; London: SCM Press), 1984.

Carneiro, R.L., "The Four Faces of Evolution", in J.J. Honigmann (ed.), *Handbook of Social and Cultural Anthropology* (Chicago: Rand McNally and Company):89–110, 1973.

Carr, D., "Reading for Unity in Isaiah", *JSOT* 57:61–80, 1993.

Carroll, R.P., "Canonical Criticism: A Recent Trend in Biblical Studies?" *ExpT* 92:73–78, 1980–1.

—— *Wolf in the Sheepfold: The Bible as a Problem for Christianity* (London: SPCK), 1991.

Childs, B.S., "Interpretation in Faith: The Theological Responsibility of an Old Testament Commentary", *Int* 18:432–49, 1964.

—— *Biblical Theology in Crisis* (Philadelphia: The Westminster Press), 1970.

—— *Exodus: A Commentary* (London: SCM Press), 1974.

—— *Introduction to the Old Testament as Scripture* (London: SCM Press), 1979.

—— "A Response", *HBT* 2:199–211, 1980.

—— "Wellhausen in English", in D.A. Knight (ed.) 1982:83–8, 1982.

—— *The New Testament as Canon. An Introduction* (London: SCM Press), 1984.

—— *Old Testament Theology in a Canonical Context* (London: SCM Press), 1985.

—— *Biblical Theology of the Old and New Testaments: Theological Reflection on the Christian Bible* (London: SCM Press), 1992.

—— *Isaiah* (Old Testament Library; Louisville, KY: Westminster John Knox Press), 2001.

—— *The Struggle to Understand Isaiah as Christian Scripture* (Grand Rapids, MI: William B. Eerdmans Publishing Company), 2004a.

—— Response to reviews of Childs' volume, *Introduction to the Old Testament as Scripture, HBT* 2:199–211, 2004b.

—— "The Canon in Recent Biblical Studies: Reflections on an Era", in C.G. Bartholomew *et al.* (eds) 2006:33–53, 2006.

Clements, R.E., *A Century of Old Testament Study* (Guildford and London: Lutterworth Press), 1976.

—— "The Unity of the Book of Isaiah", *Int* 36:117–29, 1982.

—— "Beyond Tradition History: Deutero-Isaianic Development of First Isaiah's Themes", *JSOT* 31:95–113, 1985.

Clines, D.J.A., *The Theme of the Pentateuch* (JSOTSup 10; Sheffield: JSOT Press), 1978.

—— *What Does Eve Do to Help? And Other Readerly Questions to the Old Testament* (JSOTSup 94; Sheffield: JSOT Press), 1990.

—— "Possibilities and Priorities of Biblical Interpretation in an International Perspective", *Biblical Interpretation: A Journal of Contemporary Approaches* 1:67–87, 1993.

—— *Interested Parties: The Ideology of Writers and Readers of the Hebrew Bible* (JSOTSup 205; Sheffield: Sheffield Academic Press), 1995.

—— *The Bible and the Modern World* (The Biblical Seminar 51; Sheffield: Sheffield Academic Press), 1997.

Collins, A.Y., "Persecution and Vengeance in the Book of Revelation" in D. Hellholm (ed.), *Apocalypticism in the Mediterranean World and the Near East* (Tübingen: J.C.B. Mohr [Paul Siebeck]):729–49, 1983.

Collins, J.J., "Marriage, Divorce and Family in Second Temple Judaism", in L.G. Perdue, J. Blenkinsopp, J.J. Collins, and C. Meyers, *Families in Ancient Israel* (Louisville, KY: Westminster John Knox Press):104–162, 1997.

—— "The Zeal of Phinehas: The Bible and the Legitimation of Violence", *JBL* 122:3–21, 2003.

—— *The Bible after Babel: Historical Criticism in a Postmodern Age* (Grand Rapids, MI; Cambridge, UK: William B. Eerdmans Publishing Company), 2005.

Cone, J.H., *A Black Theology of Liberation* (revised edn; Maryknoll, NY: Orbis Books), 1986.

Conrad, E. W., *Reading Isaiah* (Minneapolis: Fortress Press), 1991.

—— *Reading the Latter Prophets: Toward a New Canonical Criticism* (JSOTSup 376; London: T. & T. Clark International), 2003.

Cosgrove, C.H., *Appealing to Scripture in Moral Debate: Five Hermeneutical Rules* (Grand Rapids, MI; Cambridge, UK: William B. Eerdmans Publishing Company), 2002.

Craigie, P.C., *The Problem of War in the Old Testament* (Grand Rapids, MI: William B. Eerdmans Publishing Company), 1978.

Cripps, R.S., *A Critical and Exegetical Commentary on the Book of Amos* (2nd edn 1955; London: SPCK), 1929.

Croatto, J.S., *Biblical Hermeneutics: Toward a Theory of Reading as the Production of Meaning* (Maryknoll, NY: Orbis Books), 1987.

Cross, F.M., *Canaanite Myth and Hebrew Epic* (Cambridge, MA: Harvard University Press), 1973.

Culler, J., *On Deconstruction: Theory and Criticism after Structuralism* (London: Routledge and Kegan Paul), 1983.

Curr, H.S., "Progressive Revelation", *JTVI* 83:1–11, 1951.

Darwin, C., *On the Origin of Species by means of Natural Selection* (London: J. Murray), 1859.

Daube, D., *Studies in Biblical Law* (Cambridge: Cambridge University Press), 1947.

Davidson, A.B., *The Theology of the Old Testament* (Edinburgh: T. & T. Clark), 1904.

Davidson, R., "Some Aspects of the Old Testament Contribution to the Pattern of Christian Ethics", *SJT* 12:373–87, 1959.

—— "In Honesty of Preaching: The Old Testament Dilemma and Challenge", *ExpT* 111:365–8, 1999–2000.

Davies, A., *Double Standards in Isaiah: Re-evaluating Prophetic Ethics and Divine Justice* (London, Boston, Cologne: Brill), 2000.

Davies, E.W., *Prophecy and Ethics: Isaiah and the Ethical Traditions of Israel* (JSOTSup 16; Sheffield: JSOT Press), 1981.

—— *Numbers: New Century Bible Commentary* (London: Marshall Pickering; Grand Rapids, MI: William. B. Eerdmans Publishing Company), 1995.

—— "Walking in God's Ways: The Concept of *Imitatio Dei* in the Old Testament", in E. Ball (ed.), *In Search of True Wisdom: Essays in Old Testament Interpretation in Honour of Ronald E. Clements* (JSOTSup 300, Sheffield: Sheffield Academic Press):99–115, 1999.

—— "Reader-response Criticism and the Hebrew Bible", in R. Pope (ed.), *Honouring the Past and Shaping the Future: Religious and Biblical Studies in Wales* (Leominster: Gracewing):20–37, 2003a.

—— *The Dissenting Reader: Feminist Approaches to the Hebrew Bible* (Aldershot: Ashgate Publishing Ltd), 2003b.

—— "The Morally Dubious Passages of the Hebrew Bible: An Examination of Some Proposed Solutions", *Currents in Biblical Research* 3.2:197–228, 2005.

Dawkins, R., *The God Delusion* (London: Bantam Press), 2006.

Deidun, T., "The Bible and Christian Ethics", in B.Hoose (ed.), *Christian Ethics: An Introduction* (London: Cassell):3–46, 1998.

Desjardins, M., *Peace, Violence and the New Testament* (The Biblical Seminar 46; Sheffield: Sheffield Academic Press), 1997.

Desmond, A., and Moore, J., *Darwin* (London: Penguin Books), 1991.

Detweiler, R. (ed.), *Reader Response Approaches to Biblical and Secular Texts* (*Semeia* 31; Decatur, GA: Scholars Press), 1985.

Dodd, C.H., *The Authority of the Bible* (rev. edn; London: Nisbet & Co. Ltd), 1983.

Driver, G.R., and Miles, J.C., *The Babylonian Laws*, vol. 1 (Oxford: Clarendon Press), 1952.

Driver, S.R., *The Book of Genesis* (London: Methuen & Co. Ltd), 1904.

Dunn, J.D.G., *Unity and Diversity in the New Testament: An Inquiry into the Character of Earliest Christianity* (London: SCM Press), 1977.

—— "The Authority of Scripture according to Scripture", *Churchman* 96: 104–22, 201–25, 1982.

—— *The Living Word* (London: SCM Press), 1987.

Eagleton, T., *Criticism and Ideology: A Study in Marxist Literary Theory* (London: Verso), 1978.

Eco, U., *The Role of the Reader: Explorations in the Semiotics of Texts* (London: Hutchinson & Co.), 1981.

Eichrodt, W., Review of H.E. Fosdick, *A Guide to Understanding the Bible,* in *JBL* 65:205–17, 1946.

—— *Theology of the Old Testament* (2 vols, London: SCM Press; trans. by J.A. Baker of *Theologie des Alten Testaments,* 3 vols; Leipzig: J.C. Hinrichs, 1933–39), 1961, 1967.

Evans, C.A., "The Scriptures of Jesus and his Earliest Followers", in L.M. McDonald and J.A. Sanders (eds), *The Canon Debate* (Peabody, MA: Hendrickson Publishers):185–95, 2002.

Ewald, H.G.A., *The History of Israel* (vol. 1; trans. by R. Martineau; 2ⁿᵈ edn; London: Longmans, Green, and Co.), 1869.

—— *Die Lehre der Bibel von Gott, oder, Theologie des Alten und Neuen Bundes* (4 vols; Leipzig: F.C.W. Vogel), 1871–6.

Exum, J. C., and Clines, D.J.A. (eds), *The New Literary Criticism and the Hebrew Bible* (JSOTSup 143; Sheffield: JSOT Press), 1993.

Farrar, F.W., *History of Interpretation: Eight Lectures Preached Before the University of Oxford in the Year MDCCCLXXXV* (London: Macmillan and Co.), 1886.

Fetterley, J., *The Resisting Reader: A Feminist Approach to American Fiction* (Bloomington and London: Indiana University Press), 1978.

Fierro, A., *The Militant Gospel: An Analysis of Contemporary Political Theologies* (London: SCM Press), 1977.

Fish, S.E., *Self-Consuming Artifacts: The Experience of Seventeenth-Century Literature* (Berkeley and London: University of California Press), 1972.

—— *Is There a Text in This Class? The Authority of Interpretive Communities* (Cambridge, MA, and London: Harvard University Press), 1980.

Fishbane, M., *Biblical Interpretation in Ancient Israel* (Oxford: Clarendon Press), 1985.

Fosdick, H.E., *The Modern Use of the Bible* (London: Student Christian Movement), 1924.

—— *A Guide to Understanding the Bible: The Development of Ideas within the Old and New Testaments* (London and New York: Harper and Brothers), 1938.

Fowler, R.M., "Who is "The Reader" in Reader-Response Criticism?" *Semeia* 31:5–23, 1985.

—— *Let the Reader Understand: Reader-Response Criticism and the Gospel of Mark* (Minneapolis: Fortress Press), 1991.

Frazer, J.G., *The Golden Bough: A Study in Magic and Religion* (London: Macmillan; abridged edn of his work first published in two volumes in 1890), 1922.

Freedman, D.N., "Foreword" to M.C.Lind 1980:13–15, 1980a.

—— *Pottery, Poetry, and Prophecy: Studies in Early Hebrew Poetry* (Winona Lake, Indiana.: Eisenbrauns), 1980b.

Frye, N., *The Great Code: The Bible and Literature* (London: Routledge & Kegan Paul), 1982.

Frymer-Kensky, T., "The Strange Case of the Suspected Sotah (Num V 11–31)", *VT* 34:11–26, 1984.

Fuchs, E., *Sexual Politics in the Biblical Narrative: Reading the Hebrew Bible as a Woman* (JSOTSup 310; Sheffield: Sheffield Academic Press), 2000.

Gerstenberger, E., *Theologies in the Old Testament* (trans. by J. Bowden; London: T. & T. Clark), 2002.

Ginzberg, E., "Studies in the Economics of the Bible", *JQR*, N.S., 22:343–408, 1932.

Goldingay, J., *Theological Diversity and the Authority of the Old Testament* (Grand Rapids MI: William B. Eerdmans Publishing Company), 1987.

—— *Approaches to Old Testament Interpretation* (updated edn; Leicester: Apollos), 1990.

—— *Models for Interpretation of Scripture* (Grand Rapids, MI: William B. Eerdmans Publishing Company; Carlisle: Paternoster Press), 1995.

—— "Justice and Salvation for Israel and Canaan", in W. Kim, D. Ellens, M. Floyd, and M.A. Sweeney (eds), *Reading the Hebrew Bible for a New Millennium: Form, Concept, and Theological Perspective* (vol.1; (Harrisburg, PA: Trinity Press International):169–87, 2000.

Gordon, R.P., *1 & 2 Samuel: A Commentary* (Exeter: Paternoster Press), 1986.

Gottwald, N.K., "'Holy War' in Deuteronomy: Analysis and Critique", *Review and Expositor* 61:296–310, 1964.

Gray, M., *Rhetoric and Social Justice in Isaiah* (London and New York: T. & T. Clark International), 2006.

Greenberg, M., "On the Political use of the Bible in Modern Israel: An Engaged Critique", in D.P. Wright, D.N. Freedman, and A. Hurvitz (eds), *Pomegranates and Golden Bells: Studies in Biblical, Jewish, and Near Eastern Ritual, Law, and Literature in Honor of Jacob Milgrom* (Winona Lake, Indiana: Eisenbrauns):461–71, 1995.

Gruber, M.I., "The Motherhood of God in Second Isaiah", *Revue Biblique* 90:351–9 (reprinted in M.I Gruber, *The Motherhood of God and Other Studies;* Atlanta: Scholars Press, 1992:3–15), 1983.

Gunn, D.M., *The Story of King David: Genre and Interpretation* (JSOTSup 6; Sheffield: JSOT Press), 1978.

Gunn, D.M., and Fewell, D.N., *Narrative in the Hebrew Bible* (Oxford: Oxford University Press), 1993.

Gutiérrez, G., *A Theology of Liberation* (London: SCM Press; 2nd edn 1988), 1974.

Hahn, H.F., "Wellhausen's Interpretation of Israel's Religious History: A Reappraisal of his Ruling Ideas", in J.L. Blau *et al.* (eds), *Essays on Jewish Life and Thought Presented in Honor of Salo Wittmayer Baron* (New York: Columbia University Press):299–308, 1959.

Haran, M., "The Uses of Incense in the Ancient Israelite Ritual", *VT* 10:113–29, 1960.

Harnack, A. von, *Marcion: Das Evangelium vom fremden Gott* (Leipzig: J. C. Hinrichs), 1921.

Hayes, J.H., "Wellhausen as a Historian of Israel", in D.A.Knight (ed.) 1982:37–60, 1982.

Hayes, J.H., and Prussner, F.C., *Old Testament Theology: Its History and Development* (London: SCM Press), 1985.

Hays, R.B., *The Moral Vision of the New Testament: A Contemporary Introduction to New Testament Ethics* (London: T. & T. Clark), 1996.

Herskovitz, M.J., *Cultural Relativism: Perspectives in Cultural Pluralism* (New York: Random House), 1972.

—— "Cultural Relativism and Cultural Values", in J. Ladd (ed.), *Ethical Relativism* (Belmont, California: Wadsworth Publishing Company):58–77, 1973.

Hobbs, T.R., "An Experiment in Militarism", in L. Eslinger and G. Taylor (eds), *Ascribe to the Lord: Biblical and Other Studies in Memory of Peter C. Craigie* (JSOTSup 67; Sheffield: Sheffield Academic Press):457–80, 1988.

—— *A Time for War: A Study of Warfare in the Old Testament* (Wilmington, Delaware: Michael Glazier), 1989.

Holland, N., "Transactive Criticism: Re-creation through Identity", *Criticism* 18:334–52, 1976.

Houten, C. van, *The Alien in Israelite Law* (JSOTSup 107; Sheffield: JSOT Press), 1991.

Hunter, A.G., "(De)Nominating Amalek: Racist Stereotyping in the Bible and the Justification of Discrimination", in J. Bekkenkamp and Y. Sherwood (eds) 2003:92–108, 2003.

Inge, W.R., *Christian Ethics and Modern Problems* (London: Hodder and Stoughton), 1930.

Iser, W., The *Implied Reader: Patterns of Communication in Prose Fiction from Bunyan to Beckett* (Baltimore: The Johns Hopkins University Press), 1974.

Janzen, W., *Old Testament Ethics: A Paradigmatic Approach* (Louisville, KY: Westminster John Knox Press), 1994.

Jauss, H.R., *Toward an Aesthetic of Reception* (trans. by T. Bahti; Minneapolis: University of Minnesota Press), 1982.

Jones, G.H., "'Holy War' or 'Yahweh War'?", *VT* 25:642–58, 1975.

Jones, G. Ll., "Sacred Violence: The Dark Side of God", *JBV* 20:184–99, 1999.

Kaiser, W.C., *Toward Old Testament Ethics* (Grand Rapids, MI.: Zondervan Publishing House), 1983.

Kang, S-M., *Divine War in the Old Testament and in the Ancient Near East* (BZAW 177; Berlin: de Gruyter), 1989.

Käsemann, E., *Essays on New Testament Themes* (trans. by W.J. Montague; London: SCM Press),1964.

Kegel, M., *Los von Wellhausen!* (Gütersloh: Bertelsmann), 1923.

Kennett, R.H., "The Contribution of the Old Testament to the Religious Development of Mankind", in A.S. Peake (ed.), *The People and the Book* (Oxford: Clarendon Press):383–402, 1925.

Kermode, F., *The Genesis of Secrecy: On the Interpretation of Narrative* (Cambridge MA: Harvard University Press), 1979.

Kermode, F., and Alter, R. (eds), *The Literary Guide to the Bible* (London: Collins), 1987.

Kierkegaard, S., *Fear and Trembling* (edited and trans. by H.V. Hong and E.H. Hong; Princeton, NJ: Princeton University Press), 1983.

Kirkpatrick, A.F. *et al.* (eds), *Critical Questions* (London: S.C. Brown, Langham & Company Ltd), 1908.

Knierim, R.P., *The Task of Old Testament Theology: Substance, Method and Case* (Grand Rapids, MI: William B. Eerdmans Publishing Company), 1995.

Knight, D.A., "Tradition and Theology", in D.A. Knight (ed.), *Tradition and Theology in the Old Testament* (London: SPCK):1–8, 1977.

—— "Canon and the History of Tradition: A Critique of Brevard S. Childs' *Introduction to the Old Testament as Scripture*", *HBT* 2:127–49, 1980.

—— "Wellhausen and the Interpretation of Israel's Literature", in D.A. Knight (ed.) 1982:21–36, 1982.

Knight, D.A. (ed.), *Julius Wellhausen and his Prolegomena to the History of Israel* (*Semeia* 25; Chico, CA; Scholars Press), 1982.

Lalleman, H., *Celebrating the Law? Rethinking Old Testament Ethics* (Milton Keynes: Paternoster Press), 2004.

LaSor, W.S., Hubbard, D.A., and Bush, F.W., *Old Testament Survey: The Message, Form and Background of the Old Testament* (2nd edn; Grand Rapids, MI: William B. Eerdmans Publishing Company), 1996.

Laytner, A., *Arguing with God: A Jewish Tradition* (Northvale, NJ, and London: Jason Aronson Inc.), 1990.

Leemans, W.F., "The Rate of Interest in Old Babylonian Times", *RIDA* 5:7–34, 1950.

Lessing, G.E., *Die Erziehung des Menschengeschlechts* (Berlin: C.F. Voss und Sohn), 1780.

Levenson, J.D., *The Hebrew Bible, the Old Testament, and Historical Criticism* (Louisville, KY: Westminster John Knox Press), 1993.

Levine, B.A., *Numbers 1–20: A New Translation with Introduction and Commentary* (Anchor Bible; New York: Doubleday), 1993.

Lewis, C.S., *Christian Reflections* (ed. by W. Hooper; London: Geoffrey Bles), 1967.

Lind, M.C., *Yahweh is a Warrior: The Theology of Warfare in Ancient Israel* (Scottdale, Pennsylvania, and Kitchener, Ontario: Herald Press), 1980.

Longenecker, R.N., "Three Ways of Understanding Relations between the Testaments: Historically and Today", in G.F. Hawthorne and O. Betz (eds), *Tradition and Interpretation in the New Testament: Essays in Honor of E. Earle Ellis* (Grand Rapids, MI: William B. Eerdmans Publishing Company; Tübingen: J.C.B. Mohr [Paul Siebeck]):22–32, 1987.

Longman, T., and Reid, D.G., *God is a Warrior* (Carlisle: Paternoster Press), 1995.

Lønning, I., *"Kanon im Kanon": Zur dogmatischen Grundlagenproblem des neutestamentlichen Kanons* (Oslo: Universitets Forlaget; Munich: Chr. Kaiser Verlag), 1972.

Lüdemann, G., *The Unholy in Holy Scripture: The Dark Side of the Bible* (London: SCM Press), 1996.

Malamat, A., "The Ban in Mari and in the Bible", in A. Malamat, *Biblical Essays 1966—Proceedings of the 9th Meeting of Die Ou-Testamentiese Werkgemeenskap in Suid-Africa* (Stellenbosch):40–49, 1967.

Malina, B.J., "The Social Sciences and Biblical Interpretation", *Int* 36:229–42, 1982.

—— *Christian Origins and Cultural Anthropology: Practical Models for Biblical Interpretation* (Atlanta, GA: John Knox Press), 1986.

Mason, R., *Propaganda and Subversion in the Old Testament* (London: SPCK), 1997.

Maurice, F.D., *Patriarchs and Lawgivers of the Old Testament* (2nd rev. edn, Cambridge: Macmillan and Son), 1855.

McConville, G., "Old Testament Laws and Canonical Intentionality" in C.G. Bartholomew *et al.* (eds) 2006:259–81, 2006.

McKeating, H., "Sanctions against Adultery in Ancient Israelite Society, with some Reflections on Methodology in the Study of Old Testament Ethics", *JSOT* 11:57–72, 1979.

McKnight, E.V., *Postmodern Use of the Bible: The Emergence of Reader-Oriented Criticism* (Nashville: Abingdon Press), 1988.

McKnight, E.V. (ed.), *Reader Perspectives on the New Testament* (*Semeia* 48; Atlanta, GA: Scholars Press), 1989.

Meeks, W., *The Moral World of the First Christians* (London: SPCK), 1987.

Melugin, R.F., "Canon and Exegetical Method", in G.M. Tucker, D.L. Petersen, and R.R.Wilson (eds), *Canon, Theology, and Old Testament Interpretation: Essays in Honor of Brevard S. Childs* (Philadelphia: Fortress Press):48–61, 1988.

Mendelsohn, I., *Slavery in the Ancient Near East* (New York and Oxford: Oxford University Press), 1949.

Meyers, C., *Discovering Eve: Ancient Israelite Women in Context* (Oxford: Oxford University Press), 1988.

Milgrom, J., *The JPS Torah Commentary: Numbers* (New York: The Jewish Publication Society), 1989.

Miller, J. H., *The Ethics of Reading: Kant, de Man, Eliot, Trollope, James, and Benjamin* (New York: Columbia University Press), 1987.

Miller, P.D., *The Divine Warrior in Early Israel* (Cambridge, MA: Harvard University Press), 1973.

—— "Wellhausen and the History of Israel's Religion", in D.A. Knight (ed.) 1982:61–73, 1982.

Miskotte, K.H., *When the Gods are Silent* (trans. with introduction by J.W. Doberstein; London: Collins), 1967.

Mitchell, H.G., *The Ethics of the Old Testament* (Chicago: University of Chicago Press), 1912.

Mortimer, R.C., *Christian Ethics* (London and New York: Hutchinson's University Library), 1950.

Mosala, I.J., *Biblical Hermeneutics and Black Theology in South Africa* (Grand Rapids, MI: William B. Eerdmans Publishing Company), 1989.

—— "Reconstituting the Azanian *mišpāḥôt* (clans): Land, Class and Bible in South Africa Today", in D.Smith-Christopher (ed.), 1995:238–46, 1995.

Moyise, S., *Introduction to Biblical Studies* (2nd edn; London and New York: T. & T. Clark International), 2004.

Mozley, J.B. *Ruling Ideas in Early Ages and their Relation to Old Testament Faith* (London: Rivingtons), 1877.

Murray, R., *The Cosmic Covenant: Biblical Themes of Justice, Peace and the Integrity of Creation* (London: Sheed and Ward), 1992.

Nicholson, E.W., *The Pentateuch in the Twentieth Century. The Legacy of Julius Wellhausen* (Oxford: Oxford University Press), 1998.

—— "Theological and Religious Studies at the Founding of the British Academy", in E. W. Nicholson (ed.), *A Century of Theological and Religious Studies in Britain* (Oxford: Oxford University Press):1–27, 2003.

Niditch, S., *War in the Hebrew Bible: A Study in the Ethics of Violence* (Oxford: Oxford University Press), 1993.

Niebuhr, R., *An Interpretation of Christian Ethics* (London: SCM), 1936.

Nineham, D., *The Use and Abuse of the Bible: A Study of the Bible in an Age of Rapid Cultural Change* (London and Basingstoke: The Macmillan Press Ltd), 1977.

Noble, P.R., *The Canonical Approach: A Critical Reconstruction of the Hermeneutics of Brevard S. Childs* (Leiden: E.J. Brill), 1995.

Nogalski, J., *Redactional Processes in the Book of the Twelve* (BZAW 218; Berlin and New York: W. de Gruyter), 1993.

North, C.R., *The Old Testament Interpretation of History* (London: The Epworth Press), 1946.

—— *The Suffering Servant in Deutero-Isaiah: An Historical and Critical Study* (Oxford: Oxford University Press), 1948.

O'Donovan, O.M.T., "Towards an Interpretation of Biblical Ethics", *TynB* 27:54–78, 1978.

Oehler, G.F., *Theology of the Old Testament* (vol.1; trans. by Ellen D. Smith; Edinburgh: T. & T. Clark), 1874.

Oesterley, W.O.E, and Robinson, T.H., *Hebrew Religion: Its Origin and Development* (London: SPCK), 1930.

Orr, J., *The Problem of the Old Testament* (London: Nisbet & Co. Ltd), 1906.

Ostriker, A.S., "A Triple Hermeneutic: Scripture and Revisionist Women's Poetry", in A. Brenner and C. Fontaine (eds), *Reading the Bible: Approaches, Methods and Strategies* (Sheffield: Sheffield Academic Press):164–89, 1997.

Pardes, I., *Countertraditions in the Bible: A Feminist Approach* (Cambridge MA, and London: Harvard University Press), 1992.

Patrick, D., *Old Testament Law* (London: SCM Press), 1985.

Peake, A.S., *The Bible: Its Origin, its Significance, and its Abiding Worth* (London and New York: Hodder and Stoughton), 1913.

Pedersen, J., "Die Auffassung vom Alten Testament", *ZAW* 49:161–81, 1931.

Perlitt, L., *Vatke und Wellhausen* (BZAW 94; Berlin: de Gruyter), 1965.

Phillips, A., *Ancient Israel's Criminal Law: A New Approach to the Decalogue* (Oxford: Basil Blackwell), 1970.

—— *Deuteronomy* (Cambridge: Cambridge University Press), 1973.

Plaskow, J., *Standing Again at Sinai: Judaism from a Feminist Perspective* (San Francisco: Harper and Row), 1990.

Pleins, J.D., *The Social Visions of the Hebrew Bible: A Theological Introduction* (Louisville, KY: Westminster John Knox Press), 2001.

Poland, L.M., *Literary Criticism and Biblical Hermeneutics: A Critique of Formalist Approaches* (Chico, California: Scholars Press), 1985.

Prior, M., *The Bible and Colonialism: A Moral Critique* (Sheffield: Sheffield Academic Press), 1997.

Provan, I., "The Historical Books of the Old Testament", in J. Barton (ed.) 1998:198–211, 1998.

Punt, J., "Messianic Victims or Victimized Messiah? Biblical Allusion and Violence in *The Matrix*", in J. Bekkenkamp and Y. Sherwood (eds) 2003:139 55, 2003.

Rad, G. von, *Der Heilige Krieg im alten Israel* (Zurich: Zwingli-Verlag; ET, *Holy War in Ancient Israel*, trans. and edited by M.J. Dawn, with introduction by B.C. Ollenburger; Grand Rapids, MI: William B. Eerdmans Publishing Company 1991), 1951.

—— *Old Testament Theology: Volume One* (trans. by D.M.G. Stalker; London: SCM Press), 1975.

Rendtorff, R., *Canon and Theology: Overtures to an Old Testament Theology* (trans. and edited by M. Kohl; Minneapolis: Fortress Press), 1993.

Richardson, A., "The Rise of Modern Biblical Scholarship and Recent Discussion of the Authority of the Bible", in S.L. Greenslade (ed.), *The Cambridge History of the Bible: The West from the Reformation to the Present Day* (Cambridge: Cambridge University Press):294–338,1963.

Rodd, C.S., "Shall not the Judge of all the Earth do what is Just? (Gen. 18.25)", *ExpT* 83:137–9, 1971–2.

—— "The Use of the Old Testament in Christian Ethics", in C.S. Rodd (ed.), *New Occasions Teach New Duties? Christian Ethics for Today* (Edinburgh: T. & T. Clark):5–19, 1995.

—— *Glimpses of a Strange Land: Studies in Old Testament Ethics* (Edinburgh: T. & T. Clark), 2001.

Rofé, A., "The Laws of Warfare in the Book of Deuteronomy: Their Origin, Intent and Positivity", *JSOT* 32:23–44, 1985.

Rogerson, J.W., *Anthropology and the Old Testament* (Oxford: Basil Blackwell), 1978.

—— "Progressive Revelation: Its History and its Value as a Key to Old Testament Interpretation", *EpRev* 9:73–86, 1982.

—— *Old Testament Criticism in the Nineteenth Century: England and Germany* (London: SPCK), 1984.

—— *The Bible and Criticism in Victorian Britain: Profiles of F.D. Maurice and William Robertson Smith* (Sheffield: Sheffield Academic Press), 1995.

—— *Theory and Practice in Old Testament Ethics* (ed. M. Daniel Carroll R.; London and New York: T. & T. Clark International), 2004.

Rowland, C. (ed.), *The Cambridge Companion to Liberation Theology* (Cambridge: Cambridge University Press), 1999.

Rowland, C., and Corner, M., *Liberating Exegesis: The Challenge of Liberation Theology to Biblical Studies* (Louisville, KY: Westminster John Knox Press), 1990.

Ruether, R.R., "Feminist Interpretation: A Method of Correlation", in L.M. Russell (ed.), *Feminist Interpretation of the Bible* (Philadelphia: Westminster Press):111–24, 1985.

Said, E.W., *The Question of Palestine* (London: Vintage), 1992.

Sanders, J.A., *Torah and Canon* (Philadelphia: Fortress Press), 1972.

—— "Canonical Context and Canonical Criticism", *HBT* 2:173–97, 1980.

Sandys-Wunsch, J., and Eldredge, L., "J.P. Gabler and the Distinction between Biblical and Dogmatic Theology: Translation, Commentary, and Discussion of his Originality", *SJT* 33:133–58, 1980.

Sawyer, J.F.A., *The Fifth Gospel: Isaiah in the History of Christianity* (Cambridge: Cambridge University Press), 1996.

Schluter, M., and Clements, R., "Jubilee Institutional Norms: A Middle Way between Creation Ethics and Kingdom Ethics as the Basis for Christian Political Action", *EvQ* 62:37–62, 1990.

Schultz, A.H., *Old Testament Theology: The Religion of Revelation in its Pre-Christian Stage of Development* (2nd edn; trans. by J. A. Paterson; Edinburgh), 1909.

Schüngel-Straumann, H., "Gott als Mutter in Hos. 11", *Tübinger Theologische Quartalschrift* 166:119–34, 1986.

Schüssler Fiorenza, E., *Bread not Stone: The Challenge of Feminist Biblical Interpretation* (Edinburgh: T. & T. Clark), 1984.

—— "The Will to Choose or to Reject: Continuing our Critical Work", in L.M. Russell (ed.), *Feminist Interpretation of the Bible* (Philadelphia: The Westminster Press):125–36, 1985.

—— *Rhetoric and Ethic: The Politics of Biblical Studies* (Minneapolis: Fortress Press), 1999.

Schwartz, R.M., *The Curse of Cain: The Violent Legacy of Monotheism* (Chicago and London: University of Chicago Press), 1997.

Seitz, C.R., "Isaiah 1–66: Making Sense of the Whole", in C.R. Seitz (ed.), *Reading and Preaching the Book of Isaiah* (Philadelphia: Fortress Press):105–26, 1988.

—— "The Canonical Approach and Theological Interpretation", in C.G. Bartholomew *et al.* (eds), 2006:58–110, 2006.

Sellin, E., *Alttestamentliche Theologie auf religionsgeschichtlicher Grundlage.* Vol. 1: *Israelitisch-jüdische Religionsgeschichte.* Vol II: *Theologie des Alten Testaments* (Leipzig: Quelle & Meyer), 1933.

Silberman, L., "Wellhausen and Judaism", in D.A. Knight (ed.) 1982:75–82, 1982.

Smart, J.D., *The Interpretation of Scripture* (London: SCM Press), 1961.

—— *The Past, Present and Future of Biblical Theology* (Philadelphia: Westminster Press), 1979.

Smend, R., "Julius Wellhausen and his *Prolegomena to the History of Israel*", in D.A. Knight (ed.), 1982:1–20, 1982.

Smith, J.M.P., *The Moral Life of the Hebrews* (Chicago: University of Chicago Press), 1923.

Smith, Reverend, "Wellhausen and his Position", *The Christian Church* 2:366–9, 1882.

Smith, W. Robertson, *Lectures and Essays of William Robertson Smith* (ed. J.S. Black and G. Chrystal; London: Adam & Charles Black), 1912.

Smith-Christopher, D. (ed.), *Text and Experience: Towards a Cultural Exegesis of the Bible* (Sheffield: Sheffield Academic Press), 1995.

Spencer, H., *First Principles* (London: Williams and Norgate), 1862.

Spohn, W.C., *What are they saying about Scripture and Ethics?* (revised edn; Mahwah, NJ: Paulist Press), 1995.

Stern, P.D., *The Biblical Ḥerem: A Window on Israel's Religious Experience* (Atlanta, GA: Scholars Press), 1991.

Sugirtharajah, R.S. (ed.), *The Postcolonial Bible* (Sheffield: Sheffield Academic Press), 1998.

Suleiman, S.R., "Introduction: Varieties of Audience-Oriented Criticism", in S.R. Suleiman and I. Crosman (eds), 1980:3–45, 1980.

Suleiman, S.R., and Crosman, I. (eds), *The Reader in the Text: Essays on Audience and Interpretation* (Princeton: Princeton University Press), 1980.

Swartley, W.M., *Slavery, Sabbath, War and Women: Case Issues in Biblical Interpretation* (Scottdale, Pennsylvania: Herald Press), 1983.

Temple, F., "The Education of the World", in *Essays and Reviews* (5th edn; London: Longman, Green, Longman, and Roberts):1–49, 1861.

Terrien, S., "The Play of Wisdom: Turning Point in Biblical Theology", *HBT* 3:125–53, 1981.

Thatcher, A., *The Savage Text: The Use and Abuse of the Bible* (Chichester: Wiley-Blackwell), 2008.

Theissen, G., *Biblical Faith: An Evolutionary Approach* (trans. by J. Bowden; London: SCM Press), 1984.

Thiselton, A.C., *New Horizons in Hermeneutics: The Theory and Practice of Transforming Biblical Reading* (Grand Rapids, MI: Zondervan Publishing House), 1992.

Tollinton, R.B., *Selections from the Commentaries and Homilies of Origen* (London: SPCK), 1929.

Tompkins, J.P. (ed.), *Reader-Response Criticism: From Formalism to Post-Structuralism* (Baltimore: The Johns Hopkins University Press), 1980.

Tracy, D., *The Analogical Imagination: Christian Theology and the Culture of Pluralism* (London: SCM Press), 1981.

Trible, P., "Depatriarchalizing in Biblical Interpretation", *JAAR* 41:30–48, 1973.

—— *God and the Rhetoric of Sexuality* (London: SCM Press; Philadelphia: Fortress Press), 1978.

Trigg, R., *Reason and Commitment* (Cambridge: Cambridge University Press), 1973.

Trilling, L., *The Liberal Imagination: Essays on Literature and Society* (London: Secker and Warburg), 1951.

Vatke, W., *Die Religion des Alten Testaments nach dem kanonischen Büchern entwickelt* (Berlin: G. Bethge), 1835.

Walzer, M., *Exodus and Revolution* (New York: Basic Books, Inc.), 1985.

Warnke, G., *Gadamer: Hermeneutics, Tradition and Reason* (Cambridge: Polity Press), 1987.

Warrior, R.A., "A Native American Perspective: Canaanites, Cowboys, and Indians", in R.S. Sugirtharajah (ed.), *Voices from the Margin: Interpreting the Bible in the Third World* (Maryknoll, NY: Orbis Books):235–41, 2006.

Watson, F. (ed.), *The Open Text: New Directions for Biblical Studies?* (London: SCM Press), 1993.

Weber, M., *Ancient Judaism* (trans. and edited by H.H. Gerth and D. Martindale; Glencoe, Illinois: Free Press), 1952.

Weinfeld, M., *Deuteronomy and the Deuteronomic School* (Oxford: Clarendon Press), 1992.

Wellhausen, J., *Prolegomena to the History of Israel* (trans. by J.S. Black and A. Menzies; Edinburgh: A. & C. Black), 1885.

—— *Die Composition des Hexateuchs und der historischen Bücher des Alten Testaments* (2nd edn; Berlin: Georg Reimer), 1889.

Wenham, G.J., "Law and the Legal System in the Old Testament", in B. Kaye and G.J. Wenham, *Law, Morality and the Bible* (Leicester: Inter-Varsity Press):24–52, 1978.

—— "The Gap between Law and Ethics in the Bible", *JJS* 48:17–29, 1997.

West, G., *Biblical Hermeneutics of Liberation: Modes of Reading the Bible in the South African Context* (2nd edn; Maryknoll, NY: Orbis Books), 1995.

Whitelam, K.W., *The Invention of Ancient Israel: The Silencing of Palestinian History* (London and New York: Routledge), 1996.

Whybray, R.N., *Wealth and Poverty in the Book of Proverbs* (JSOTSup 99; Sheffield: Sheffield Academic Press), 1990.

Wiles, M.F., *The Divine Apostle: The Interpretation of St Paul's Epistles in the Early Church* (Cambridge: Cambridge University Press), 1967.

Wilson, R.R., "Approaches to Old Testament Ethics", in G.M. Tucker, D.L.Petersen, and R.R.Wilson (eds), *Canon, Theology, and Old Testament Interpretation: Essays in Honor of Brevard S. Childs* (Philadelphia: Fortress Press): 62–74, 1988.

Wright, C.J.H., *Living as the People of God: The Relevance of Old Testament Ethics* (Leicester: Inter-Varsity Press), 1983.

—— *Walking in the Ways of the Lord: The Ethical Authority of the Old Testament* (Leicester: Apollos), 1995.

—— *Old Testament Ethics for the People of God* (Leicester: Inter-Varsity Press), 2004.

—— "Response to Gordon McConville", in C.G. Bartholomew *et al.* (eds), 2006:282–90, 2006.

—— *The God I Don't Understand* (Grand Rapids, MI: Zondervan), 2008.

Wright, G.E., *The Old Testament Against its Environment* (London: SCM Press), 1950.

—— *God Who Acts: Biblical Theology as Recital* (London: SCM Press), 1952.

—— *The Old Testament and Theology* (London and New York: Harper and Row Publishers), 1969.

Wright, G.E., and Fuller, R.H., *The Book of the Acts of God: Christian Scholarship Interprets the Bible* (Garden City, NY: Doubleday & Company, Inc.), 1957.

Zenger, E., *A God of Vengeance? Understanding the Psalms of Divine Wrath* (Louisville, KY: Westminster John Knox Press), 1996.

Index of Biblical References

Index of Subjects

Index of Modern Authors